NARRATIVE

OF A

VOYAGE TO THE SPANISH MAIN,

&c. &c. &c.

BICENTENNIAL COMMISSION OF FLORIDA

Governor Reubin O'D. Askew, *Honorary Chairman*
Lieutenant Governor J. H. Williams, *Chairman*
Harold W. Stayman, Jr., *Vice Chairman*
William R. Adams, *Executive Director*

Dick J. Batchelor, Orlando
Johnnie Ruth Clarke, St. Petersburg
A. H. "Gus" Craig, St. Augustine
James J. Gardener, Fort Lauderdale
Jim Glisson, Tavares
Mattox Hair, Jacksonville
Thomas L. Hazouri, Jacksonville
Ney C. Landrum, Tallahassee
Mrs. Raymond Mason, Jacksonville
Carl C. Mertins, Jr., Pensacola
Charles E. Perry, Miami
W. E. Potter, Orlando
F. Blair Reeves, Gainesville
Richard R. Renick, Coral Gables
Jane W. Robinson, Cocoa
Mrs. Robert L. Shevin, Tallahassee
Don Shoemaker, Miami
Mary L. Singleton, Jacksonville
Bruce A. Smathers, Tallahassee
Alan Trask, Fort Meade
Edward J. Trombetta, Tallahassee
Ralph D. Turlington, Tallahassee
William S. Turnbull, Orlando
Robert Williams, Tallahassee
Lori Wilson, Merritt Island

NARRATIVE

OF

A Voyage to the Spanish Main,

IN THE

SHIP "TWO FRIENDS;"

The occupation of Amelia Island, by M'Gregor, &c.—Sketches of the
Province of East Florida;

AND

ANECDOTES ILLUSTRATIVE OF THE HABITS AND
MANNERS OF THE SEMINOLE INDIANS:

WITH AN

Appendix,

CONTAINING

A DETAIL OF THE SEMINOLE WAR,

AND THE

EXECUTION OF ARBUTHNOT AND AMBRISTER.

A FACSIMILE REPRODUCTION
OF THE 1819 EDITION, WITH AN
INTRODUCTION AND INDEX
BY *John W. Griffin.*

BICENTENNIAL FLORIDIANA
FACSIMILE SERIES.

A University of Florida Book.

University Presses of Florida.
Gainesville / 1978.

BICENTENNIAL FLORIDIANA
FACSIMILE SERIES,
published under the sponsorship of the
BICENTENNIAL COMMISSION OF FLORIDA,
SAMUEL PROCTOR, *General Editor.*

A FACSIMILE REPRODUCTION
OF THE 1819 EDITION
WITH PREFATORY MATERIAL, INTRODUCTION,
AND INDEX ADDED.

NEW MATERIAL COPYRIGHT © 1978
BY THE BOARD OF REGENTS
OF THE STATE OF FLORIDA.

PRINTED IN FLORIDA.

Library of Congress Cataloging in Publication Data

Main entry under title:

Narrative of a voyage to the Spanish Main in the ship Two Friends.

(Bicentennial Floridiana facsimile series)
"A University of Florida book."
Photoreprint of the ed. printed for J. Miller, London.
  1. Florida—History—Spanish colony, 1784–1821.
  2. Amelia Island—History. 3. Two Friends (Ship).
  4. Venezuela—History—War of Independence, 1810–1823. 5. Seminole War, 1st, 1817–1818.
  6. Arbuthnot, Alexander, 1748?–1818. 7. Ambrister, Robert Christie, 1785?–1818. I. Series.
F314.N23 1978   975.9'03   78-9785
ISBN 0-8130-0416-0

GENERAL EDITOR'S PREFACE.

So many fantastic, almost unbelievable things have happened in Florida in the nearly half millennium since Europeans first made landfall along her eastern coast that the history of this state reads like an exciting tale of adventure. Explorers, conquistadors, Indian traders, freebooters and slavers, land speculators, runaway slaves, bounty hunters, cattlemen, farmers, all have moved across Florida's stage. Some remained only briefly; others put down roots and established themselves permanently.

Florida's history is older than that of any other American state. In 1976 when the nation was celebrating its two-hundredth birthday, Florida could look back on a historic period that began with the Cabot voyages of the 1490s and Ponce de León's landing in 1513. Even before the time of the American Revolution, the flags of Spain, France, and Britain had flown over fortresses and settlements in East and West Florida. This long history has often been marred by bloodshed, violence, and terror.

During her earliest years, Florida was caught up in the great wars which shook the empires of Europe. Alliances, conspiracies, and an assortment of treaties continued to change the map of Florida and to threaten her sovereignty. In 1763, in the peace agreement ending the Seven Years' War, Spain transferred Florida to English control. Two decades later, at the close of the American Revolution, East and West Florida were retroceded to Spain, and her king's royal banners continued to fly over the land until sovereignty was transferred to the United States in 1821.

During these years, while Florida remained under Spanish control, land-hungry Americans cast covetous eyes on the territory that lay south of Georgia and the St. Marys River. The Second Spanish Period was a time for plots and counterplots, for conspiracies, and for all kinds of illegal activity. Northeast Florida—Amelia Island and Fernandina—was very much involved in these affairs and became caught up in one of the most incredible incidents in the state's history. The Amelia Island Affair, as it came to be known, began in June 1817, when Gregor MacGregor, a Scotsman and a veteran of the Napoleonic Wars in Europe who had fought with Miranda and Bolívar to free Venezuela, landed at Fernandina. He claimed the island in the name of the republics of Venezuela, New Granada, Mexico, and Rio de la Plata. The Spanish garrison surrendered without firing a shot, and MacGregor raised his own resplendent flag over Fernandina, the Green Cross of Florida, a St. George's Cross in green on a white field.

MacGregor, who had arrived with a full wardrobe of uniforms and medals, was only the first of the colorful adventurers who became involved in that area of Florida at the time. His frenetic antics are included among the intriguing incidents described in this volume, *Narrative of a Voyage to the Spanish Main in the Ship "Two Friends,"* which has been edited by John W. Griffin and is being published in the Florida Bicentennial Facsimile Series. Ruggles Hubbard, high sheriff of New York City, and Jared Irwin, former congressman of Pennsylvania, followed MacGregor into Fernandina. They arrived in August 1817, just about the time that MacGregor was sailing north to search for funds and support. Close on the heels of this pair of inept Americans came the pirate Luis Aury, who raised the flag of the Republic of Mexico over the area. At this point, Florida's turmoil had reached a point no longer tolerable to the United States. When an American naval squadron moved into position to protect the landing of United States troops, Luis Aury quickly hauled down his flag and departed without firing a shot. The Amelia Island Affair had ended, but the troubles detailed in the narrative of the adventures of the *Two Friends* continued. The stage was already set for still another colorful episode in Florida's history, but this time it was to the west of the Suwannee River.

The Seminoles, then living in North Florida, felt threatened by the ever advancing line of American settlements, and their rising hostility endangered the frontier. Andrew Jackson arrived from Tennessee to take personal charge of the campaign against the Indians. Leading a force of army regulars, Georgia militia, and friendly Creeks, Jackson moved down the Apalachicola River, captured St. Marks, and struck out against the Seminole villages along the Suwannee River. He captured two Britishers, Alexander Arbuthnot and Robert Ambrister, and charged them with inciting the Indians to border warfare. Ambrister was shot and Arbuthnot was hanged. Jackson then moved west against Pensacola where hostile Indians were being armed and trained by the English. After occupying the town and forcing the surrender of Fort Barrancas, he returned to his home in Tennessee. Thus ended the First Seminole War.

These incidents created a major controversy in the United States and for nearly a month Congress debated whether to censure General Jackson. When Spain also protested, her forts and Pensacola were returned. These events, as it turned out, were steps leading to the Adams-Onís Treaty which transferred Florida to American control. These are also among the incidents which the unidentified Narrator recounts in detail in the *Narrative of a Voyage to the Spanish Main in the Ship "Two Friends."*

This is one of the twenty-five rare and out-of-print Florida volumes dealing with various aspects of Florida history which are being published by the University Presses of Florida in cooperation with the American Revolution Bicentennial Commission of Florida. The purpose of Floridiana Bicentennial Facsimile Series is to make available to the citizens of Florida, and to people everywhere, the story of this state's rich and colorful history. Each volume is being edited by a recognized scholar, such as John W. Griffin who holds his degrees from the University of Florida and the University of Chicago. He taught at Florida State University and for many years was an archeologist with the Florida Park Service and the National Park Service. He served as executive historian for the St. Augustine Historical Society and was director of both the Historic St. Augustine Preservation Board and the Historic Key West Preservation Board. Mr. Griffin helped to found the Florida Anthropological Society; he twice served as its president and was editor of its journal, *The Florida Anthropologist*. He has also played an active role in the Florida Historical Society, twice serving on its board of directors. His best known book is *Here They Once Stood: The Tragic End of the Apalachee Missions* which he co-authored with Mark F. Boyd and Hale G. Smith (University of Florida Press, 1951). He is also the author of many articles on Florida and Southern Indians and on archeology, which have been published in professional and scholarly journals.

SAMUEL PROCTOR.
General Editor of the
BICENTENNIAL FLORIDIANA
FACSIMILE SERIES.

University of Florida.

INTRODUCTION.

THE Amelia Island Affair began late in June 1817 with the seizure of Fernandina in the extreme northeastern corner of Spanish East Florida by the Scottish adventurer Sir Gregor MacGregor, representing several South American insurgent governments. It ended six months later with the occupation of the island by military forces of the United States, and the dispersal of MacGregor's successors. The Narrator of the volume *Narrative of a Voyage to the Spanish Main in the Ship "Two Friends"* tells of some of these hectic events, but in this introduction one must flesh out the context of his first-hand observations in order to reach some understanding of what was going on and why.

Since before the turn of the nineteenth century the Napoleonic Wars had kept Europe in a nearly constant state of turmoil, which subsided only after the Battle of Waterloo in 1815. Spain had been heavily drawn into conflict in 1804, providing a rich field for repeated insurrections in her New World empire.[1] With the energies of the Mother Country so dissipated, Spanish Florida remained weak and unprotected throughout this second period of Spain's possession of the territory. The young and land-hungry United States had also been tangentially involved in the European upheaval through her acquisition of Louisiana in 1803 and her participation in the War of 1812.

In Britain the coming of peace was accompanied by readjustment and economic depression. Many men of the young officer class found themselves impoverished, unemployed, and restless. To some of these men the revitalization during 1816 and 1817 of movements for independence in Spanish South America seemed to fill a need. In particular, the renewal of Simón Bolívar's efforts in Venezuela was attracting attention in Britain, and agents busily recruited officers to serve in the armies of the Insurgents. Their appeals were to promotion, glory, and riches, although some responded to the ideological goals of the Insurgent cause. The Narrator in this volume, which is being republished as a facsimile, while acknowledging the more avaricious motives of some of his companions, presents himself as a lover of rational liberty, suffering from the loss of a parent, and in "some circumstances of a painful and distressing nature" over which he had neither control nor influence.

The anonymous author of the narrative identifies himself only as "the narrator." A contemporary reviewer noted, "whatever may be the reasons which induce this writer to conceal his name, he has so distinctly marked himself . . . that he may be easily identified and recognized by any of the many persons who were present at the various scenes which he describes."[2] Yet no attribution of authorship is given in the *British Museum General Catalog of Books*, nor in the *National Union Catalog of Imprints*.[3]

It is tempting to read something into the statement that the book was published for John Miller. There was a John Miller who in 1820 wrote a two-volume biography of his brother, General William Miller. This John Miller was a veteran of the Napoleonic Wars and otherwise qualifies for the role, but there is no available proof. And, on the other hand, there was a nineteenth-century London bookseller named John Miller, who may well have been in business in 1819.[4] Withal, the author of *Narrative of a Voyage to the Spanish Main* . . . remains anonymous.

There is some internal evidence concerning the Narrator. It is known that he was a young British officer, a veteran of the Napoleonic Wars, educated, and well read in the law.[5] In his relations with his companions on this adventure he seems to have been somewhat of a "loner," although he went out of his way to help some of them. He seems to have felt himself superior to many of his associates, at least by holding himself to a more rigorous code and disparaging many of their actions. Toward Americans he displayed ambivalence, apparently liking some of them on a personal basis while holding to a general anti-American attitude. A similar attitude toward Englishmen was of course common among Americans of the time. He found praiseworthy certain aspects of Spanish culture, such as the treatment of slaves. In short, he was not untypical of his nation, class, and time, and even without further personal documentation one may feel that one knows him well enough to allow for that personal bias which is certain to creep into any account.

The Narrator, one of a party of eighty officers enrolled to serve in the armed forces of Venezuela, was packed aboard the 250-ton ship *Two Friends*, which left England July 31, 1817. They were bound for the island of Margarita, off the coast of Venezuela, and the first landfall was to have been St. Thomas, then in the Danish Virgin Islands. However, they had left port poorly supplied; food, wine, and tempers grew short. The essentially self-serving nature of most of those embarked on the enterprise became apparent. There is the vain and pompous McDonald, who had already assumed the rank of colonel and had provided himself and his subordinate officers with lavish dragoon uniforms. McDonald is one of the few of the party whom the Narrator identifies by name; he appears time and again throughout the story, but never in a very favorable light.

The *Two Friends* put into Madeira because of the sad state of her provisions, and most of the party seem to have spent the days and nights in uncontrolled revelry and fighting, to the disgust and anger of the local authorities. In fact, the Narrator notes that subsequent ships bound on a similar mission were refused permission to land their passengers.

The internal frictions continued on the next stage of the voyage; food supplies were again inadequate, but most of the officers had obtained adequate private stocks of spirits. McDonald and the ship's captain quarreled. But, at last, anchor was dropped at St. Thomas. And there everything fell to pieces. The promised agent of Venezuela was nowhere to be found. Ugly rumors circulated which dispelled much of the glamor which had surrounded the revolutionary cause. McDonald was irritating local authorities as well as his own companions.

The enterprise seemed doomed even before the *Two Friends* slipped out of port one night, carrying with it a few of the group who happened to be on board, and the belongings of others who had not carried them ashore. Some of the men followed toward South America by other means in the hope of regaining their possessions; many others booked passage back to England on various ships. Insofar as most of the party were concerned, the voyage of the *Two Friends* to the Spanish Main was over.

But for the Narrator and twenty-nine of his companions a new adventure beckoned. They had learned that Sir Gregor MacGregor had occupied Amelia Island off northeast Florida. The American consul at St. Thomas had encouraged them to throw in their lot with their countryman who was serving the Insurgent cause. McDonald and some of his men were among the group, and, considering his statements even up to this point, one wonders why the Narrator decided to participate. Whatever the reason, the Narrator and the others departed St. Thomas sometime around October 10, 1817, in the American schooner *Mary* bound for Amelia Island and Fernandina by way of Turks Island.

Spain had regained control of Florida from England by treaty in 1783 and had reoccupied East Florida in the following year. From the beginning, this Second Spanish Period was more nominal than effective. Aside from the governor, his establishment, and the garrison, the population remained largely non-Spanish. In and near St. Augustine were a number of Minorcans, survivors and descendants of the Mediterranean colony planted first at New Smyrna during the British occupation. The majority of the plantation owners, ranchers, and farmers of the out-country were of English or Anglo-American extraction.[6]

Faced with a weak political and military presence, Spain had been forced to accept the reduction of her territory in West Florida.[7] In 1795 came the loss to the United States of all lands north of the thirty-first parallel, although it took the Spanish three years to pull back their frontier force to the agreed-upon boundary. The sale of Louisiana to the United States in 1803 ended all hope that Spain could hold onto Florida for very many more years. In 1810 came the proclamation of the Republic of West Florida, and on October 27 President Monroe announced America's claims to the territory from the Perdido to the Mississippi as part of the Louisiana Purchase. By 1813 the frontier was definitely set at the Perdido, the present western boundary of the state of Florida.

As the United States steadily encroached on the western Spanish lands, Governor Juan Vicente Folch wrote on December 2, 1810, that he would yield West Florida to the United States unless support reached him within a month, by January 1. This move resulted in quick action in Washington. Congress by secret act on January 15, 1811, authorized the president to occupy the Floridas peaceably if delivered by local authorities, or forcibly if necessary to prevent seizure by a foreign power.

Attempts were made almost immediately to gain Florida under the terms of this act. President Madison named doughty seventy-two-year-old General George

Mathews of Georgia as the agent to secure the Floridas for the United States. In March, Mathews made his contacts with Governor Folch at Pensacola, but in the meantime the Spanish official had changed his mind; he had received orders and promises of support which negated his earlier offer.

Mathews then shifted his theater of operations to East Florida, using St. Marys, Georgia, as his base. The plan was to foster an East Florida rebellion, supported of course by expected substantial aid from the Georgia side of the border. Once the independence of the area had been declared, and the territory offered to the United States through Mathews, the armed forces of the United States could be brought into the arena.[8]

The first requirement was a resident of Florida who would act as leader of the rebellion. Such a person was found in John Houstoun McIntosh, an East Florida planter recognized as a Spanish subject. Other Anglo-Americans in the area also agreed to join the Patriots, as those in the movement came to be called.

On March 13, 1812, on the south bank of the St. Marys River, McIntosh and nine other Florida residents promulgated a manifesto of independence from Spain, invited citizens of Florida to join them, and raised their own Patriot flag. They were accompanied at these ceremonies by over seventy Americans. McIntosh was elected commissioner of the Patriot group, and offered General Mathews the small parcel of Spanish land presently occupied, to be held for the United States.

The initial plan had been to move across the St. Marys, bypass Fernandina, and attack St. Augustine. But both the army and navy commanders of the United

States units along the St. Marys were reluctant to provide immediate support. The Patriots then moved against nearby Fernandina, which capitulated without resistance on March 17. The Spanish officer in command, and all nine of his soldiers, surrendered when his small battery was approached by five American gunboats, Commodore Hugh Campbell obviously having had a change of heart.

The Patriots marched south and by March 25 were encamped within two miles of the Castillo de San Marcos. The following day McIntosh demanded the surrender of St. Augustine, but Governor Juan de Estrada refused even to confer with him. Returning to Fernandina, McIntosh ceded to the United States the territory of East Florida to the walls of the Castillo, through the agency of General Mathews. This opened the door for Mathews to request the aid of United States troops, and Lieutenant Colonel Thomas Adam Smith with a hundred men arrived at the Patriot camp before St. Augustine by April 12.

At this juncture the situation reached the stage of acute embarrassment for the administration in Washington, forcing the president to repudiate General Mathews and to replace him with Governor David B. Mitchell of Georgia. It was a paper move; Washington still hoped for success in Florida. Mitchell was ordered to see to the orderly evacuation of Americans from Spanish Florida, and he took his time about the process.

But the Spaniards were impatient. On May 16 they drove the Patriots from their camp at Moosa Old Fort on the outskirts of St. Augustine. On June 11, Sebastian Kindelan arrived as the new governor, accompanied by a force of trained soldiers, and demanded that Colonel Smith withdraw from Florida.

Then, on June 18, 1812, the United States declared war on England. But Congress refused to support the occupation of Florida. During the summer, the Seminoles actively joined the Spaniards in attacks on the Americans, and in turn several deep thrusts into Spanish territory were made by American militia. The combined Indian and Spanish pressure became so great that the American forces retired north of the St. Johns River. During that same summer, in a further attempt to legitimize the East Florida operation, the Patriots wrote a constitution for the Territory of East Florida and elected John Houstoun McIntosh as director of the territory. Congress remained adamant, and under considerable pressure the administration finally ordered the complete evacuation of United States forces. The final contingent left Fernandina on May 6, 1813.[9] For over a year units of the United States Army had been deployed deep within Spanish East Florida.

The East Florida situation remained unsettled, but the major activity had switched back to West Florida. The War of 1812 was in progress, and a slackening of the European action permitted England to give more attention to the American conflict. In 1813 the British began supplying arms and encouragement to the southeastern Indians, in particular to the Creek, with most contacts being made through the Spanish Floridas. This eventually resulted in Andrew Jackson's brief occupation of Pensacola in late 1814, and the episode of the American attack on the so-called Negro Fort on the Apalachicola River in 1816.[10] Following the end of the War of 1812, and the cessation of direct British intervention, a short period of relative quiet settled on the Floridas. But it was only relative, and definitely brief.

In East Florida, the failure of the Patriot Rebellion did not lead to a wholesale withdrawal of the basically Anglo-American settlers. A plan of local government worked out in 1816 between Governor Kindelan and the inhabitants seems to have been an effective device. Three districts were set up: a Fernandina, or Northern, District from which Amelia Island itself was excluded, an Upper St. Johns District, and a Lower St. Johns District. Commissioners for the Northern District were George J. F. Clarke, Zephaniah Kingsley, and Henry Yonge. The plan called for local magistrates and a militia. Thus, considerable autonomy was gained by the inhabitants, while the Spanish crown retained their allegiance. The apparent success of this system probably accounts for some of the lack of enthusiasm with which most inhabitants greeted the Insurgent occupation of Amelia Island the following year.

Fernandina had mushroomed as a community, following the United States Embargo Act of 1807 and the prohibition on the importation of slaves in 1808. Located, as it was, across a narrow body of water from the United States, with access to many tidal streams in the marshy estuarine environment, Fernandina was an ideal location for a variety of licit and illicit activities. The deep and capacious harbor could hold any number of ships.

By 1811 the settlement had experienced such a degree of unplanned and unregulated growth that Spanish Governor Enrique White had ordered surveyor George Clarke to prepare a plan for the town. Streets were platted, a plaza delineated, and buildings moved where necessary to conform to the regularized town plan. Warehouses, taverns, a hotel, shops, and homes took their places in the growing community.

By 1817 Fernandina must have appeared much as it did in 1821 when James Forbes described it: "The town consists of about forty houses, built of wood, in six streets, regularly intersecting each other at right angles, having rows of trees (Pride of India) and a square, with a small fort of eight guns, fronting the water. Several of these houses are two stories high, with galleries, and form a handsome appearance."[11]

Fort San Carlos had replaced the smaller gun position that had been in place at the time of the Patriot War. Located on a high bluff overlooking the water, it was a demilune, or half-circular structure, of earthen ramparts with planked platforms for the guns. The land face was closed with a palisade and a gate. The garrison strength had been raised to fifty-four officers and men.[12]

It was this settlement, with a population of less than two hundred permanent inhabitants, which was about to become the focus of yet another incursion into Spanish Florida. But this time the impetus stemmed little, if at all, from actions of the United States.[13] General Sir Gregor MacGregor was just past thirty years of age when he embarked on his Florida adventure. He had entered the service of the Venezuelan revolutionaries in 1811, and had risen steadily under Miranda and Bolívar until in 1816 he had been promoted to the rank of General of Division. But even though he was married to a niece of Bolívar, he experienced and sensed the rising tide of prejudice against foreign officers in the South American insurgent armies. It was apparently to establish a career of his own that he traveled to the United States in 1817 and began negotiations in Philadelphia with three emissaries of revolutionary governments: Pedro Gual of New Granada and Mexico, Lino de Clemente of Venezuela, and Martin Thompson of Rio de la Plata. The result was a commission dated March 31, 1817, for the purpose of liberating East and West Florida, while observing the neutrality laws of the United States.

MacGregor apparently believed that the United States government would be pleased with his planned operation, and he intended to encourage Floridians to join the United States. In view of the interest of the United States in the Floridas, this was perhaps not an unwarranted assumption. He may have had some informal indications of support at the outset of the adventure. It is remembered that the American consul at St. Thomas had been the one to encourage the British officers to join the expedition.[14]

A high proportion of the army which MacGregor raised was American, recruited in Baltimore, Charleston, and Savannah. The men were, however, mostly products of the waterfront, and included the customary seaport mix. The promise of cheap land in the territory to be conquered provided a major inducement. MacGregor had a force of about 150 when he reached the mouth of the Altamaha River on the coast south of Savannah, but many drifted away before he actually moved into Florida.

Greatly exaggerated accounts of the number of his adherents preceded MacGregor, so that when he and fifty-four followers landed on June 29 and marched on

Fernandina and Fort San Carlos they met no resistance.[15] The Spanish commander, Don Francisco de Morales, with a larger force in a fortified position, surrendered without firing a shot. The Spaniards were permitted to return to St. Augustine where the wrath of Governor José Coppinger, himself an army colonel, must have seemed more terrible than the threat of enemy arms.

MacGregor's flag, a green St. George's Cross on a white field, flew above Fernandina, and he issued a proclamation heralding his victory as a blow for the independence of South America. He established a post office, and ordered a printing press which upon arrival began to spew forth proclamations and currency. He entered into negotiations with privateers and less savory sea rovers for the use of the port and the disposition of their prizes. Reports began to filter northward branding Fernandina as a slave-importing and smuggling base.

Attempts to secure the support of the inhabitants of northeast Florida failed. They were not impressed by MacGregor's blow for independence, as measured on the one hand by the form of self-government they were enjoying and on the other by the past history of incursions into their territory. MacGregor did, however, force the abandonment of the post of San Nicholas at the Cowford on the St. Johns River.[16]

Promised supplies, funds, and reinforcements did not arrive, at least not in any quantity. Former Pennsylvania congressman Jared Irwin joined the group on August 28, becoming second in command.[17] Another addition was the former high sheriff of New York City, Ruggles Hubbard, who arrived in his privateering brig *Morgiana*, flying the flag of Buenos Aires. But even these accessions to the cause did not greatly improve the steadily deterioriating situation. MacGregor's own personality may have been a significant factor in his failure; the Narrator speaks of his "arbitrary and unconciliating conduct." When information arrived concerning an impending attack upon Fernandina by Spanish forces from St. Augustine, MacGregor resigned his command on September 4, leaving the affairs of Fernandina in the hands of Hubbard and Irwin. They were determined to stand and fight, supported by the guns of the *Morgiana*. MacGregor's portion of the Amelia Island affair had lasted but slightly over two months.

On the day that MacGregor left office, the U.S. brig *Saranac*, Captain John H. Elton, dropped anchor in American waters nearby with orders to search every vessel entering the St. Marys River and to seize those bearing slaves. Apparently the United States government had decided quite early that the situation at Fernandina bore watching, since Elton's orders, which he had received in New York, were dated July 16.[18] The *Saranac* remained on station for the remainder of the Amelia Island affair, and Elton may be identified as the "Captain E." to whom the Narrator refers on several occasions.

Governor Coppinger had amassed a force fully competent to effect the recovery of Fernandina, but Spanish law prohibited him, by virtue of his office, from assuming active field command. Had it been otherwise, the Narrator contends, the outcome of the attack would have been far different. But as it was, the expedition was placed in the hands of a major of the Regiment of Cuba. His command consisted of about three hundred men, almost equally divided between regular black troops of the Regiment of Cuba and men of the Florida militia. The men of both groups, according to the Narrator, were brave and steady soldiers. Several boats with light artillery accompanied the army.[19]

The Spanish force moved without difficulty to within range of the guns of the Insurgents, and on September 10 was sheltered behind a rise of ground when a sudden cannonade erupted, which killed two soldiers and wounded others. Despite the pleading of his officers, the major in command ordered an immediate retreat to St. Augustine. For the second time the frustrated Spanish governor faced an incompetent subordinate. The major was immediately imprisoned, and then court-martialed, but he was found guilty of an error in judgment, rather than of cowardice. For the duration of the Amelia Island affair, Coppinger took no further military action.

Only a week after the Spanish debacle, on September 21, a new element was added to the Fernandina scene. It was Luis Aury, under commission from an already defunct revolutionary Republic of Mexico, with two of his own privateering vessels and a prize ship. He had come at the urging of the same Pedro Gual who was one of the signers of MacGregor's commission and had expected to join the Scottish adventurer. MacGregor met him aboard ship at the mouth of the St. Marys and gave him full authority to move on Fernandina.

The French-born and virtually illiterate Aury had risen to command of the navy of New Granada during 1813 and 1814, and since that time had assembled his own private fleet as a privateering force. In the fall of 1816 he had established a base in Spanish territory at Galveston

Island, modeled on the establishment of Jean Lafitte at
Barataria. From here he had operated under the flag of
the Republic of Mexico before shifting his base of operations farther south to Matagorda Bay. Lafitte, in turn,
moved into the abandoned Galveston Bay location. In
many ways Lafitte and Aury were cut from the same
mold. It is perhaps this similarity which lies behind the
persistent, but undocumented, latter-day statements of
the presence of Lafitte himself in early Fernandina.

Aury reached an agreement with Hubbard and Irwin.
Hubbard would remain civil governor, while Aury
would become commander-in-chief of the military and
naval forces, with Irwin as his adjutant-general. The flag
of Mexico was raised over Fernandina, and Aury's substantial crew of ruffians, including about 130 piratical
Haitian mulattoes, became the dominant force on Amelia
Island. Hubbard soon became dissatisfied with the arrangement and began to attempt to force Aury out. Thus
was born what came to be called the "French" and the
"American" parties on Amelia.

While things were still in this tense state, the Venezuelan privateer *America Libre* arrived in port on October 4 bearing Pedro Gual, the fiery South American
journalist Vicente Pazos, and a number of European officers, including Augustin Codazzi, Augusto Gustavo
Villaret, and Maurice Persat. With this additional support, Aury replaced Hubbard as civil governor, naming
Pedro Gual in his stead. Hubbard's group took up arms,
but were quickly crushed by the French party. On October 19 Hubbard died from a fever, and Aury's group
was fully in power. The combined land and naval forces
amounted to about four hundred men and five armed

vessels, a very considerable increase over a month before.[20]

It is at this point that one again picks up the first-hand account of the Narrator. Arriving on October 25, he and his fellow British officers were first met by a boat crew of the American brig *Saranac*, engaged in their assigned task of preventing smuggling. Then they were greeted by Captain Liers of the *Morgiana*, Hubbard's ship. Captain Liers took the Narrator and several others ashore and introduced them to Aury. There, for the first time, they learned that MacGregor had departed, and were further informed by Aury that he was already overstocked with officers. And as they began to understand the general composition of the town, disillusionment set in. Apparently not realizing the true strength of the French party, they began to plot with some of the Americans to overthrow Aury. Irwin, however, would not cooperate, and in disgust the Narrator and some others left Fernandina and crossed over to the town of St. Marys in Georgia, abandoning the Insurgent cause.

The Narrator had been in St. Marys only three days when he was asked to return to Fernandina to defend a British naval officer who was to be tried for treason. Seemingly this was a result of the continued plotting both before and after the Narrator had departed Amelia Island. McDonald had set up a third, a British, party, and with some defections from the American party had in effect strengthened Aury's hand. On November 5 Aury declared martial law, banished members of the American party, and arrested some of the British officers.

The trial itself provides an additional insight into the power struggle. Captain Liers was the first president of the court-martial, but when he appeared to be leaning toward the Narrator's case, perhaps because of his earlier identification with Hubbard and the American party, Aury ordered him to embark and appointed replacements to the panel. Nevertheless, the Narrator won his case by securing the sentence of banishment for his client. Arrested after a fist fight with McDonald, the Narrator himself was banished from the Floridas, a punishment which amused him.

Once back in St. Marys the Narrator received an invitation from Governor Coppinger to visit St. Augustine, presented by the surveyor-general of East Florida, probably George J. F. Clarke. This journey and a second one early in 1818 to the same city provide most of the interesting insights of the Narrator on conditions in Spanish East Florida late in the Second Spanish Period.

With his power consolidated, Aury moved forward in several areas. Prize vessels and merchantmen continued to fill the harbor. By November 1, prize goods valued at $500,000 had been disposed of in Fernandina, and there was a report that more than a thousand slaves had been sold into Georgia. In another area he was being helped substantially by Vicente Pazos. All of Aury's proclamations and letters were undoubtedly from the hand of this man, who was also instrumental in drafting the resolutions for the election of nine representatives to draw up a plan for the creation of the Republic of the Floridas. Pazos also became editor of *El Telégrafo de las Floridas*, a newspaper published on the island.

Insofar as the government of the United States was concerned, however, matters on Amelia Island were going from bad to worse. There was much concern over the establishment of the port as a smuggling base. Among others, John Houstoun McIntosh, the titular leader of the earlier Patriot uprising, wrote on October 30 about the deplorable conditions at Amelia and suggested breaking up Aury's establishment.[21] There were many such complaints. But an even stronger reason existed for the eviction of Aury. The entire incident had become an annoying third element in the negotiations between Spain and the United States on the cession of the Floridas. Whereas the route of sanctioned revolutions had earlier served its purpose, the United States now preferred to proceed by diplomatic negotiation.

At a meeting of the cabinet on October 31 the Amelia Island situation was discussed, a decision was reached, and President James Monroe immediately ordered the secretary of the navy to dispatch a squadron to join the army forces under the command of Major James Bankhead in evicting Aury from the island. The actual orders went forward on November 12 and 14. Those to Bankhead were simply to take possession of Amelia Island in cooperation with the naval force. Commander J. D. Henley was directed to take command of the U.S.S. *John Adams* and proceed with the brigs *Enterprise* and *Prometheus* and the schooner *Lynx* to the St. Marys River, where he would find the brig *Saranac* and gun-boat No. 168. He was then to cooperate with a landing force that would occupy Amelia Island.[22]

President Monroe informed Congress on December 2 of his actions, while the representatives in Fernandina were still busily working on the fundamental rules for their new democratic government. Lino de Clemente in Philadelphia dispatched a letter to Amelia Island as soon as he heard the news from Washington. Consternation reigned, and many left the island to enroll in other campaigns elsewhere.

So there was really no surprise at the appearance of the United States squadron, nor at the joint message of Henley and Bankhead on December 22 informing Luis Aury that they were directed to occupy Amelia Island. Pazos wrote a very passionate and interesting reply for Aury, but it was really a declaration of capitulation. On December 23, 1817, American forces entered Fernandina. Soon thereafter the long secret act of 1811 was released for publication, revealing to the general public for the first time the basis for many of the actions taken by the United States in this and previous incursions.[23]

All of the insurgents did not leave at once; the Narrator found a dispirited group still there when he revisited the place in mid-January 1818. Aury arrived in Charleston in mid-March and was promptly arrested on an old piratical charge, but it was dismissed.[24] He was last heard from cruising off the north coast of Cuba in 1820. Others involved in the Amelia Island Affair had spread far and wide by the end of January, and the Narrator tells of McDonald's fate in his concluding chapter. MacGregor was rumored to be planning a descent on Tampa Bay, and while this never materialized, fear of it was one factor in the 1818 campaign of Andrew Jackson.

The Amelia Island Affair was ended. The flags of several nations and pseudo-nations had flown over Fernandina in a brief half-year. And one of the remarkable things is that during the entire tumultuous episode only two men were killed in action, the unfortunate Spanish soldiers in the abortive attack in September. Perhaps it is this relatively bloodless aspect, coupled with the panoply of exotic revolutionary regimes, the romance of privateering, and the undoubtedly colorful personalities, which has led some to characterize the entire proceedings as comic opera. There is something of the intrigue of mythical principalities about it, yet to those who participated it was a deadly serious business. Motivations from crass to noble moved the actors, but in the end it was only the United States which could be regarded as a winner. Although Spain protested the occupation, it could be pointed to as a service to the crown, while at the same time it constituted a veiled threat.

Only one other major event was to create an overt snag in negotiations between Spain and the United States, and that was the intrusion once again of Andrew Jackson into the peninsula in the spring of 1818. As early as the previous summer reports were heard that the Seminole were gathering and that British agents were once again supplying them. The previously mentioned rumor of a possible second MacGregor assault was also known. Action on both sides of the border between Indians and Americans erupted and the secretary of war ordered action against the Seminole, even into Florida. Jackson was later to argue that President Monroe authorized him to take possession of the Floridas, and the total truth of this matter is still controversial.

Jackson crossed into Florida on March 10, 1818, moving down the Apalachicola and building Fort Gadsden before taking over Fort St. Marks from the Spaniards. In a whirlwind campaign as far east as the Suwannee River, he hit at the Seminole and captured two

British subjects, Alexander Arbuthnot and Robert Christie Ambrister. Following a court-martial, both men were executed on April 29. Moving on, Jackson turned westward and in late May occupied Pensacola, before returning home. This entire episode is known as the First Seminole War.

The ensuing official and public clamor swept the nation. Spain protested strongly, and in the United States cabinet only John Quincy Adams supported Jackson's actions. Congressional debate went on for twenty-seven days, but four motions to vote censure were refused. The forts and Pensacola were returned to Spain, and negotiations proceeded.

It was the execution of the two British subjects which most incensed the Narrator. The events may have been taking place while he was still touring the United States, but he does not say. His long appendix is basically made up of the documentary record of the court-martials of Arbuthnot and Ambrister, and in fact the reprinted documents parallel exactly those printed in *Niles' Weekly Register*, to which he undoubtedly had access.[25] To the body of the documentation he adds a bitter denunciation of Jackson, an appraisal of the legal proceedings, and an appeal for England to vindicate her honor. The British government, however, lodged no formal protest.

In spite of, or some would say perhaps even because of, the Jackson incident, a treaty of cession was finally signed on February 22, 1819, the same year in which the *Narrative of a Voyage to the Spanish Main in the Ship "Two Friends"* appeared in print. After a second ratification two years later, the United States took formal possession of the Floridas in the summer of 1821, and Andrew Jackson was appointed the first territorial governor.

Having run full cycle on the military and political events of the Second Spanish Period of Florida, it is now time to examine the Narrator's contribution to our geographical, social, and cultural understanding of the time. Usually, when the Narrator is dealing with events he neglects descriptive detail, but he does at times insert rather lengthy descriptive passages. Some of this occurs in the sections dealing with Madeira and St. Thomas, while Chapters 8 through 10 of the *Narrative* provide most of the descriptive material on the land and people of Spanish Florida. These chapters revolve around the two trips from the northern boundary to St. Augustine, with travel overland one way on each trip. The Narrator describes countryside, plantation life, simple graziers' quarters, towns, and people, and in so doing provides the reader with some of the best information for this period of Florida history.

On his second visit to St. Augustine, after a tiring ride from the head of the North River, he approached the darkened city. He wrote: "The clock was striking ten as I reached the foot of the draw-bridge; the sentinels were passing the *alerto*, as I demanded entrance; having answered the preliminary questions, the draw-bridge was slowly lowered." In this writing the Narrator provides in a single sentence the only two doubts concerning his objectivity in reporting. First, the matter of the clock: The most likely location for a clock would have been the Parish Church, now the Cathedral, but no clock was listed in the 1798 accounting of expense for the building, nor is it shown in Ramón de la Cruz's elevation of the facade drawn in 1821.[26] Perhaps there was a clock elsewhere, although it seems unlikely, or perhaps one should interpret the striking of the clock as a literary figure of speech used by the Narrator.

The drawbridge is a more difficult problem to dismiss. The Narrator not only mentions reaching it but also seeing it slowly lowered. The problem is that there never was a drawbridge at the City Gate of St. Augustine. A careful review of the contemporary engineers' reports leaves us no doubt about the question. Could the Narrator have confused one of the drawbridges of the Castillo de San Marcos? Repairs in 1817 *may* have put the ravelin drawbridge of the Castillo back into operation, but the main drawbridge was definitely still in a fixed position because of its deteriorated condition.

Even if the ravelin drawbridge was functioning, it would make no sense for the Narrator to be presenting himself for entrance at that location. To reach that point he would already have passed through the City Gate, which was the control point. And the ravelin drawbridge led only to the inside of the Castillo, which was certainly not where the governor was. Apparently the Narrator was in error on this point. He did not arrive at a drawbridge and have it lowered for him; he appeared before the City Gate and it opened for him. Twenty-three miles on horseback are probably enough to dull anyone's recollection. An issue is made of this not to discredit the Narrator, for there are few other, if any, points of actual observation that one can challenge. His account is, however, the apparent source for all later statements concerning a drawbridge at the City Gate.

At any rate, having gained the city, the Narrator presented himself once again to Governor Coppinger with whom he had apparently established quite friendly relations on his earlier visit. He doubtless visited with him on several occasions, and on one of these, on the basis of circumstantial evidence, he probably encountered an interesting group of young American visitors to St. Augustine.

A party of naturalists representing the young Philadelphia Academy of Natural Sciences had come south to Spanish Florida that winter, traveling with a royal passport to insure their passage in the uncertain times. The group was headed by William Maclure, an older philanthropist and geologist who had sponsored the party. He was already the author of a pioneer work on the geology of the United States. The younger members were artist and naturalist Titian Peale, naturalist and philologist George Ord, and entomologist and conchologist Thomas Say, who was also the great-grandson of John Bartram. All were destined to become prominent leaders in nineteenth-century natural science.

But at the time of this account, the three young men had left Maclure in camp on the St. Johns River and had sloshed through the wet winter swamps from Picolata to St. Augustine. They were tired, dirty, and wet when they presented themselves that night at Governor Coppinger's house. The guards detained them on the ground floor because the governor was entertaining one or more British officers upstairs. It was apparently a rather long wait before they were ushered upstairs into the presence of Coppinger and his still seated guests.

The initial greeting was icy, with Coppinger haughtily demanding their business, but the atmosphere changed dramatically when the Spanish passport with its royal seal and signature was presented. Still, quarters for the trip could not be found, "until the British officer said, at their boarding house they might possibly be accommodated and sending, they got rooms for the party."[27] Of course, the writer cannot prove that the Narrator was that British officer. Yet, how many British officers were being entertained by Governor Coppinger in February 1818?

While in St. Augustine the Narrator saw his first Indians, and to his own observations he added those of "a gentleman of the province" to provide a sixteen-page portion of the narrative. This section is a valuable document in Seminole ethnography in the pre-American period. Of interest is the origin myth involving the creation of Man by the Great Spirit by means of modeling and firing him from clay. The successive firings to produce the black, white, and Indian racial stocks implies, of course, a knowledge of the three, and hence cannot be pre-Contact.[28]

The Narrator locates the village of Cowford as on the south side of the St. Johns River, presumably near the post of San Nicholas (pp. 133–37). And, one must take issue with his botany on page 138 when he states, "the root *mandihoca*, from which the *cassava* flour is made, is found in every direction." He was probably seeing *Smilax*, since it certainly was not *Manioc* and even *Zamia* does not grow in the area north of the St. Johns.

But now it is time for the Narrator himself to take over and present his story with that inimitable flavor to be found only in a contemporary account.

JOHN W. GRIFFIN.

Key West.

NOTES

1. See John Lynch, *The Spanish-American Revolutions, 1808–1826* (New York: W. W. Norton, 1973) for a full account.
2. *The Edinburgh Monthly Review*, Edinburgh, 2 (August 1819): 309–33. The reviewer, himself anonymous, objects to the anonymity of the Narrator. While not challenging the testimony of the book, the reviewer expresses an "unfavourable disposition" toward the author. To the contemporary reviewer the appendix is the most important part of the book, a view opposite to that taken in this introduction. We do concur with the reviewer when he says (p. 312): "It is hardly worth while to quarrel very much with the title page of any book; and yet we are greatly dissatisfied with that of the volume before us. Unless East Florida be called the *Spanish Main*, there is no 'voyage to the Spanish Main'; nor was the voyage to Florida made in the ship *Two Friends*, since it appears from the narrative, that this ship carried the author only to the island of St. Thomas in the West Indies...."
3. Only the 1819 edition is mentioned; apparently there were no others.
4. *Dictionary of National Biography*, s.v. Miller, William. See also S. Austin Allibone, *A Critical Dictionary of English Literature and British and American Authors*, vol. 2, 1898.
5. His legal background is made apparent on p. 102 of the narrative.
6. For the first years of the Second Spanish Period see Helen H. Tanner, *Zéspedes in East Florida, 1784–1790* (Coral Gables, Fla.: University of Miami Press, 1963).
7. The general account of border difficulties is mostly drawn from standard secondary sources such as Charlton W. Tebeau, *A History of Florida* (Coral Gables, Fla.:University of Miami Press, 1971) and J. E. Dovell, *Florida: Historic, Dramatic, Contemporary*, 4 vols. (New York: Lewis Publishing Company, 1952).
8. For the East Florida Rebellion and related events see Rembert W. Patrick, *Florida Fiasco: Rampant Rebels on the Georgia-Florida Frontier, 1810–1815* (Athens: University of Georgia Press, 1954).
9. *Niles' Weekly Register* 4 (May 29, 1813): 216.
10. The Negro Fort episode is recounted in many places, but for a good account see Mark F. Boyd, "Events at Prospect Bluff on the Apalachicola River, 1808–1818", *Florida Historical Quarterly* (October 1937).
11. James Grant Forbes, *Sketches, Historical and Topographical, of the Floridas* (New York, 1821; facsimile ed., University of Florida Press, Gainesville, 1964). Pride of India trees usually meant the chinaberry.
12. Partial excavation of Fort San Carlos is reported by Hale G. Smith and Ripley P. Bullen, *Fort San Carlos*, Florida State University Notes in Anthropology, vol. 14 (Tallahassee, 1971).

13. Unless otherwise noted, the account of the Amelia Island Affair is drawn from the *Narrative* itself and from the following sources: T. Frederick Davis, "McGregor's Invasion of Florida," *Florida Historical Quarterly* 7 (July 1928): 3–71; Richard G. Lowe, "American Seizure of Amelia Island," *Florida Historical Quarterly* 45 (July 1966): 18–30; Charles H. Bowman, Jr., "Vicente Pazos and the Amelia Island Affair, 1817," *Florida Historical Quarterly* 53 (January 1975): 273–95; and Bowman, "Vicente Pazos, Agent for the Amelia Island Filibusters, 1818," *Florida Historical Quarterly* 53 (April 1975): 428–42.

14. The *Narrative*, p. 53. On p. 87 the Narrator also states that Colonel Posen, United States Army, was MacGregor's second in command, but Francis B. Heitman, *Historical Register and Dictionary of the United States Army* (Washington, 1903) lists no one by the name of Posen. Closest is Thornton Posey, who was honorably discharged as a lieutenant colonel in 1815.

15. The Narrator is in error when he gives the date of occupation as July 9.

16. MacGregor proclaimed its capture, *Niles' Weekly Register* 12 (August 9, 1817): 376. A temporary abandonment by the Spanish garrison is noted by T. Frederick Davis, *History of Jacksonville and Vicinity, 1513 to 1924* (St. Augustine, 1925; facsimile ed., University of Florida Press, Gainesville, 1964), p. 36.

17. Our Narrator has him as a former congressman from Vermont; other sources say New Jersey. Pennsylvania is correct, however, for the then forty-nine-year-old native of Georgia who had served as colonel of the Fifth Rifle Regiment in the War of 1812, before serving in the 13th and 14th Congresses. See *Bibliographic Directory of the American Congress, 1774–1949* (Washington, 1950).

18. *Niles' Weekly Register* 13 (January 24, 1818).

19. In using the Narrative as a source, we must remember that it is a mixture of primary observation and second-hand material. All of Chapter VI on the MacGregor period predates the arrival of the Narrator, and in it he seems to state that the Spanish attack took place before MacGregor's departure, when in fact it occurred almost a week after that event.

20. Bowman, "Vicente Pazos and the Amelia Island Affair," pp. 280–82. The Narrator nowhere mentions Gual or Pazos.

21. *Niles' Weekly Register* 13 (January 3, 1818): 301–4.

22. *Niles' Weekly Register* 13 (January 24, 1818): 346–52.

23. *Niles' Weekly Register* 13 (January 10, 1818): 315–16.

24. *Niles' Weekly Register* 14 (April 4, 1818): 92–93.

25. *Niles' Weekly Register* 15 (December 12, 1818): 270–81.

26. I am deeply indebted to Luis Arana, National Park Service historian at the Castillo de San Marcos National Monument, St. Augustine, for information and discussion of the clock and the drawbridge.

27. Jessie Poesch, *Titian Ramsay Peale, 1799–1885, and His Journals of the Wilkes Expedition* (Philadelphia: American Philosophical Society, 1961). I am grateful to Mrs. Betty Bruce, Monroe County Library, Key West, Florida, for calling this reference to my attention.

28. A major portion of the Seminole data has been reprinted and annotated. See John W. Griffin, "Some Comments on the Seminole in 1818," *Florida Anthropologist* 10 (November 1957): 41–49.

NARRATIVE

OF A

VOYAGE TO THE SPANISH MAIN,

&c. &c. &c.

NARRATIVE

OF

A Voyage to the Spanish Main,

IN THE

SHIP "TWO FRIENDS;"

The occupation of Amelia Island, by M'Gregor, &c.—Sketches of the Province of East Florida;

AND

ANECDOTES ILLUSTRATIVE OF THE HABITS AND MANNERS OF THE SEMINOLE INDIANS:

WITH AN

Appendix,

CONTAINING

A DETAIL OF THE SEMINOLE WAR,

AND THE

EXECUTION OF ARBUTHNOT AND AMBRISTER.

" Nihil est aptius ad delectationem lectoris quam temporum varietates, fortunæque vicissitudines."

London:

PRINTED FOR JOHN MILLER, BURLINGTON ARCADE, PICCADILLY.

1819.

PREFACE.

The following narrative was compiled at the request of several friends, desirous of possessing a detailed account of the ill-fated expedition, in which the narrator was engaged.

The narrator has left untouched, the merits of the original question, between the Insurgents of Spanish America, and the parent state, fully aware of his incompetence to determine a subject of such grave importance, merely animadverting upon the conduct of the cause, and its probable progress, with the view of explaining his motives, for dissuading his countrymen from giving implicit credit to the specious promises and false representations of interested individuals.

The cause of Venezuela, has been too much identified in the public mind, with that of Buenos Ayres. Forgetful of the vast distance separating those provinces, the variety of climate, and the marked characteristic distinctions of their inhabitants, the British public has considered them as one people, actuated by a common motive, and capable of similar exertions.

On the European continent, a space far more limited, presents nations totally dissimilar, in habits, language, and feelings. How then can we imagine the people of Spanish America, who are avowedly less enlightened from the nature of their government, and their Colonial restrictions, than the people of Europe, capable of a simultaneous effort in support of the cause of freedom, and appreciating the advantages of rational liberty.

The occupation of Amelia Island, is inserted as a part of the cause of South America, because it emanated from a scion of the Venezuelan republic, and was subsequently supported by a pretended agent of that of Mexico, a republic which never had any other than ideal existence.

The account of East Florida, and the peculiar habits of the Seminole Indians, has followed as a matter of course in the progress of the narration, though not properly entitled to be classed with the avowed object of this publication, the narrator, however, hopes that the novelty and interest of the subject may plead his apology for the insertion.

For the Appendix and observations on the Seminole war, and the murder of our unfortunate countrymen, Arbuthnot and Ambrister, by the fiat of General Jackson, the narrator feels it unnecessary to offer an apology. The high and important character of his countrymen, their national honour and personal security, compromised by this barbarous act of a vindictive foreigner, will sufficiently interest their feelings, and relieve him from the charge of intrusion.

The narrator warns his countrymen from admitting too credulously, the statements of the North American Commissioners, who were sent out by their government, to ascertain the progress and prospects of the Insurgents; not that he would for one moment hazard a suspicion of the integrity of those Gentlemen, to whom the commission was entrusted, or a doubt that they have given any other than their impressions, but on account of the peculiar circumstances under which they visited the various States of South America. Their mission was expected by the Insurgents, who were fully advised of the nature and importance of their visit, avowed by the President of the United States in his message to Congress, as a prelude to the recognition of South

American independence, by the North American Union, which would follow their report, if favourable to the existence of those infant republics. That the Insurgents would give the most imposing character to their establishments, could not be doubted. We find the American flag received by them, with all that glitter and parade, the established usage of recognised governments. From the Insurgent Chiefs, every thing relative to their resources and objects was learnt, and the prejudices of the commissioners, in favour of their own federative system of government, flattered by the assurance, that those infant republics would copy and adopt their institutions.

The narrator commits this narrative to the public, aware of its numerous imperfections, relying upon their liberal interpretation of his motives and expressions.

CONTENTS.

CHAP. I.

Introductory matter. - - - - - - - - PAGE 1

CHAP. II.

Arrive at Portsmouth—the general feeling in favour of our objects—delay of the ship in taking in wines, &c.—fabricated reports to induce our embarkation—consent to proceed to Madeira for our wine—embark—foul wind drove us about the channel—fair wind—vanity of my comrades—false expectations of the generality of the adventurers—state of the ship's provisions, miserable—near Madeira the captain endeavours to avoid going into that island—arrive off Madeira, and make the passage of the Deserter Rocks—attempt to land in the boat, fired at—endeavouring to anchor after sun-set, fired at—land at Madeira—duel—description of Funchal and the surrouning hills—muleteers—equestrianism—the soi-disant chamberlain of Austria—visit the monastery of Dominican friars, and the nunnery—folly and excesses of my comrades—sapient opinions of M'Donald—assumed rank of our heroes—discover a dangerous character—embark for St. Thomas's - - - 10

CONTENTS.

CHAP. III.

Sail from Madeira—quarrel between M'Donald and the captain—meet a patriot privateer—enter the tropic of cancer—disgusting ceremony of shaving—opposed by some of the passengers—trade winds—beauty of the clouds in those latitudes—disputes and quarrels—duel between O. and the Irish apothecary—its farcical termination—Christophe and his drinking party, their ludicrous exhibitions—make the land, the island of Barbuda—St. Bartholemew's, Sabra, St. Kitt's, Sombrero, and Nevis—the Virgin Gordas, St. John's, Tortola, and open the view of St. Thomas's—beautiful appearance of the West India islands—St. Thomas's—state of our provisions. - - - - - 31

CHAP. IV.

Land at St. Thomas's—silly conduct of M'Donald—our disappointments—reported state of affairs on the Spanish main—wounded officers from the insurgents—the Two Friends sails clandestinely—miserable account of the schooner that preceded us—the death and dispersion of her passengers—fatal duel—several determine to proceed to Amelia island, others to return to England—hire an American schooner for Florida—*permitted* to embark, by orders from the governor of Santa Cruz—loyal refugees from the Spanish Main, their misery—description of the island of St. Thomas's—the pirate Black Beard, his story—dignity ball—a death. - - - - - - 40

CHAP. V.

Departure from St. Thomas's—arrive at Turk's island—manner of making salt—Americans permitted an intercourse—M'Donald's folly—quit Turk's island—attack upon the town at night—our outrage—visited by the magistrates—M·Donald's proposal to carry the fortress of Port Plate in St. Domingo—his plans, their absurdity—dying dolphin—a calm—sharks, one taken near the gulph stream, see a sail, suppose her a spaniard—determine to take her—hoists American colours—

CONTENTS.

M'Donald's disappointment—he boards her in full costume—frightens the captain's wife and child—make the coast of East Florida—supposed off St. Mary's river—M'Donald and his satellites land—discover we had mistaken the entrance of the St. John's for that of the St. Mary's—apprehensive that M'Donald and his party are taken by the Spaniards—arrive at Amelia island—Commodore Aury in command—M'Gregor gone to the Bahamas—escape and arrival of M'Donald at head quarters—decline employment at Amelia. - - - 65

CHAP. VI.

Account of the expedition of M'Gregor against Amelia Island—its capture—M'Gregor forms a depot for privateers—his financial difficulties—expedition of Spanish troops from St. Augustine against M'Gregor, their defeat—the Spanish commander tried by a court-martial—schisms among M'Gregor's forces—arrival of Commodore Aury—Aury agrees to pay the debts of the Amelian treasury, upon being made commander of the forces—Mr. Hubbard, civil governor—M'Gregor assigns his command to Aury, and retires—Aury's impolitic system towards the Americans. - - - - 81

CHAP. VII.

M'Donald's dishonourable conduct—meditated revolution in Amelia—proposed coalition of English and Americans against the French party of Aury—Colonel Irvin refuses to co-operate—determine to quit Amelia—arrive at St. Mary's in Georgia—sickness at St. Mary's and the dreadful endemic at Charlston—requested to defend a British officer on trial at Amelia, for high treason—arbitrary proceedings of the court-martial—prisoner ordered for transportation—sent off to the Morgiana brig—quarrel and personal contest with M'Donald—arrested by the adjutant-general—garrison in a state of alarm—confined under a corporal's guard—unpleasant situation of

CONTENTS.

PAGE.

one of my friends—embarked for St. Mary's and banished the republic of the Floridas—arrive at St. Mary's—a party of Americans at St. Mary's waiting an opportunity to revolutionize Amelia—offered ample encouragement to join them—invited by the governor of East Florida to visit St. Augustine—engage a passage for St. A.—oblige Colonel Irvin to apologize to my friend the Lieutenant—embark for St. Augustine. 98

CHAP. VIII.

Sail for St. Augustine—friendly reception of the governor and inhabitants—description of St. Augustine—the fort of St. Mark's—Catholic the established religion—Protestants admitted to citizenship—climate—former state of the province of East Florida—Americans excluded from holding land—society of St. A.—beauty of the women—attempt of the Americans against St. A.—their defeat and dispersion—obtain a grant of land—treatment of negroes superior to other slave states—offer to retake Amelia Island. - - - - 116

CHAP. IX.

Depart for St. Mary's—pass through the Royal road—overtaken by a storm—sleep at a grazier's—suspicious character of our host—murder committed by his two sons—arrive at the village of Cowford—description of that part of the river St. John's—party of back-woodmen—they remain with us as guards against the apprehended attack of Aury's gang—illness of one of my companions—his recovery—kidnapping of negroes—character of the people on the back frontier of Georgia—pursue our route across the St. John's—disappointed of a breakfast—way-laid and fired at—one of the assailants wounded—proves to be their guide—arrive at a grazier's, good fare—proceed on our journey and arrive on the confines of Okufenokey—badness of the roads—arrive at St. Mary's—find my fellow-passengers from

CONTENTS.

England wind bound—death of one of the party—embark for Charlston. - - - - - - 129

CHAP. X.

The Americans take possession of Amelia—embark for that Island—fallen fortunes of the patriots—ball given by the officers of the United States navy—proceed for St. Augustine—pass the St. John's River to the plantation of a friend—the scite of the town of St. John's—account of Rolle's Town—the object of the founder—proceed to another plantation—method of cultivating cotton and rice—agreeable life of a planter—set forward for St. Augustine—the carnival—the Seminole Indians—their habits—anecdotes respecting them, illustrative of their manners and feelings—the barbarous character of the war carried on by the Americans against them—General Jackson—anecdotes respecting him—depart for Charlston. - - - 147

CONCLUDING CHAPTER.

Arrival of the *Two Friends*, at Margaretta—the reception by the Commander, General Aresmendez—the captain of the *Two Friends*, proceeds up the Oronoco—the ship quits Margaretta, and escapes to Aux Cayes—four of her passengers ascending the Oronoco, are taken by the Spaniards—the unemployed passengers, at Margaretta, sent off the Island—M'Donald proceeding up the Oronoco, is shot by the Indians, with one of his companions—meet in the United States, officers, who had quitted the Insurgent cause—Foreigners omitted in the accounts of their battles, and the jealousy that opposes their progress—Sir Gregor M'Gregor's policy—his present plan to join Aury—their probable objects—The importance of Venezuela to the Spaniards—the danger of the climate, and its influence upon Europeans—the declining state of the Insurgents—titles of nobility, their influence on the Creoles—Morillo recruits from among the Creole population—treatment of French officers, at Buenos Ayres—the general ignorance in

CONTENTS.

PAGE

England respecting the state of the contest in Venezuela—the Morning Chronicle, the sole channel of information—the independance of South America, desirable to the British—favourable disposition of the United States to South American independance—their probable motives: 183

APPENDIX.

CHAP. I.

PAGE

The Seminole war—execution of Arbuthnot and Ambrister, &c.

ERRATA.

N. B. The reader is requested to observe, that from an oversight of the printer, the references from the notes are made to the *manuscript* instead of the *printed copy*: they should stand as follows—

Note A page 27.
B 36.
C 79.
D 84.
E 107.
F 148.
G 149.
H 175.
I 180.

Page	line		
15	6	*for* Shackaes,	*read* Shackoes.
17	12	*for* alleviations,	*read* alleviation.
18	20	*for* Southerns,	*read* Southern.
30	1	*for* these,	*read* they.
46	4	*for* progres,	*read* progress.
81	13	*for* priaries,	*read* prairies.
130	26	*for* covertion,	*read* covert on.
133	4	*for* rose,	*read* arose.
136	1	*for* yomime,	*read* yomini.
——	3	*for* unabled,	*read* unable.
178		the last line to be read first.	
186	1	*for* from those,	*read* by those.
190	8	*for* take,	*read* stake.
192	7	*for* foreign manufacture,	*read* foreigners manufacture.
197	3	*for* evince,	*read* evinces.
210	5	*for* W. W. Webb,	*read* W. W. Bebb.
277	7	*for* were,	*read* was.

(*To face page* 313.)

NARRATIVE, &c.

CHAP. I.

INTRODUCTORY MATTER.

THE contest between Spain and her South American possessions had long excited the lively interest and generous sympathy of the British public, and they deemed holy the arduous struggle of the Insurgents to throw off the sovereignty of the parent State, confidently anticipating that the revolution would terminate in favour of a people armed against the most oppressive tyranny, and the most revolting superstition.

Without examination, and indeed without information upon this interesting and important subject, they permitted their characteristic warmth of heart to reject the suspicions and doubts that justice demanded, and prudent enquirers would have investigated and entertained.

Increased by the peculiar circumstances of the times, this tide of feeling was at its height. The tranquil state of the political communities of Europe had withdrawn the public attention from a contemplation which had by turns agitated, agonized, and delighted their sensibilities. This feverish state of existence, nourished by twenty-five years of constant aliment, could not be subdued by a sudden revulsion, but required temporary sustenance, and gradual reduction; and they eagerly dwelt upon the struggles of South America, as a fruitful source from which to minister to their diseased appetites. Availing themselves of this critical juncture, the friends and partisans of the Insurgents caught at the public prepossession in their favour, and announced, with pompous exultation, battles which had never been fought, and victories which had never been gained. The Spaniards, whom the inconstant public had lauded with the highest commendation for bravery and patriotic devotion in their resistance to the invasion of their country by Napoleon Buonaparte, were now, in their transatlantic contest, stigmatised as cowards in every battle, and dastards in every flight. The mistaken policy of Spain induced her to look upon the farrago of lies and nonsense, with which the columns of some of our journals teemed, with cold indifference; opposing only that contemptuous silence which may disarm an individual of malice, but can never influence a people, instead of meeting those statements with the refutation of facts. That nation has yet to learn, that the pen is more powerful, and its operation more extensive, than the swords of thousands, however just the cause of their espousal.

The reduction of the army and navy, at the conclusion of the war, had thrown from employment numbers of young and ardent spirits; and the fatigue of indolence which followed the dissipations of the capital, and the exhaustion of their resources, called for some new object to occupy their time, and interest their feelings.

An individual, calling himself Don Luis Lopez Mendez, from the Caraccas, and his co-adjutor, a Mr. W. Walton, a citizen of North America, acted as agent and interpreter to the republic of Venezuela; the latter, whose name had been already known to the public as the author of a work upon St. Domingo, published to the world a captivating account of the resources of a continent highly interesting, though little known to European society, and an exposé, presented by him, to the Prince Regent, upon the state of South America, excited the public curiosity, and induced them to receive with confidence, and to admit without suspicion, the pompous fictions of his brain. Their subordinates, acting in the same spirit of deception, sought with eager anxiety individuals to support their system, and aid their resources; and the road of honour and promotion was offered in captivating colours to the ambition and cupidity of the unemployed of both army and navy. Adventurers, for in this land of credulity there is no want of daring enthusiasm and enterprize, flocked to the standard of those pseudo Patriots, devoting themselves with an energy worthy of a better fate, to the emancipation of the enslaved population of Venezuela and Caraccas.

The loss of a beloved parent, and some circumstances of a painful and distressing nature, over which I had neither controul nor influence, induced me to seek relief to my feelings in absence from my country; and this contest, which my prejudices in favour of rational liberty had led me to respect, caused me to listen with attention to proposals at once imposing and seductive; hoping in their reality, and consulting my wishes for absence, I joined the party who were to embark at Portsmouth in the ship *Two Friends;* determined, notwithstanding the enthusiasm of the moment, to investigate the cause before I would so far commit myself as to become identified with it, and one of its supporters. To detail this infatuated enterprize, to describe the miseries of my comrades, and our disappointments, is the object of the present narrative, hoping, at the same time, that it may deter others from becoming the victims of credulity, and the devoted instruments of wicked and unprincipled men, who would willingly make the bodies of their generous allies steps to their ambition and power.

A publication of this kind has been long called for, but absence has withheld me from acquitting myself of a debt, that, as an individual, I owe to society. To arrest the tide of infatuation which still flows, and threatens with destructive influence more of the generous and enterprising of my country—to lessen its force, if not to controul its current, is as much as an individual can hope from his solitary testimony.

Out of eighty passengers on board the *Two Friends*, many have sunk under their accumulated sufferings to rise no more; others, whose minds were not sufficiently strong to encounter the frowns of fortune, and the desolation of their hopes, have, from the despondency of feeling, and pressure of misfortune in the loss of reason, lost the sense of calamity. Some were doomed to wander about the West India Islands in abject misery, exposed to the destructive influence of climate, and the horrors of famine, until the generous kindness of Admiral Harvey induced him to furnish many of those victims with passages to England. In my progress through the United States of America, I have seen those who are perhaps destined by this calamitous adventure, to eternal separation from that home dear to every Englishman; scarcely twenty have joined the cause of South America, and many of that unfortunate number were of the least respectable, whose misfortunes, follies, or indiscretions had concurred to impel them to self banishment from their country, and to seek, in the dangers of distant and destructive climes, relief to the misery, and refuge from the pains of retrospection.

With feelings at once ungenerous and unjust, some of the public journalists have lavished abuse and falsehood upon the characters and motives of those, who deemed it more consistent with their honor to abandon the cause of despotism and deception, than to support that system in the prostituted names of liberty and patriotism; that their charges and vituperative calumnies have not been repelled with indignation, and their accusations refuted with equal publicity by those who have earlier returned, is to me a matter of equal surprise and regret.

I may assert, without fear of contradiction, that there never assembled such a number of young men as were collected for this unfortunate expedition, whose appearance was more favourable, and whose energies, if properly controuled and directed, would have redounded higher to their own honour, or the credit of the country that gave them birth; but unfortunately for their hopes and anticipations, many were abandoned to the guidance of a weak and contemptible adventurer, or left to the influence of their own wayward feelings. Can it be a subject of surprise that those ardent young men, unrestrained by prudence and reflection, who had been accustomed to the strict discipline of Lord Wellington's army, and to the undisputed severity of the navy, should be guilty of excesses unwarrantable, and highly discreditable, and for which an apology is impossible? In the relation of facts, I am well aware there will be found much to condemn, much to censure in their conduct; but I do not come before the public as their advocate—I do not ask of the severe moralist to relax his system of ethics in favour of those unfortunate, deluded, and erring individuals, but their sufferings and disappointments (for they have amply expiated their offences) demand that charity of opinion, that sympathy enjoined by the doctrines, and recommended by the example of the author of christianity.

Juvenile vitium regere non posse impetum.

The agent to the Insurgents of Venezuela had promised to those who were willing to join the standard of the republic, on their arrival in Venezuela, an additional step in rank to that held previously by the individual in the British army and navy; the pay and allowances of the various grades were distinctly stipulated, and were no trifling baits to those adventurers, the greater part of whom had solely to depend upon their pay for existence; in addition to which, he asserted his authority to promise each, on arrival at head quarters, or the place of debarkation on the Spanish main, or Island of Margaretta, the sum of two hundred dollars, payable by the republican government, to cover the expences out. His myrmidons had chartered a ship of 250 tons, called the *Two Friends*, in which passages were engaged at forty pounds each person, for which the owners agreed to provide a sufficiency of live and other stock, and to allow one pint of wine, half a pint of spirits, and a bottle of porter per day. Our first destination was the Island of St. Thomas's, where we were to meet an accredited agent from Venezuela, whose instructions were to direct our future proceedings, and designate the port of debarkation, to which an insurgent vessel of war was to convoy and protect us from the ships of the enemy; to anticipate this arrangement, Mendez asserted he had dispatched instructions to the government he represented.

After a long and tedious delay in the river, the *Two Friends* sailed for Gravesend, where several of her passengers embarked, and proceeded in her for Portsmouth; at that port by far the greater number were waiting to join.—From that period my narrative commences.

CHAP. II.

Arrived at Portsmouth—the general feeling in favour of our objects—delay of the ship in taking on board wines, &c.—fabricated reports to induce our embarkation—consent to proceed to Madeira for our wine—embark—foul winds drive us about the channel—fair wind—vanity of my comrades—false expectations of the generality of the adventurers—state of the ship's provisions miserable—near Madeira the Captain attempts to avoid going to that Island—arrive off Madeira, and make the passage of the Deserter Rocks—attempt to land in the boat, fired at—endeavouring to anchor after sun-set, fired at—land at Madeira—duel—description of Funchal and the surrounding hills—Muleteers—equestrianism—the *soi-disant* Chamberlain of Austria—visit the Monastry of Dominican Friars and the Nunnery—folly and excesses of my comrades—sapient opinions of M'Donald—assumed rank of our heroes—discover a dangerous character—embark for St. Thomas's.

On reaching Portsmouth, I found that the ship-agent and several of my companions had preceded me, and were anxiously awaiting the arrival of the ship from the Downs, where she had been several days detained by adverse winds. The streets of Portsmouth were crowded by my fellow adventurers, whose courage and devotion to the interests of oppressed human nature were designated as magnanimous and generous in the extreme; the extensive plains of South America were already, in idea, rendered smiling, and their population free and happy, by their philanthropic exertions, and the energies of the Insurgent armies: to doubt their complete success was at once deemed treason against liberty, and infidelity to a sacred cause, peculiarly the care of heaven.

Many days succeeded the arrival of the ship at Portsmouth, with little prospect of departure; the parties interested in her equipment had engaged here to take in their stock of wines, &c.; and we were anxiously and daily waiting our orders to embark; but the poverty of the parties, and their want of credit, uniting with their duplicity, created numerous delays and excuses: at one time, bonds could not be procured for the exportation of the wine, &c.; at another, stores were not obtainable; in the meantime, the small resources of my comrades were exhausted, and several were arrested for debt, while others, in secresy and retirement, avoided the durance vile which awaited their discovery. Profiting by their distressed situation, those unfeeling parties interested in the vessel circulated reports with industrious exertion, calculated to alarm their victims, and to induce them upon any terms to quit their country. Accounts were daily fabricated in, and forwarded from London, stating that our government had resolved to arrest the progress of the adventurers, who, in this event, saw the frustration of their darling hopes, and the total annihilation of their splendid expectations. Alarmed, as was expected, the majority were urgent to sail, and importuned the captain to quit the coast of England, in spite of a prevailing foul wind, rather than encounter the danger of delay, upon condition that we should stop at Madeira for those supplies so important to our health and comfort. This was the point the ship owners desired to gain, and they were in consequence liberal of their promises of compliance.

At ten o'clock on the evening of the 31st of July, 1817, the pilot went off to the ship, to carry her from the coast; all was hurry and confusion, and the appearance of the cabins presented a second chaos; the floors were strewed with beds, bedding, trunks, and packages of every description; upon these sat, smoking and drinking, those thoughtless adventurers, celebrating in noisy mirth their escape. About two o'clock in the morning a light but favourable breeze carried us beyond the floating light at St. Helen's. In the hurry of embarkation, three of our comrades had been left behind, and we were anxiously expecting their arrival, and fearful of our ability to stand off and on for them; when the favourable breeze subsided, and was succeeded by an adverse

South-Wester. We were, in consequence of this change, obliged to make long tacks to clear the Isle of Wight: in the meantime the pilot quitted us, promising, if possible, to bring off our luckless comrades :—The sun had nearly sunk in the West, and the hopes of seeing our companions were gradually diminishing, when the preconcerted signal from the pilot-boat assured us of their approach; the sails were immediately furled, and we hove to, to await their arrival. They had been joined by another adventurer, who had arrived only that morning from London, to increase the victims of our ill-fated expedition.

Adverse gales continued for several days, and we were driven about the channel, at the mercy of a tempestuous sea, alternately threatened with destruction under the Bill of Portland, and upon the rocky coasts of Capes Barfleur and La Hogue: to this succeeded a calm off Falmouth, which was followed by a strong North-Wester, carrying us into the Bay of Biscay, where we were several days tossed about, exposed to that dangerous navigation. Cape Ortugal frowned upon our course, and our anxiety to escape the high and rocky coast of Spain was increased by the fear of being obliged to seek shelter in a harbour of that nation. The object of our voyage, we doubted not, was already known to the Spanish government, and that they would attempt to arrest our progress was readily believed.

The sun had for several days withheld the cheering influence of his beams; despondency appeared to settle upon the minds and spirits of our party; the fates received their share of malediction, and not a saint in the calendar escaped the memories, and alternate prayers, and denunciations, of our good Catholics; when the exhilarating cry—" she comes up three points," roused our torpid faculties, and once more gave tone to our existence.* The gloom at length dispersed, and the god of day once more irradiated us with his presence, the animal spirits of my comrades returned with his beams, a display of military equipments glittered on the quarter-deck, and each seemed anxious to court the approbation of those around him, by splendid dresses, and highly polished arms. This vanity, the excusable and harmless folly of youth, was particularly conspicuous in those who formed the officers of a regiment of lancers, to be raised and commanded by a Mr. M'Donald, one of our fellow passengers, who was re-

---

* This nautical expression implies that the vessel will lie three points of the compass nearer her course.

ported to have served under the Spanish General Ballasteros, in the Peninsula war, with the rank of major of brigade. Their dresses were certainly handsome, green dragoon jackets, trimmed with silver lace, and faced with scarlet; epaulettes, with the rising sun of Venezuela: shackaes mounted with silver lace and gold cord, and surmounted with a yellow and blue plume, their saddles, &c. correspondently handsome. It was evident they had formed high anticipations of the resources of the republic, and had pictured to themselves Oriental splendour and enjoyment. These delusive hopes were not confined to the subaltern officers, but occupied the vivid imagination of their commander, who could not be persuaded to moderate his ambition by those who viewed the enterprize as they were likely to realise it. One of our steerage passengers, a low Irishman, who had served with some rank in the rebellion of Ireland, was the most successful in satirising their follies, and dissipating the airy phantoms of those brainless adventurers. He ridiculed their parade of military appointments, laughed at their gay equipments, telling them he should have to show them into the field—" By Jasus, give me a pike, or a half pike, and I'll be a better commander than any of ye! Was'nt I at

Vinegar-hill, where ye dars'nt show your noses—'twas too hot for ye."*

In the early part of our association, I was led to suspect there were but few induced to enter the cause of Spanish America, from motives of attachment to the principles of liberty; that suspicion was soon confirmed, and I found by far the greater part were uninfluenced by feelings so honorable. Driven from their country to avoid the fatigue of inaction, or the solicitations of their injured and clamorous creditors; alike to them whether they were to fight for or against his Catholic Majesty; whether they were to loosen or rivet the chains of slavery; enough for them, that there was an object of enterprize, and that they were to be far removed from the dunning of tradesmen, and the precincts of a prison.

The foul weather which succeeded our embarkation had soured their dispositions; betraying their natural feelings, even the most circumspect could not escape the general desolation. Disputes and quarrels followed each other in rapid succession; but in fact the miseries we endured were enough to de-

---

* This man, at St. Thomas's, hired himself as a negro-driver.

stroy the little philosophy we possessed. Two days had exhausted our fresh beef and vegetables : the salt provisions were hard and rancid, and had been purchased at the sales of condemned naval stores; our biscuit was worm-eaten and mouldy; and the few pigs provided for our passage, were as yet too transparent, and too nearly resembling carrion to excite our appetite. Without wine, and without spirits; reduced to the necessity of drinking sour, and foul porter; crowded together in a ship too small for our number, and little calculated for the voyage; without even the most trifling alleviations to our misery, it is to all surprising that we escaped contagious disease.

Such was our lamentable situation as we approached the latitude of Madeira; our proximity to that Island gave new energies to our existence, and the renovation we expected from our visit, already gave us (in idea), a foretaste of its advantages. It was now, for the first time, that our captain began to express his doubts of the propriety of proceeding to the island of Madeira, alleging as an excuse for his fears, that this departure from the course of his voyage, would vitiate his insurance, and deprive his owners of the protection of their policy. This was, however, evidently a pre-concerted pretext to avoid the engagement of his owners, and was doubtless a part of his instructions ere we left Portsmouth. The prospect of increasing misery, and the destruction that would have attended our progress through the warmer latitudes, had we pursued our voyage without wines, &c. determined us to insist upon his carrying the ship into the island; the fear of being deprived of her command, alone induced him to comply with our resolves.

The dawn of that morning, which presented to our ardent gaze, a view of the island of Madeira, was hailed with the most heartfelt satisfaction; the base of that beautiful island was enveloped in clouds; its lofty summits alone were seen as if floating upon the vapour, suspended between heaven and the ocean. It was, indeed, a spectacle worthy of the pencil of a painter, and the splendid imagination of a poet. The Deserter Rocks lay before us, presenting the dangerous experiment of a passage through the two southerns, to the alternative of continuing at least one day longer at sea. The day was extremely auspicious, and the wind sufficiently strong to warrant the risk of the attempt. These rugged rocks, rising abruptly from the bosom of the ocean, on either side of the narrow channel, which in its broadest part could not exceed three lengths of the ship, presented their barren and craggy precipices to our view, as if frowning on our temerity. All were in breathless anxiety, not a whisper even disturbed the heaving of the lead, and the warning voice of the man on the forecastle, directing the steersman, passed uninterrupted. We made in safety this dangerous passage, which is but seldom attempted, and three cheers testified our satisfaction. Towards the close of day we were nearing the anchorage ground in Funchal Bay; but the wind becoming light and adverse, a party of our comrades manned the ship's boat, in order to anticipate the arrival of their friends. As they came within the range of the guns, a shot from the battery warned them to desist, and obliged them to await the arrival of the pratique-boat, which slowly approached from the shore. The officer demanded from whence we came, and if provided with bills of health: this precaution had not been taken by our captain, unaware of the necessity, as we were direct from England; the officer, in consequence of the omission, refused permission to land, and stated it was too late to visit the ship for examination, but promised to board her early in the morning. This refusal annoyed them extremely, and many were for landing in spite of the interdiction; the attempt was made, when another shot from the battery, directed with better aim, within a few feet of the stern of the boat, warned those daring spirits once more to desist. The courage of the party began to cool upon this close application of advice, and they retired with reluctance, cursing the island and its inhabitants for their disappointments. M'Donald was one of the luckless party : in the bitterness of his resentment, he expressed a hope that he should be at no distant period ordered to reduce the island to the power of the independents, when he resolved to make the governor, and others in authority, repent his present annoyance. Out of humour, and impatient for the morrow, they returned on board, doubly mortified by the attempt, and its failure; the ship still stood in, the day had already closed when we prepared to anchor; two shots from the batteries that flank the town and protect the bay, now saluted us; one passed over our bows and the other through our rigging. These we afterwards found were fired in consequence of our attempt to anchor after sunset, contrary to the regulations of the port. We then stood off for the night, and in the morning having again reached the anchorage ground, the pratique officers relieved us from our thraldom.

Arrayed in all the glitter and parade of war, the

greater part of the passengers disembarked. Naval and military uniforms, gaily shone along the narrow streets of the town of Funchal, exciting the wondering gaze of the inhabitants, and the taverns were put in requisition to satisfy our craving appetites.

An affair of honour between a tall Irish officer of the 60th regiment, who had rendered himself extremely disagreeable to us all, and a wild thoughtless master's mate, created a little interest and variety to our conversation; they exchanged two shots without effect, when the seconds interfered, and terminated the affair, without detracting from the courage of either.

The island of Madeira, composed of a cluster of high hills, rises abruptly from the sea, forming at its base a considerable semi-circular bay. The cultivation of the hills, from their steep ascent, is in terraces, or ridges, presenting to the water, a bright, pleasing, and variegated landscape, adorned with vineyards and flower-gardens, intersected with groves of orange and other fruit-trees, at that time in full bearing, from which our tables were daily supplied, with the finest grapes, peaches, pears, oranges, and figs, of most delicious flavour.

The town of Funchal, situated at the base of the hills upon the bay, defended by two strong batteries at the extremities, is of tolerable extent ; the houses are generally built of stone, of cumbrous solidity, but like all old towns, and particularly those of the European continent, the streets are narrow, crooked, and ill designed, the houses wanting that neatness and uniformity so completely our own in England. Comfort, indeed, has seldom existence with foreigners, the word, as well as its meaning, is alike unknown in their language.— Some, however, of the residences of the merchants, and persons of condition, situated above the town, are handsomely constructed, and externally bear marks of taste.

The salubrity of the air, which has long rendered this island celebrated for the cure of pulmonary complaints, gives a degree of elasticity to the animal spirits, of which they are not susceptible in more northern regions, and of which I was fully sensible. Many unfortunate invalids were here, endeavouring for a time to cheat the tyrant death of his victims, though pale and emaciated, presenting merely the outline of the " human form divine;" they entered into our feelings, and dwelt upon our objects with lively interest, and would gladly have exchanged their inaction and crutches, for the rude assaults and weapons of war. Much, it is said, depends upon the state of the invalid on arrival; if the disease has reached a certain stage, the air rather accelerates, than retards the progress of destruction, from the constant excitement of the nerves, and the consequent exhaustion of the system; but in cases merely incipient, the atmosphere, by its stimulating properties, enables the invalid to throw off those vicious humours which otherwise destroy the lungs. This opinion upon the properties of the climate was given me by a professional friend, of some celebrity, and I think his hypothesis appears entitled to respect.

The lower orders of the people, retaining the traces of their Portuguese origin, are swarthy, dark, and dirty, their abodes the receptacles of filth and vermin. The women of the higher ranks have some pretensions to beauty, their black and expressive eyes, shining through their long dark eye-lashes, are more striking than seductive; the men, on the contrary, as if nature had exhausted her bounty on the other sex, are spiritless, idle, and demoralised, while the mountaineers, from their laborious habits and occupations, are active, vigorous, and enterprising.

We had not been long arrived at our hotel ere we were offered horses, mules, and asses, for hire, to ride up the mountains; the muleteers crowded about us, urgent in their offers, and were not to be refused. Some of our aspiring heroes mounted and displayed a variety of equestrianism, not to be exceeded in ridiculousness at an Easter hunt; a train of muleteers followed on foot, urging the speed of their unfortunate animals, with long Bamboo canes. Some of those ardent spirits, determined to evince their prowess, and to rehearse the dreadful charges they were to make among the enemies of liberty in South America, rushed down the steep streets at full speed, and suddenly checking their rozinantes, were precipitated from their saddles to the ground, and rose with broken heads and bloody faces, the objects of derision and contempt, to the astonished population. Never in my life did I witness such extravagant follies, such madness, as was daily, nay, hourly, presented by my comrades, giving but a sad *presentiment* of the issue of our enterprize. Their credulity, uniting with their ignorance of human nature, rendered them the ready listeners and believers of every tale, however extravagant. One evening, some of our adventurers met at their hotel a person to whom they listened with grave and gratified attention, who by half sentences, mysterious hints, and significant shrugs, excited their opinion in favour of his assumed importance, insinuating that he was an emissary from Maria Louisa, charged with communications to the Ex-Emperor at St. Helena. His *patois* French could not conceal the peculiar accent of a Scotchman; when charged with being a native of that country, he parried, but in vain, our enquiries, calling himself a German; and so convinced was one of my comrades (less credulous than his companions), of the fellow's impudent assumption, that he ordered him to quit the room, as an impostor and a blackguard. This pretended chamberlain to his Imperial Majesty of Austria (for he claimed that honour among other distinctions), did not feel his courage sufficiently elevated to contradict the charge, by a public display either of his personal prowess, or of his official documents; but sneaked off to that insignificance from which he had but recently emerged.

We visited the monastry of Dominican Friars, a heavy gothic structure, little indebted to external ornament; the fathers were preparing for dinner, the refectory was plain, and simply furnished; the tables were laid with clean, though coarse cloths, each cover garnished with a piece of bread, a cucumber, and a napkin. The arrangement bore evident marks of abstemiousness, but I presume their cells boasted the luxury of good wine, and other commensurate advantages, to compensate for those external marks of self denial. They politely shewed us the curiosities of their monastry, and their holy relics, and would have described their miraculous effects and influence, had we understood their language, and desired their information. In various recesses, screened from vulgar eyes by silk and other curtains, were misshapen wax figures of our Saviour and his virgin mother, the latter decked out in spangled gauzes and satins, hooped petticoats, and all the paraphernalia of the birth-day dresses of our high dames of the last century. The holy fathers approached these sanctuaries with slow and measured steps, and in half whispers (denoting their awe and veneration), informed us that they represented the immaculate virgin and her holy son. Our religious feelings were not elevated by those spectacles, our piety was displaced by pity and contempt, for the mass of human nature imposed upon by those absurd symbols of religion. We were not admitted to the grate of the convent, which is situated high upon the hill; in vain *le boit tournant* presented a collection of beautiful artificial flowers, pictures, and works of embroidery, our object was to see the secluded beauties of nature, and we testified our disapprobation at the exclusion, by refusing to become purchasers of their works ; the fair originals were far more interesting to our curiosity.

But for the folly of my comrades, and the constant danger incurred by their mad excesses, I could have passed many days on this interesting island, which daily presented new subjects for investigation and inquiry. It had thus early become dangerous to venture out after night-fall, unless well armed, in consequence of the repeated fracas in which those foolish young men were engaged with the inhabitants; to quell those disturbances the guard was frequently summoned. The British consul, with a zeal extremely considerate, though convinced of their criminality, actively exerted himself in palliating their offences, to the ruling authorities, and in appeasing the popular indignation excited by the unrestrained and uncontroulable licentiousness of those juvenile adventurers, who appeared to have but just made their *entré* into life. The hope that active service, and strict discipline, when arrived at our destination, would curb their too buoyant spirits, alone reconciled the discreet part of my companions to a continuance with them. The islanders of Madeira will long remember the turbulent passengers in the *Two Friends.**

---

* See note A.

The agent for Venezuela had, as has been previously stated, promised a step in rank to those who engaged in the service of the republic. Many taking advantage of these expectations, exceeded even the bounds of his engagements; colonels, majors, and captains, were in great profusion. lieutenantcies and ensigncies were beneath the dignity of those aspiring heroes, none of whom ever held higher rank in the army than captains, and few in the navy the rank of lieutenants. The latter were commodores, while master's mates and midshipmen determined to become post captains and commanders. Such were the elements to compose an army and a navy to give liberty, and to direct the energies of the extensive countries of South America: their sentiments were as hostile as their expressions, to purposes so honourable. M'Donald, who had already assumed the rank of colonel, talked of laying waste whole provinces with the sword, in order to give them liberty. The law of the strongest was to him the law that ought to govern, and he calculated upon becoming one of the executive, as soon as he should present himself at the seat of government. If he ever obtains the object of his ambition, the people will find their friends more oppressive than their enemies. He was a weak and uneducated man, and his appointment to command was an example of the indiscriminating character of the agent of the republic. Vanity was a ruling passion, and the adulation of some of his sattelites had so far procured his favor, that he was lavish of his promises of distinction, when his rank would enable him to bestow honours and command: he had pre-determined that General Bolivar, the dictator of the republic, would establish a military order of merit, of which he felt assured of becoming a grand cross! Such were the vagaries of his brain, and such the man destined to lead an army to the field!

On the eve of embarkation, an incident of an unpleasant nature exposed to us a dangerous companion, in the person of a young man, a lieutenant in the navy, who, on several occasions had rendered himself obnoxious to many of us. On this occasion he intruded himself into the company of a select party, who desired his absence, and although repeatedly requested, refused to withdraw; fatigued with his obstinacy and his insolence, two of our party were obliged to use coercion in his expulsion. Encouraged by those, who either were, or pretended to be ignorant of his real character, he sent challenges to those who were active in expelling him;

these were about to give him the *amende honorable,*
when a passenger, who had been hitherto restrained by motives of delicacy, and feelings of
compassion towards him, perceiving the extremity
to which he was proceeding, charged him publicly
with crimes of a flagrant nature, by the commission
of which his life was forfeited to the laws of his
country. The charge was minutely examined, and
as clearly substantiated, and the wretched individual
consigned to merited ignominy.

The captain having taken on board a small quantity of wine, &c. by no means adequate to our
promised allowance, we were under the necessity
of forming ourselves into messes, and of taking on
board private stocks of wine, spirits, fruit, &c. to
increase our comforts, and to lessen the inconveniences inseparable from our situation, for the
crowded state of the ship, menaced us with danger
in the warmer latitudes. We were in all 80 passengers, 30 of whom were in the steerage; but
equality appeared the prevailing sentiment, if
I might be allowed to judge, from the coarseness of
their manners, and the familiarity of their language.

CHAP. III.

Sail from Madeira—quarrel between M'Donald and the Captain—meet a patriot privateer—enter the tropic of Cancer—disgusting ceremony of shaving—opposed by some of the passengers—trade winds—beauty of the clouds in those latitudes—disputes and quarrels—duel between O. and the Irish Apothecary; its farcical termination—Christophe and his drinking party, their ludicrous exhibitions—make the land; the island of Barbuda—St. Bartholomew—Sabra, St. Kitt's, Sombrero, and Nevis—the Virgin Gordas, St. John's, Tortola, and open the view of St. Thomas's—beautiful appearance of the West India islands—St. Thomas's—state of our provisions.

Scarcely had we returned on board, and prepared for our departure from the island of Madeira, ere several of my companions, flushed with wine and ardent spirits, were lavish in their abusive phraseology to each other, charging their comrades with neglect and other offences, while on shore. Bitter in their animadversions, and loud in their menaces, reason appeared altogether to have deserted us; the captain mad, and drunk as his passengers, irritated with fancied injuries and insults, stormed and raged about the quarter-deck, launching his invectives upon all who approached him, and had the temerity to threaten to put some of those around him in irons for mutiny. This threat, the most absurd that could be offered to a set of daring young men, heedless of consequences, impatient of the least controul, and whose passions were not subjected to the influence of reason, recoiled upon him with redoubled fury, and they were about to make him the victim of his own menaces, when springing on one side of the quarter-deck, he attempted to throw the ship's papers overboard. Aware of the danger of our situation, a young midshipman caught those important documents, and preserved us from the fear of detention. Overcome by the violence of his passions, and exhausted by their influence, we conveyed him below, and succeeded in procuring comparative tranquility. The principal cause of this disgraceful scene was attributable to some altercations between the captain and M'Donald. Considerable party feeling had existed from the early part of our voyage, owing to the assumed consequence of the latter, who imagined himself our commanding officer, demanding our respect for his authority. In this, however, he by no means succeeded, all were anxious to retain their liberty, until the service to which they were devoted, should require their obedience. Our want of wine and spirits, had hitherto kept in a state of quiescence, those hostile feelings, which now raged with increased fury from their long suppression, and the influence of intoxication.

If the charges of the captain were well founded, too much cause appeared for his accusing M'Donald of ingratitude; the latter had been arrested at Portsmouth on the eve of our embarkation for thirty pounds; this sum he had not the means of paying, and even Mendez refused to advance the small amount upon the credit of his colonel's appointment. In this situation the captain had generously advanced the money, and taken him from a prison and the destruction of his golden prospects. It is unnecessary to comment upon this statement; it is altogether dependent upon facts, and I am well aware that little confidence is to be reposed in the assertions of the captain.

Two days after our departure from Madeira, we fell in with a patriot schooner, under French colours, with a large brass gun, mounted upon a swivel carriage midship. She ran along-side; but seeing us full of men, for our curiosity had manned every part of the ship, the captain contented himself with asking the longitude, and before we could put any questions in return, she hauled her wind and stood from us. Her compliment of men and her force were evidently disguised, and the gun midship was partly concealed by a tarpaulin; not more than eight men were visible on deck; she was very sharp built, and went to windward with surprising rapidity, and in a short time totally disappeared below the horizon.

On entering the tropic of Cancer, the senseless and disgusting ceremony of shaving, so often described and reprobated, was imposed upon many who had never visited those latitudes. This ceremony, on entering the tropics, is an extension of the same disgusting custom on passing the line. It generally happens that passengers are too few to make any serious resistance; from these circumstances it has grown into established precedent, and is constantly resorted to, as the means of levying contributions of grog in favor of the sailors. Some of our comrades, however, indignant at the idea of submission to a degrading operation, resolutely determined to resist every attempt to subject them to its endurance, and armed with pistols, placed themselves at one end of the cabin, threatening with death those who should endeavour to coerce them. Neptune and his tritons were at all hazards inclined to risk the consequences, rather than suffer an invasion of their rights, but a promise of additional grog from those who feared the desperate courage of both parties, appeased the watery god, and reprieved our indignant companions.

Running down the trade winds our progress was steady, and little variety occurred to chequer our course. The appearance of the clouds in those latitudes is extremely beautiful and extraordinary; in a picture the generality of people would ascribe to the imagination of the painter their various shapes and prismatic colouring, like detached masses of rocks they floated in the blue æther, presenting the boldest shades and outlines. The air was highly rarified, and our spirits experienced an expansion unknown to us before.

Wine, the monotony of our course, and the want of objects to excite and claim attention, impelled us into frequent disputes and quarrels. Scarcely a day passed undisturbed; many were the affairs of honour awaiting adjustment on our arrival at St. Thomas's. One of a ridiculous character occurred, which I cannot omit to mention: a young Irishman, with an O preceding his name, doubtless, of true Milesian descent, tenacious of his fancied honour, and emboldened by the influence of the Tuscan grape, challenged upon some frivolous pretence, an Hibernian apothecary to meet him as a gentleman; those who were present at the fracas, desirous of procuring a little relief to the tedium of our existence, proposed an immediate settlement of the dispute in the usual way, under the lee of the long boat. The decks were accordingly cleared, and the combatants assigned their allotted stations. The heroic O, to evince the superiority of his courage, and his high sentiments of honor, stripped to the buff, above the waist, awaiting the fire of his adversary, no less than six shots were exchanged without effect, when the spectators, fatigued with this mock heroic scene, burst into a loud laugh, and assured the combatants that they had merely been exchanging corks; poor O, the only one not in the secret, sobered by the farce, sneaked off to his birth, to escape the general mirth; poor fellow! he was really harmless, and his eccentricities were of the amusing kind. He had purchased in London a set of Irish bag pipes, and we had designated him with the title of Bolivar's piper general : his blunders, the proverbial errors of his country, made him the constant subject of mirth, and amused many of our otherwise weary hours.*

Scenes both laughable and deplorable, daily occurred to us. A party of six, principally naval officers, had purchased at Madeira (for their private stock), one hundred and eighty gallons of spirits;

---

* See note B.

this quantity for their number was enormous, but in order to reduce it, they were daily, nay, hourly drinking. One of them who acted as their chief, and to whom they had given the appellation of Christophe, presided at their orgies, and though drunk as his companions, preserved over them extraordinary influence: some of their performances were extremely ludicrous. The chief had swung his hammock between the shrouds and the mizen stay, elevated at least seven feet above the deck; at his feet, suspended in the netting, hung a cask of spirits; in his hand he held a speaking trumpet, the ensign of command, and the channel of his orders; his *subjects* were seated round a table below him, while one echoed his orders by the sound of a bugle. On the other side of the quarter deck, in a less elevated, though similar situation, swung his second in authority, whose redundant humour heightened the absurdity of their exploits. Christophe, from his airy throne, commanded all those who approached the limits of his empire, to partake of his bounty, and he never failed to pledge them with equal quantities. It is a matter of surprise that he escaped destruction from this course of dissipation; he was a fine young man, and his excesses were much to be lamented;

he had served as a lieutenant in the navy in the American war, and was wounded in the Chesapeake in the ill conducted attack upon Craney Island, near the entrance of James's River.

On the 24th of September, early in the morning, the welcome sound of "land on the lee bow" roused us from our beds, and we crowded the deck, anxious to view the long desired islands of the West Indies: from the flat appearance of the land, we imagined it to be the Island of Barbuda. In the course of the day we made those of St. Bartholomew, Sabra, St. Kitts, Sombrero, and Nevis, and the following day sailed along the coasts of the islands of the Virgin Gordas, St. John's, Tortola, and opened the entrance of the Danish Island of St. Thomas, the desired port of destination. The passage through the Caribbee Islands is extremely beautiful and picturesque, in the distance they rise like black clouds on the surface of the water, and on a near approach, their variegated shape and bright green delights the eye, and enlivens the prospect.

About sun-set we entered the harbour of St. Thomas, and cast anchor, our hearts beating anxiously with various hopes, and agitated by numerous conjectures respecting our ultimate destination, happy in having thus far arrived towards the scene of action. On every account this arrival was fortunate, had we continued at sea many days longer, we must have suffered still more severely. Our private stocks were consumed, the ship's salt provisions were mouldy, decayed, and nearly exhausted, and the few miserable pigs, with which the poverty of the owners compelled them to supply the ship, were long since devoted to appease our craving appetites. Such was our deplorable situation on board, when we prepared for disembarkation!

CHAP. IV.

Land at St. Thomas's—silly conduct of M'Donald—our disappointments—reported state of affairs on the Spanish main—wounded officers from the insurgents—the *Two Friends* sail clandestinely—miserable account of the schooner that preceded us—the death and dispersion of her passengers—fatal duel—several determine to proceed to Amelia Island, others return to England—hire an American schooner for Florida—*permitted* to embark, by orders from the governor of Santa Cruz—loyal refugees from the Spanish main, their misery—description of the Island of St. Thomas's—the pirate Black-beard, his story—dignity ball—a death.

It had been generally agreed to proceed on shore with the utmost circumspection, aware that our objects ought not to be avowed to the government of an island friendly to Spain. But determined to sport his newly acquired rank, and to strut in his gay uniform, the silly M'Donald resolved to brave our opinions and to adopt his proceedings to his own sentiments, senseless vanity! which had nearly cost us our liberty, as it did our comfort, and rendered us the objects of suspicion and distrust during our stay upon the island. Landing with a few of his satellites, he paraded his name before the commandant with his assumed rank and consequence, telling that gentleman, that he was commissioned by the Prince Regent to precede some British regiments on the eve of embarkation for South America, at our departure from England, and to assure the patriots of the lively interest felt by his Royal Highness and the British nation, in their ardent struggle for independence. Astonished at this intelligence, so irreconcileable with the usual policy of one friendly nation to the revolted subjects of another, and doubting the extent of British interference, and of M'Donald's powers and information, the commandant expressed his surprise at the statement, and requested perusal of his papers; these M'Donald is said to have promised, but prudently avoided the detection and exposure, by withdrawing from observation and enquiry.

The commandant, indignant at this proceeding, estimating us by the standard of this weak man, who called himself our leader, dispatched a schooner for instructions to the governor of Santa Cruz, upon which the command of this island is dependent.

Ashamed of the conduct of M'Donald, who had thus compromised our characters and feelings, and disgusted with an association so little flattering to our discernment, many withheld from paying their respects to the commandant, and in private lodgings avoided the individual by whom we had been dishonored; he, in the mean time, was occupied in writing to General Bolivar, a tirade of nonsense, describing the misery of our voyage and the disrespectful conduct of the captain, praying his excellency to refuse him and his ship employment in the republican service. These dispatches were afterwards forwarded to Angostura ; of their influence I have yet to learn.

We had waited at our hotel with some impatience, the appearance of the accredited agent of Venezuela, when a gentleman who had previously arrived upon the same unfortunate enterprize, and under similar instructions, came to inform us that no such agent was to be found on the island, nor had there been one from the republic. The object of our enterprize soon circulated through the town, and many of the merchants and other respectable residents hastened to relieve our minds from the pains of fruitless expectation, sympathising in our distressed situation, and lamenting the deception that had decoyed us from our country, to embark in a cause both despicable and dishonourable. This intelligence came upon us like a clap of thunder, involving in darkness and destruction our golden day dreams, and prostrating in the dust all our brilliant anticipations. This *splendid* republic, which the vivid imaginations of its agents had displayed in all the seductive colouring of pomp and glory, was now reduced to a few bands of itinerant free booters, calling themselves patriots and champions of their country, a distinction to which they were as much entitled as the roving marauding Arabs of the desert.

Bolivar, whose devotion and *amor patria* we had been taught to admire as a splendid imitation of the heroic and noble Romans of the best ages of that commonwealth, was described as a mere bravo, coarse, cruel, arbitrary, and vindictive, devoting to destruction all who opposed his power, or questioned the policy of his measures. Alike insatiable in ambition and vanity, sacrificing the advantages of victory and the pursuit of successes, to the parade of celebrating a triumph. Disgusted with the system of one less formidable to his enemies, than dangerous to his friends, whose darling passions menaced with destruction their legitimate hopes, and the objects of their co-operation, the respectable leading characters of Venezuela had retired from the contest, leaving to the worst part of the insurgents the issue of a revolution, which had dawned with the brightest promise, but now foreboded the most distressing results. Fortress after fortress submitted again to the power of Spain, while provinces followed each other in rapid succession, seceding from the cause, abandoning the wild, trackless, and extensive deserts of the interior, to the irregular bands of insurgents.

A variety of circumstances, perhaps unequalled in the annals of popular insurrections, had led to the revolutionary movements in Venezuela and Caraccas, and at one time gave promise of consistence and stability; but the restless turbulencies of Bolivar, and the schismatic divisions of the army, had brought discredit upon their objects, and had disorganised their arrangements; Generals Piar and Morales were already in open defiance to the authority of their chieftain. The former, a mulattoe, had collected to his standard those people of colour whom the royalist and insurgent chiefs, had at various times, in the madness of exasperation and revenge, manumitted and armed: with these it was feared he meditated repeating the horrid scenes which had swept away the white population of St. Domingo, and given birth to a black empire in the west.

The mass of the population of the Spanish Main, though well endowed by nature, were described as yet unprepared both by habits and feelings, for the enjoyment of rational liberty and independence;

blind, bigotted, and infatuated, they were rendered the ready victims of the priesthood, and the instruments of designing men. The native clergy, disaffected to their government by their exclusion from the higher offices of the hierarchy, panting for an opportunity to throw off the yoke of Spain, had, early in the revolution, exerted the influence of their ghostly direction, to withdraw the people from their allegiance, and to become the supporters of their apostacy.

But the timely overtures of the court of Madrid, whose counsellors well knew the tempers and influence of the priesthood, uniting with the calamitous earthquake of the Caraccas, which nearly destroyed that important city, and engulphed thirty thousand of its inhabitants in the bowels of the earth, recalled the disaffected by thousands back to the royal standard, terrified with the belief that this calamity was an evidence of the anger of offended heaven.

Not a single fortress on the sea coast remained in the possession of the Insurgents, except the island of Margaretta, whose few miserable inhabitants had experienced the horrors of war, inflicted equally by friends and enemies, six times had this ill-fated island changed masters. The revolting cruelties that disgraced both sides of the contest, and the vacillating character of the people, presented formidable and insurmountable difficulties to the progres of independence.

The town of Angostura, situated two hundred miles above the mouths of the river Oronoco, was designated as the seat of the Insurgent government; the approach to which, was both difficult and dangerous. This solitary possession in the interior, was the point of concentration for their armies during the inclement seasons: and the misery of those shut up in a place so limited may be readily conceived; beef was almost the only article of sustenance. The poverty of their resources, and the cupidity of the North American traders, had deprived them of the power of purchasing flour and other essential articles of support. The most formidable part of their troops were irregular bodies of cavalry, wrapt in blankets by day, which served them for covering at night; their services, like those of the Cossacks, better calculated for the destruction of a dispersed enemy, than to procure a victory. Their equipments were in every way wretched : shoes were known only as luxuries to the superior officers of the army, while the inferiors were reduced to the necessity of swathing their feet in the reeking skins of their slaughtered animals. Liberty was the delusive war cry, while the chieftains exercised the authority of despots over their wretched dependants, characterising the warfare rather that of partisans, than of patriots.

Such was the cause, and such were its supporters, for whom Britons were about to fight and sacrifice existence, without the ties of kindred or of country, for a people jealous of our interference, enemies of our religion, and incapable of appreciating the generosity of our motives: going forward, to become identified with them, appeared, I confess, a species of Quixotism unworthy of us; yet, to recede, was to many extremely difficult.

We were at first willing to ascribe to exaggeration those gloomy and disgusting descriptions; but the numerous victims of that ill-fated contest, who were here, maimed in the service of the insurgents, and abandoned by them, without succour and without support, because they had ceased to be useful, attested too strongly the facts we had collected. The concurrent testimony of those merchants interested in the opening of the trade of the Spanish main, was enough to dissipate the doubts and suspicions of the most sceptical.

"What must we now do?" was the important and unanswered query of my comrades as they met one another in the streets of St. Thomas's, the victims of despair. Insensible to the dangerous fervid beams of the mid-day sun, they were seen traversing with hurried and irresolute steps the neighbouring hills, unconscious of their imprudence: to return to England was to encounter mortification, to go on to the Main was madness; but it was necessary to resolve upon something, as our resources were rapidly diminishing.

The owners of the *Two Friends* had engaged to convey us to the island of Margaretta, or to Angostura. The deceptions practised by them, and the state of the ship's provisions, have already been noticed. Our arrival in the warm latitudes had reduced the few remaining casks of beef and pork to decay; the salt fish had become putrid. The poverty of the captain, and his want of credit on the island, forbade his purchasing supplies, so imperatively necessary for the remainder of the voyage. In order to pay his current expences, he had sold a quantity of the ship's stores of rigging, water-casks, &c. Such was the situation of the ship, while we wavered in opinion respecting the future; when one morning we were informed that the *Two Friends*, taking advantage of the night, had slipped from her anchorage, and had clandestinely sailed without paying the harbour dues, carrying off the clothes and equipments of several of our comrades, who had not had the prudence to anticipate this event; few of our original number were on board, and those were impelled by circumstances, to submit to their untoward destiny.

A chooner, full of passengers, on the same disastrous enterprize, had preceded us from England a few weeks: she was still at St. Thomas's on our arrival, about to be sold to defray her port charges. The ill-fated victims she had brought were dispersed in every direction, and many had fallen sacrifices to the climate and their desponding feelings; their voyage had in many respects exceeded the misery of ours, and their privations had been greater. Induced to quit England by similar artifices, and upon similar promises to those used with us, they sailed professedly for Madeira. By false reckonings and observations, the captain contrived to pass to leeward of that island, but the naval officers on board soon detected the deception. Indignant at this dishonourable treatment, they took the command of the vessel, bestowing on the wretch the punishment of flogging for the treachery of his conduct. Being too far to the south to reach Madeira, they bore away for the Canary Islands, where they arrived in a most destitute condition, reduced to half rations, and obliged to drink the water in a state of putridity. At these islands their limited resources confined them to absolute necessaries for the remainder of their voyage to St. Thomas's. Their accumulated sufferings both of body and mind, were here increased by the new calamity which awaited them. Driven almost to desperation, without money and without friends, they wandered about the streets of St. Thomas's, unmindful of the pernicious influence of the night air, and without protection from the burning heats of the day; their clothes, their equipments, in fact every thing of value, was devoted to the purchase of food, and to obtain ardent spirits, in the indulgence of which they sought alleviation to their miseries. These resources were soon expended, their debts accumulating, and their situations without hope. To relieve their present wants the Danish commandant assigned them lodgings in the fort, on condition of remaining within its walls, a measure rendered necessary by their imprudent exposure to the climate, until opportunities should occur to send them down to the Spanish main.

Some of those unfortunates who could not bear the idea of confinement, wandered about the country, dependant upon the casual humanity of the planters for sustenance through the day, and exposed unsheltered to the fatal atmosphere by night.

A young man, a surgeon, who had been attached to the army of Lord Wellington, of good abilities, and well known to me in England, condemned to this wretched state of existence, was found one morning, by the side of the road, in a burning and delirious fever; by the evening his struggles and his life were terminated, and his unfortunate body consigned unpitied to the earth. Let it be remembered, that on this island there are many English and other European families; that they were insensible witnesses to the sufferings of those unfortunate young men, permitting them to linger and to die, unpitied and unaided. Whatever their sentiments of the cause in which they were embarked, whether they approved or condemned it, the duties of humanity and christian charity demanded from them, in those moments of desolation to their hopes, assistance and advice; but to the dishonour of our national character, abroad our countrymen have none of that sympathy so distinguishable in the people of other nations; we are in fact denationalized.

An event of a melancholy character occurred the morning succeeding that on which we landed at St. Thomas's, which distressed us even more than our own disappointments. A fine young man, a naval officer, of highly respectable family and connections, who had been many years detained a prisoner at Verdun, of an excellent disposition, and much humour, celebrated as *un bon raconteur*, though unfortunately addicted to infidelity in matters of religion, fell a victim to his misplaced attachment to M'Donald. Impelled by him to offer a gross insult to a young man, whose susceptibility was equalled by his courage, a challenge was the consequence of the outrage, and with his life he atoned for his offence. He went out with two adversaries under similar circumstances, and produced by the same influence; on the first fire the ball of his antagonist penetrated his right side, lacerated the intestines, and lodged near the left groin; he lingered until the evening, and died in great pain. Before he went to the field, he felt a presentiment of his approaching fate, and so expressed himself to his second; he met his adversary's fire with perfect coolness, and it is only to be lamented that his courage was tested in an affair so little flattering to his memory. He certainly deserved—though I sincerely deplored the severity of his fate, poor fellow! to his mistaken confidence and friendship, may be ascribed this fatal conclusion. With difficulty the manner of his death was screened from the police; the laws respecting duelling are there very severe, and rigidly enforced. To his remains we paid the last melancholy duties: borne to the grave by his comrades under the union jack; he was consigned to our common parent, lamented and pitied; while he, for whose caprice he had sacrified existence, avoided this last tribute of respect to his memory, as he did his repeated requests to see him while he yet lingered in the arms of death, pleading as an excuse for his absence the influence of feeling!

Straightened in our resources, and reduced to the necessity of selling some of our equipments, we saw nothing but misery in the attempt through another channel, to proceed to the Spanish main, from which we might not easily retire.

M'Gregor, it was known, had made a descent upon the confines of East Florida, and had established himself at Amelia Island, where he invited to his standard recruits, for the purpose of reducing the Spanish garrison of St. Augustine, the only supposed obstacle to his subjection of the whole province. The American consul, acting in the spirit of his government, whose ambitious views had long desired the possession of that important boundary, recommended our joining the forces of M'Gregor.

and readily assisted our wishes to do so. Sick of
the scenes at St. Thomas's, and of the prospects
on the Spanish main, I adopted the resolution of
several of my companions, and consented to proceed to Amelia Island, where we anticipated meeting under the banners of a countryman; a cause
and a service more worthy of our co-operation. Its
proximity to the United States was to me an additional motive, as I could easily quit the association,
if their views and actions were not accordant with
my feelings. In consequence of this determination
we hired the American schooner, *Mary*, Captain
Lane, of 170 tons burthen, destined for Turk's
Island to load salt, and from thence engaged to
convey us to Amelia Island.

Some of our fellow passengers now resolved to
return home, and engaged passages direct to England, while others returned by the route of Philadelphia and New York; those whose clothes had
been carried off by the *Two Friends*, were reduced
to the sad necessity of following her to the Spanish
main, to obtain their restitution.

By this time the schooner dispatched by the commandant of St. Thomas's to Santa Cruz, had returned with instructions from the Governor of that
island, respecting us; his directions were, that we

might be *permitted* to embark : a softened expression for dismissal.

The motives of the Danish governor were apparent, and his conduct perfectly justifiable; he by no means committed a breach of hospitality by desiring our absence, but adopted a just measure of self-preservation. The Island of St. Thomas's is principally dependent upon the Spanish Island of Porto Rico, a few hours sail distant, for provisions; civility to us, as the avowed partisans of the Insurgents, would undoubtedly have given umbrage to the ruling authorities of that island, and they might have been induced to withhold supplies of the last importance to the existence of their neighbour. To the folly of M'Donald must be ascribed the disagreeableness of our situation; had he acted as we wished and advised, no notice could have been taken of our objects, but we should have experienced the courtesy due to strangers.

The Island of St. Thomas's furnished an asylum to numerous families, refugees from the Spanish main; a part of the town was exclusively occupied by these unfortunates, who had in many instances escaped with mere existence; their misery was indeed extreme. The appearance of the island from the sea is certainly beautiful; its high green hills and savannas, variegated with fields of Indian corn and sugar canes, interspersed with the cocoa and broad leaf plantain tree. At its base stands the town upon three gentle eminences, the harbour in the form of a horse shoe; its extremities defended by a battery. The houses, like those of other tropical regions, are spacious and airy, calculated to relieve the severe heats of the climate. The products of this island are inferior to most others of the Carribbee Isles, and by no means numerous; its principal importance is ascribable to its being a free port, from whence the North Americans, the most enterprising of commercial adventurers, carry on a valuable trade with the Spanish main and their own States. I found the temperature of the night air excessively relaxing, my sleep disturbed by the noisy flight of the musquitoes; but the heat of the day was relieved by the regular sea breezes.

The white inhabitants, either from the effects of climate, or from their habitual indolence, or perhaps the combination of those enemies to health and vigour, have sallow complexions, lank, and uninteresting in appearance. The negroes and mulattoes, on the contrary, are well formed, light, and agile, with an elasticity in their step and action, not to be found in the more favoured colour, and far

superior to the African slaves in the United States
of North America.

Upon a small hill, commanding the town, are the
ruins of a castle, once the residence and defence of
the celebrated pirate Black Beard, the scourge and
terror of those seas: little now remains but the le-
gend, to remind us of its once terrific owner, whose
exploits are yet remembered in the neighbouring
islands, particularly in the Bahamas, where his establishment was of a more important character. Of
this daring pirate, M'Kinnon, in his tour through the
British West Indies, and Bahama Islands, relates
the following:—

" This extraordinary man had united in his fortunes a desperate and formidable gang of pirates,
styling himself their commodore, and assuming the
authority of a legitimate chief. Under a wild fig-
tree, the trunk of which still remains, and was shewn
to me in the eastern part of the town, he used to sit
in council among his banditti, concerting or pro-
mulgating his plans, and exercising the authority of
a magistrate. His piracies were often carried on
near the English settlements on the coast of North
America, where he met with extraordinary success.
Perhaps in the history of human depravity, it would
be difficult to select actions more brutal and extra-

vagant than Black Beard's biographer has recorded of him. As the narrative to which I allude is generally credited, and bears strong internal evidence of truth, it may be amusing to mention a few particulars of a man who was for some time considered as sovereign of this island.*

"In person, as well as disposition, this desperado John Teach, who was a native of England, seems to have been qualified for the chief of a gang of thieves. The effect of his beard, which gave a natural ferocity to his countenance, he was always solicitous to heighten, by suffering it to grow to an immoderate length, and twisting it about in small tails, like a ramilies wig; whence he derived the name of Black Beard. His portrait in time of action, is described as that of a complete fury; with three brace of pistols in holsters, slung over his shoulder, like bandoliers, and lighted matches under his hat, sticking out over each of his ears. All authority as well as admiration, amongst the pirates, was conferred on those, who, committing every outrage on humanity, displayed the greatest audacity and extravagance. Black Beard's pretensions to an

---

* New Providence, the Chief of the Bahama Islands, and the seat of their government.

elevated rank in the estimation of his associates, may be conceived from the character of his jokes. Having often exhibited himself before them as a dæmon, he determined once to show them a hell of his own creation. For this purpose he collected a quantity of sulphur and combustible materials between the decks of his vessel; when kindling a flame, and shutting down the hatches upon his crew, he involved himself with them literally in fire and brimstone. With oaths and frantic gestures he then acted the part of the devil, as little affected by the smoke as if he had been born in the infernal regions; till his companions, nearly suffocated, and fainting, compelled him to release them. His convivial humour was of a similar cast. In one of his ecstasies, whilst heated with liquor, and sitting in his cabin, he took a pistol in each hand; then cocking them under the table, blew out the candles, and, crossing his hands, fired on each side at his companions: * one of them received a shot, which maimed him for life. His gallantry also was of the same complexion as this vein of humour. He had fourteen wives, if they may be so called; but his

---

* One of the guests, who related this anecdote, perceiving what was likely to happen, adroitly took himself off.

conduct towards one of them appears to have been too unfeeling and unmanly, to admit of description.

"The English government, having determined to clear the sea of these ruffians, directed some ships of war to effect that purpose in the early part of last century. Black Beard at that time was lurking in a small vessel in the creeks and shallows of an inlet near Cape Hatteras, in North Carolina. But the chief magistrate of that province having long connived at his robberies, the sufferers gave information to the governor of Virginia, and the naval force on that station was directed to assist in the extermination of the pirates. The intrepidity displayed in this service by a lieutenant of the name of Maynard, at least equal to that of the rover, and in a better cause, deserves a circumstantial detail.

"From the nature of Black Beard's position, in a sloop of little draught of water, on a coast abounding with creeks, and remarkable for the number and intricacy of its shoals, with which he had made himself intimately acquainted, it was deemed impossible to approach him in vessels of any force. Two hired sloops were therefore manned from the Pearl and Lime frigates in the Chesapeake, and put under the command of the gallant officer before named, with instructions to hunt down and destroy

this pirate, wherever he should be found. On the
17th of November, in the year 1718, this force,
sailed from Jame's River, and in the evening of the
21st came to an inlet in North Carolina, where
Black Beard was discovered at a distance, lying in
wait for his prey. The sudden appearance of an
enemy preparing to attack him, occasioned some
surprise; but his sloop mounting several guns, and
being manned with twenty-five of his desperate
followers, he determined to make a resolute defence;
and having prepared his vessel over night for action,
sat down to his bottle, stimulating his spirits to
that pitch of frenzy, by which only he could rescue
himself in a contest for his life. The navigation of
the inlet* was so difficult, that Maynard's sloops
were repeatedly grounded in their approach; and
the pirate, with his experience of the soundings,
possessed considerable advantage in manœuvring
which enabled him for some time to maintain a
running fight. His vessel, however, in her turn,
having at length grounded, and the close engagement becoming now inevitable, he reserved her
guns to pour in a destructive fire on the sloops as

---

* Occacocke Inlet, a little south of Cape Hatteras.

they advanced to board him. This he so successfully executed, that twenty-nine of Maynard's small number, were either killed or wounded by the first broadside, and one of the sloops for a time disabled. But notwithstanding this severe loss, the lieutenant persevered in his resolution to grapple with the enemy, or perish in the attempt. Observing that his own sloop, which was still fit for action, drew more water than the pirates, he ordered all his ballast to be thrown out, and, directing his men to conceal themselves between decks, took the helm in person, and steered directly on board of his antagonist, who continued inextricably fixed on the shoal.

" This desperate wretch, previously aware of his danger, and determined never to expiate his crimes in the hands of justice, had posted one of his banditti with a lighted match over his powder magazine, to blow up his vessel in the last extremity. Luckily in this design he was disappointed by his own ardour and want of circumspection; for as Maynard approached, having begun the encounter at close quarters, by throwing upon his antagonist a number of hand granadoes of his own composition, which produced only a thick smoke; and conceiving, that from their destructive agency, the sloop's deck had been completely cleared, he leaped over her bows, followed by twelve of his men, and advanced upon the lieutenant, who was the only person then in view. But the men instantly springing up to the relief of their commander, who was now furiously beset, and in imminent danger of his life, a violent contest ensued. Black Beard, after seeing the greater part of his men destroyed at his side, and receiving himself repeated wounds, at length, stepping back to cock a pistol, fainted with the loss of blood, and expired on the spot. Maynard compleated his victory, by securing the remainder of these desperate wretches, who were compelled to sue for mercy, and a short respite from a less honourable death at the hands of the executioner."

Curiosity led me one evening, with some of our party, to what is called in the West Indies a dignity ball; a term of derision applied to the assemblies of people of colour, of whose *inferiority*, and degradation in the scale of humanity, we were not then sensible. The various shades from the jet black to the clear brunette, were whirling in the giddy dance, arrayed in silks, satins, spangled gauzes, and all the frippery of European fashions, decorated with a profusion of imitation pearls, and other trinkets; good order and decency prevailed, in this motley association, and they were no mean imitators of their white neighbours. They received us with the utmost courtesy, and appeared highly gratified with our visit, which they requested us to repeat.

Having completed our arrangements for departure, and on the point of embarkation for Amelia island, another casualty occurred to us, in the death of a young officer of the 43rd Regiment, who had served in the ill conducted expedition of our troops against New Orleans, a fine and promising young man, a general favorite, from his uniformly good disposition, fell a sacrifice to the fever of the Island, produced by imprudently taking off at one draught a a bottle of claret, while in a state of profuse perspiration. We had scarcely time to pay to his remains the last duties of humanity, ere we were hurried on board to avail ourselves of a favorable wind.

CHAP. V.

Departure from St. Thomas's—arrive at Turk's Island—manner of making salt—Americans permitted an intercourse—M'Donald's folly—quit Turk's Island—attack upon the town at night—our outrage—visited by the Magistrates—M'Donald's proposal to carry the fortress of Port of Plate, in St. Domingo—his plans, their absurdity—dying dolphin—a calm—Sharks, one taken—near the Gulph stream, see a sail, suppose her a Spaniard—determine to take her—hoists American colours—M'Donald's disapointment—he boards her in full costume—frightens the captain, wife, and child—make the Coast of East Florida—supposed off St. Mary's river—M'Donald and his satellites land—discover we had mistaken the entrance of St. John's, for that of St. Mary's—apprehensive M'Donald and his party are taken by the Spaniards—arrive at Amelia Island—Commodore Aury in command—M'Gregor gone to the Bahamas—escape and arrival of Mac Donald at head quarters—decline employment at Amelia.

AFTER bidding a hasty adieu to the few of our unfortunate comrades left at St. Thomas's, by the treachery of the captain of the *Two Friends*, who had carried off their cloaths, and who had now no other alternative than to follow the ship; we embarked, in all thirty, for the Island of Amelia, glad to escape the scene of our severe disappointments, and exhilarated by the new hopes our present prospects created. A brisk and favorable gale, bore us from the West Indies, and in

F

five days carried us to the British settlement of Turk's Island, one of the Eastern of the Bahama Isles. This Island is little more than a sand bank, but its importance arises from the quantity of sea salt raked at certain seasons of the year in the salt pans. The salt pans are formed on a flat part of the Island, subject to the influx of the sea, through a narrow channel. After having deposited a certain quantity of water, the further ingress of the sea is prevented by an embankment. The water in the pans being exposed to the fervid heat of the sun, soon granulates, and deposits by evaporation, a chrystalisation of sea salt. This salt is divided by certain head rights, among those resident on the Island, before the tenth day of February, this privilege induces a number of periodical settlers from others of the Bahama Islands, who retire with the conclusion of the season.

The Americans, who are as well as other foreigners, excluded by our colonial policy from trading with our Islands, in vessels not under the British flag, are permitted an intercourse with this island, under their own, for the sole purpose of carrying off this produce; and here our captain had arrived to load a cargoe for Mobile, to which he was destined after landing us at Amelia Island.

M'Donald who had become one of our fellow passengers, under the impression that his Scottish origin would fraternize him with his countryman Sir Gregor M'Gregor, mortified by the events which had occurred, and dissipated his brilliant prospects while at St. Thomas's, had hitherto kept tolerably quiet, little disposed to assume that consequence, he knew few of us inclined to support; but his vanity getting the better of his temporary prudence, returned with renewed ardour, as we approached the shores of Turk's Island, and he once more cloathed himself in the garb of war. Mounted on wretched horses, miserably caparisoned, he and his shadow, a young man we had designated his *Aid du Camp*, were seen urging their unfortunate animals over the barren sandy hills, the objects of curiosity and surprise, to the few miserable inhabitants. This vanity, though perfectly harmless, did not fail to excite in his companions, contempt for the silly ambition of one, selected to conduct the fortunes of war.

After a detention of four days, in which we compleated our loading of salt, we bade adieu to the settlement of Turk's Island, and were already at the close of day, at a considerable distance from the town, when our course was staid, and the

schooner directed again towards the island. The
long-boat was now hoisted out and manned, and
twelve of our comrades completely armed sprang
into her, and pulled off for the shore. This military
equipment was a subject of curiosity to those not
in the secret, and we were anxiously asking
an explanation of such hostile movements,
when firing was observed along the eastern extremity of the town, succeeded by the ringing of bells,
beating of drums, and all the bustle attendant upon
surprise and invasion. Lights were now moving in
every direction, and the inhabitants were evidently
in a state of general alarm. It was only then that
our imperative demands produced an explanation
from the captain, who began to feel the danger of
his situation. He stated that one of our comrades,
enjoying the supposed hospitality of an inhabitant,
had been defrauded of four doubloons. The character of his host was extremely doubtful, and on
application to the Magistracy for redress, he avoided
the inquiry, and absconded into the country. Under the impression that he would return to his house
when aware of our having sailed, this armed party
had gone on shore to claim and enforce restitution;
their detection we imagined had given rise to those
hostile appearances, and we were now anxious to

aid their escape. For this purpose we hoisted a lanthorn as a signal at the topmast, to guide and induce their return. Although those coercive measures were by no means justifiable, yet their criminality was palliated by their peculiar and confined circumstances, and the offence of the individual against whom their predatory expedition was directed, and we could not refrain from wishing them successful in their object. In about an hour they returned to the vessel, celebrating their success in noisy mirth, and towing along a boat, the object of their triumph, which they had cut out, and asserted to be the property of the individual from whom they sought to obtain indemnity. Scarcely had they secured their prize, and our course been renewed, when it fell a perfect calm, which continued through the night. Our evil destiny uniting with the tide, had carried us the following morning back within five miles of the shore, from whence we had no doubt but some application would be made, to explain the motives of our alarming descent the preceding night. Towards noon we observed a large row-boat, displaying at her stern the British ensign, making towards us, which we rightly conjectured the bearer of the civil authorities of the island, prepared to compel restitution of our unlawful capture. Some of our daring spirits were for resistance, determined to maintain their acquisition by further violence; but the superior prudence of the moderate part of our fellow passengers, restrained, in some measure, the turbulencies of those thoughtless adventurers. On a nearer approach of the boat we discovered the judge and a respectable merchant and magistrate of the island, unattended by any force capable of coercion. They testified their surprise and regret at our hostile proceedings, expressing their hopes that they were not, for the honour of British officers, conceived in the spirit of piracy; evidently ignorant that we had gone so far as to commit depredation upon the property of the island. They at length discovered the extent of our criminality, and claimed restitution of the boat; declaring that it was not the property of the individual against whom our predatory excursion was directed, but the sole means of sustenance to a poor fisherman, whose family depended upon it for existence. Deaf to the claims of justice and humanity, and obstinately bent upon retaining their unlawful prize, those buccaneers resolutely refused to listen to the demands of the magistrates. Though warned of the criminal character of their proceedings, and of the consequences that might result, they pertinaciously resisted the advice and intreaties of the moderate party, who were too few to compel their submission. Our visitors reluctantly withdrew from the unavailing discussion, declaring they would cause the transaction to be laid before the proper authorities in England, where it was doubtless met by deserved reprobation.

Soon after the departure of our visitors a favourable breeze enabled us to renew our course. From that moment the small moderate party were the objects of suspicion and distrust, and the empty shadow of a Colonel no longer concealed the worst traits of his character; endeavouring by every means he could devise to lesson their influence and excite the animosity of their comrades; but firm in their principles and resolves they resisted the united efforts of M'D. and his myrmidons. Their contempt for this silly pretender was increased by the knowledge of his real character and former circumstances. One of the party had long recognized this *soi disant* Brigade-Major, as a private raised in the regiment to which he belonged, from the ranks to the commission of an ensign, and his subsequent removal to a foreign corps, in which he had not attained higher rank than a lieutenancy. I am willing to believe that his former good conduct had recommended him to promotion, but his elevation had certainly deranged and dissipated his pretensions. He had amused us with various feats of his *high* family, and of his own prowess, evidently the fabrication of his distempered brain.

An American captain, than whom there are none less celebrated for pertinaceous adherence to truth, had at Turk's Island amused our Quixotic colonel with a description of the immense treasures contained in the small Spanish fortress of Port of Plate, in the Island of St. Domingo, and had stimulated M'Donald's ambition to undertake its reduction.— Big with the importance of the enterprize, and anticipating certain success to our efforts, and his consequent elevation to the honours of supreme command, either in Amelia or Venezuela, this redoubted hero proposed our attempting its reduction, and for that purpose summoned a council of war, composed of his satellites, who instantly proffered their assistance, and the ship master, eager to avail himself of every advantage, the hazard of our persons might procure him, readily consented to the enterprize. But our party, though small, was too important in the scale of force to be omitted, and M'Donald was reduced to the mortifying necessity of asking our concurrence.— Feeling the want of authority attending our proceedings against the dominions and property of Spain, as we were not yet enrolled in the service of the Insurgents, and aware that we should be liable to be treated as pirates, even by our own government, if detected, we determined to oppose the project, at the same time desirous of ascertaining the extent of M'Donald's powers, and his information on the subject, we professed a partial acquiescence, and requested inspection of his commission. He produced the appointment of Mendez, who had constituted him colonel commandant of a regiment of lancers, to be raised in Venezuela, under his inspection and direction, contending that it was a sufficient authority for his attempting the reduction of the fortress. We next desired to know his plans. The American captain had described the fort of inferior strength, and that it was the invariable practice of the governor and other officers of the garrison to visit all vessels on their arrival in the port; these he proposed to lure on board by disguising the compliment of our crew, to detain them as hostages, until a handsome ransom should be offered for their liberation. Such was the sum and substance of his information and plans, to reason with one capable of forming such projects, and making such proposals, was to encounter the loss both of time and argument; we consequently declined participation, and demanded not to be compromised by his measures, but to be landed on some friendly shore. Our rejection did not deter those daring spirits from the attempt, but the reflection that they were without arms and ammunition, to carry the fort, in the event of resistance, having only their swords and pistols, to contend with the enemy's cannon, compelled those ardent adventurers to abandon the alluring prospect.

We again pursued our course to the gulph stream. As we approached it, the variety and quantity of fish surprised us. Dolphins were seen in numbers, sporting across our bows with the velocity of thought, displaying their lovely and variegated colouring.— Our boatswain harpooned one, and gave us the novel, and celebrated spectacle, of a dying dolphin. The rapid succession of colours, and the strong tints of each change, conveyed a painful sensation, when we reflected that our gratification was procured by the severe sufferings of the animal. We were visited with a calm which continued two days; those who have never experienced the misery of a similar situation, are incapable of furnishing their imagination with a just idea of the desolation of feeling it produces: most willingly would I have exchanged our quiet, for rude gales, and mountain billows.—

Sharks surrounded our vessel regaling themselves by rubbing their slimy bodies against the sides. The mate seizing a favorable opportunity, plunged a harpoon through the body of one of the most considerable; with difficulty we got him on board, from head to tail he measured nine feet three inches. The struggles of the animal, even when deprived of his tail, were extremely powerful, menacing with destruction all who approached him, and exciting our apprehension that he would destroy the bullworks of the schooner. The tail, the only part of this enormous fish at all palatable, was soon served up, well broiled, upon our table, and to those who were reduced to salt provision, this unexpected supply of fresh fish was by no means unacceptable.

We were now fast approaching the edge of the gulph stream, when one evening we descried a distant sail making towards us. The sanguine hopes of my comrades instantly determined her to be a Spanish ship, bound from Havanna to Cadiz, laden with a valuable cargo of coffee, indigo, sugar, &c., which they resolved to capture, and so far did they calculate the certainty of their anticipations as to reckon the amount of prize money. On her near approach we were directed to conceal our numbers to avoid creating alarm. Some of us were I apprehend discovered, for she seemed to hover in doubt as to our real character; but to the mortification of those ardent sons of adventure, on closing, she displayed the American ensign. M'Donald, annoyed at this discovery, yet determined to pay the captain a visit, and that his aspect might be more impressive, attired himself in his military costume: poor Jonathan could scarcely believe his visitants were friends, particularly when Mac, laying a brace of pistols on the cabin table, exclaimed in the discordant tones of his country—" Haud ye ben a Spaniard I haud brought ye change for your doubloons." With trembling apprehension the poor Yankee offered him the remnant of a bottle of brandy, while his wife, who was lying in the cabin with her infant, endeavoured to appease the little squaller; so much had the terrific appearance of Mac frightened the urchin.

On the fourteenth day of our departure from St. Thomas's we made the coast of East Florida, and imagining we were off the river St. Mary's, on the confines of that province, and Georgia, we made signal for a pilot. Our *gallant* Colonel with some of his party prepared to disembark, anxious to present himself to the authorities at Amelia, to apprise them of the importance of his character and pretensions. We saw them land, and were urgent with our Captain to follow them: this however he refused without the assistance of a pilot, whose non-arrival at sun-set obliged us to stand off until the following morning, which not having brought our comrades or the pilot, we demanded why we were delayed making for the river. Thus pressed, the Captain acknowledged his suspicion that he had mistaken the entrance of the St. John's for that of St. Mary's river, in consequence of his neglect to take a solar observation the preceding day. Supposing this to be the case, we doubted not but that our comrades had been taken prisoners by the Spaniards, and were conveyed to the fortress of St. Augustine. Little as M'Donald deserved our commiseration, we regretted that fate which had equally involved his companions, who we knew to be misled by a mistaken confidence in the man, and an unwillingness to entertain the suspicions he merited. At twelve o'clock our error was demonstrated, and our course directed for the St. Mary's river, which we entered about sun-set, and were visited by a boat from the United States brig of war "*Saranac*," stationed in the American waters of the river, to protect their trade, and to prevent smuggling from Amelia. Captain

Liers, the commander of the "*Morgiana*" insurgent privateer, under the flag of Buenos Ayres, soon after came on board ; with him several of us disembarked, and were presented to commodore Aury, whose reception was extremely civil, but the appearance of those around him, by no means favourably impressed us with the cause. To our mortification we learnt that M'Gregor had quitted the island, and had gone to the Bahamas, his views and future proceedings were alike matters of secrecy to the remaining authorities, with whom it was evident he had not maintained the best intelligence.— Aury having ascertained our number and description, expressed his regret that we had not brought privates as well as officers to his standard, he was already overstocked with the latter, who were in consequence obliged to do duty alternately in the ranks, and on the guards of the garrison.

Scarcely had we risen from a supper laid for us in the house of the Commodore, and were preparing to retire to the quarters assigned us, when M'Donald and his friend arrived at Fernandina, the town of Amelia, disappointing our expectations of hearing that he was encaged in the fortress of St. Augustine. We learnt that in passing the bar of the St. John's, the boat had been upset, but the party had contrived to escape unhurt to Talbot Island : from the courtesy of a planter they obtained refreshment and refuge through the night, and the following day, M'Donald and his *aid* were provided with horses and a guide to Fernandina. The residue of the party remained to bring the boat through the narrow channels dividing the islands of Talbot, Nassau, and Amelia, from the main land of East Florida.*

The expression of our countenances soon conveyed to Mac the little gratification we felt at his escape, and we were mutually indifferent as to the concealment of our feelings. Aury, on discovering the schism that prevailed, was anxious to ascertain the cause of its existence. An explanation ensued, followed by the declaration and determination of the moderate party, not to serve the republic, if M'D. was permitted to bear the rank he anticipated from his appointment by Mendez. We had not then seen the wretched party with whom we proposed to congregate, nor were we aware of the debased character of those pseudo patriots : but the following morning convinced us of the little honour to be gained in the cause, and exhibited the heterogeneous character of its supporters.

---

* See Note C.

M'Donald finding that at Amelia he could not hope to realize those honours, his ambitious imagination had created, applied to Aury for a passage to Venezuela, resolved to venture on that desperate service, since to return to England was far more formidable. The Commodore, alarmed by the turbulent spirits we had manifested since our landing, and conscious of the little respect we entertained for his buccaneers, seemed eager to promote the wishes of those of the party who were disposed to withdraw; to some few however, he offered employment, but as they were among the most respectable, his proposals were declined.

CHAP. VI.

Account of the Expedition of M'Gregor against Amelia island—its capture—M'Gregor forms a depot for Privateers—his financial difficulties—expedition of Spanish troops from St. Augustine against M'Gregor, their defeat—the Spanish Commander tried by a court-martial—schisms among M'Gregor's forces—arrival of Commodore Aury—Aury agrees to pay the debts of the Amelia treasury, upon being made Commander of the Forces—Mr. Hubbard, Civil Governor—M'Gregor assigns his command to Aury, and retires—Aury's impolitic system towards the Americans.

THE occupation of Amelia island, by M'Gregor and his small party, adds one to the many proofs of the degeneracy of the Spanish character. It is truly lamentable to see a high minded and gallant people, compromised by the imbecility, to use the most softened expression, of their commanders.

The province of East Florida, from its peculiar situation upon the boundary line of Georgia, the most southern of the United States of America, had long allured the cupidity of that nation, whose governors are ever warily alive to their political interests.

Independent of the rich soil and luxurient priaries, the superiority of the climate, the immense forests of live oak, cedar, cypress and pine, more highly estimated than any in the southern states of the union, rendered available by the numerous intersections of navigable streams, this province possesses an important political character, from its situation upon the gulph stream, through which all vessels from the coasts of the gulph of Mexico, and the islands of the West Indies, are obliged to pass, unless they hazard the windward passage, which is often extremely dangerous, and always difficult. In time of war, exposed to the swarms of privateers which the numerous inlets of East Florida will permit them to fit out, it will be scarcely psssible for a single vessel to escape capture from the Americans, and not all the navy of Great Britain would be equal to the protection of her trade through this important channel; added to this, it will give to the Atlantic states of the union a decided influence over those of their western territory, uniting their destinies by a gordian knot, which the latter will never be able to sever. But while this province remains in the possessession of a foreign power, the union of North America will want one of the most important links to the chain of their security.

The bays of Appalache and Tampo, and Charlotte's harbour, on the west of this province, are admirably situated for naval stations; particularly the bay of Tampo, capable of receiving the whole of the British navy.

The ambition of the United States to obtain an empire on the sea, and to oppose a successful rivalship to our undisputed sovereignty on that element, has rendered them peculiarly alive to those advantages; and they have tried every measure that cunning, conciliation, or threats could suggest, to obtain the cession of this desirable province from the dominion of Spain, who is not forgetful, that on her retention of this peninsula, depends much of the security of her transatlantic possessions.

We cannot feel surprise at this ardent aspiration of the Americans, after a territory so peculiarly important to their quiet and security, and which will give consistence and stability to their vast and increasing empire.

England is, perhaps, the only power that could successfully dispute the possession of this province with the Americans; and from her maritime character, she is, perhaps, next to Spain, the only nation materially concerned in the question of its occupancy. Naval pre-eminence is our legitimate ambition, to preserve which we should sacrifice every other consideration of influence. Our insular situation, our habits, our impressions, and our constitution even, make a navy, if I may use the expression, the offspring of our soil; less expensive than an army, it can never like the latter, menace our liberties, but will always be ready to protect our honour, and hurl the thunders of vengeance upon our distant foes. America, like a young eagle that has already tried her strength, is now trimming her beak and talons, to pounce upon the sleeping lion. That she would even hazard another war with England, for the possession of Florida, appears by the spirit of the secret resolution, and act of congress, of the 15th of January, 1811, by which "the president is fully empowered to occupy any part, or the whole, of the territory lying east of the river Perdido, and south of Georgia, in the event of an attempt to occupy the said territory, or any part thereof, by any foreign government or power;" and by the same resolution and act, "he may employ any part of the army and navy of the United States, which he may deem necessary, for the purpose of taking possession of, and occupying, the territory aforesaid, and in order to maintain therein, the authority of the United States." This secret authority was only promulgated on the 10th of January, 1818, after the seizure of Amelia island, and in consequence of that measure.*—That the government of the United States should

---
* See note D.

hold such language as this, controlling the rights of Spain, and permitting to that nation, a mere qualified possession of the soil, proves the estimated value and importance of the stake.

M'Gregor, disgusted with the system pursued by General Bolivar, (whose niece he had married,) foreseeing from the disunion of the insurgent chiefs of Venezuela, and the little confidence they inspired in the respectable and enlightened class of society in that division of Spanish America, the present ruin of the popular cause, and the remote possibility of its recovery, quitted the patriot service on the main, and directed his attention to the United States, with whose views upon the Spanish provinces of the Floridas, he was well acquainted; and assured by their emissaries that a descent upon them from the union, would not be opposed by the executive of that government.

Having collected several adventurers to his standard in the northern states, and raised some funds for his enterprise, he proceeded to Charlston; here numbers of respectable young men, who had imbibed a military spirit during the war with Great Britain, and were thrown out of employment by its termination, readily tendered their aid and assistance; but the impolitic expression of his feelings in favour of negro emancipation, deemed a species of political heresy in the slave states, joined to his arbitrary and unconciliating conduct, soon detached them from his cause, and obliged M‘Gregor to seek for succour and assistance, in the more enterprising and less scrupulous community of Savannah.

The mercantile establishment of C. and Co. of that city, relying upon the successful issue of M‘Gregor's expedition, purchased of his anticipated conquest over the province of East Florida, 30,000 acres of land, at one dollar per acre, and induced several of their friends to contribute to his support.

With these supplies, and the remnant of his associates, in all about 150, M‘Gregor concentrated at the entrance of the river Altamaha, in Georgia, on which stands the flourishing settlement of Darien. Much time was consumed in the equipment of his forces, and numerous defections led to the further diminution of his partisans, from a want of confidence in his military talents, and the imperative system of European discipline, little suited to the genius and feelings of a people, whose militia create their officers by popular suffrage, thereby controlling that independence of character, so highly important to the enforcement of military duty, and dangerous to the interests of the individual who shall feel it necessary to resort to rigid measures of coercion.

The expedition being at length in a sufficient state of forwardness to undertake its object, a partner in the house of C. and Co. already the holder of some landed property in Amelia, with the view of anticipating events, preceded them to that island, and by representing to the inhabitants a magnified and fabulous account of M'Gregor's forces, who he described as 1000 strong, and every way equipped to secure their objects, prepared their minds to forego its defence, and to lessen the confidence of the Spanish commandant in the means of resistance.

On the 9th of July, the little band of M'Gregor, attended by two schooners and a few row boats, passing the shores of Cumberland island, at the entrance of the river St. Mary's, anchored in the Spanish waters of Amelia, disembarking in all about sixty muskets, under the very guns of the fort of Fernandina, and two block houses intended as a defence for the rear of the town. M'Gregor, assisted by Colonel Posen, of the United States army, as second in command, led his little band over a swamp, which divided the point of debarkation from the town, plunged up to their knees in mud, exposed to the means possessed by the Spaniards of totally annihilating them. To the cowardice of the Spanish commandant, and not to the talents of M'Gregor, must be attributed their success; for in this, the latter displayed an excess of folly in exposing his troops to the possible hostility of the garrison, which did not, as it happened, offer a single *coup de canon* of resistance from the fort, and only one gun was fired from the block house, and that without the orders of the commandant.

Possession of the fort and town being thus easily obtained, the prisoners were immediately sent to the main land, whence they retired upon the fortress of St. Augustine, to the no small astonishment and mortification of the governor of the province, who immediately directed a court-martial to try the commandant and second in command, on a charge of cowardice, which resulted in condemning the chief to death, and the second to imprisonment. But as it is necessary to transmit the decision of all courts-martial through the captain general of Havanna for approbation to the king of Spain, it is anticipated from the consequent delay, that some act of grace, in which his Catholic Majesty indulges upon every important occasion, such as the birth of a prince, &c. may include them with other culprits.

M'Gregor feeling himself firmly seated in his conquest, and acquiring daily some addition to his forces, began to arrange the system upon which its extension over the whole of the Floridas was to be founded; invited the insurgent privateers to make the Island of Amelia the depot of their prizes, and the vent of their cargoes. This acquisition of a port upon the Atlantic, and so near to the United States, was an object of the last importance to those swarms of Buccaneers who infest that ocean, and the islands of the West Indies, under the various flags of the republics of Mexico, Buenos Ayres, Venezuela, and others; who thereby avoided the danger and delay attending the carrying of their captures through the Gulph of Mexico to the Spanish Main, or to Galveston at the entrance of the river Trinity, where Lafite and his piratical gang had established a similar depot. Upon the cargoes of these prizes, the government of Amelia levied an impost of sixteen and a half per cent, upon the gross amount of sales, together with charges of admiralty courts, &c. for the current expences of the establishment, and for the purpose of replenishing their military chest, already too much exhausted to warrant a further progress in their meditated conquest of the provinces; the important prelude to which was the reduction of the fortress of St. Augustine, the seat of the government of East Florida, defended by a brave and tried soldier, Colonel Coppinger, whose loyalty to his sovereign was unquestionable. This subject occupied their attention, claiming the utmost consideration.

The people of the province of East Florida had evinced but little inclination to become associated with those who usurped the title of patriots, and who had no possible claim to that distinction, aliens alike in kindred and country; some few only who were contiguous to the seat of the intruders, listening to their fears, and desirous of protecting their little property, sacrificed the evidence of their feelings to their interested motives, by this dissimulation escaping the destruction that would otherwise have inevitably overtaken them.

The fiscal system of the occupiers of Amelia still lingered in poverty, and their resources, both in men and money, were as yet unequal to any enterprise beyond the walls of their garrison; various were the means suggested, and as often found fruitless in their attempts, to raise the consequence of their establishment, and the importance of their contemplated acquisitions. The people of the

United States, shrewd though speculative, seeing no immediate prospect of gain, and doubtful of the capacity of those at Amelia to obtain any serious and valuable results to their enterprise, withheld the promised assistance, and denied even to furnish them with the funds already raised for their necessities.

In the midst of this desolation, threatened with bankruptcy in their finances, and destruction to their plans, Colonel Irvin, formerly an officer in the American Militia, and a member of Congress for the State of Vermont, who had been appointed Adjutant-General, succeeding the retirement of Colonel Posen, was created chief of the Amelian treasury, and in that character issued notes negotiable upon the faith of the government. This experiment for a time supported their tottering credit, though it did not meet the ensuing difficulties.

Their financial embarrassments however began to throw discredit upon M'Gregor's party, and the people of the neighbouring state of Georgia, who supplied the garrison with provisions, &c. grew impatient under the factitious mode of payment, and at length positively refused to furnish rations unless paid for in specie. Private loans were then resorted to, and every expedient, however destructive, seized upon to support their tottering credit.

The Spanish governor of St. Augustine, apprised of every movement of the Buccaneers, waited with impatience a naval co-operation which had been promised from Havanna, for the purpose of destroying these intruders; but the characteristic delay of Spanish operations, for a long time baffled his hopes and lessened his confidence in their aid. This gentleman, the son of an Irishman, inheriting the native gallantry of his paternal ancestry, who had rendered himself, while a subaltern, conspicuous in the Peninsula, was rewarded for his bravery by his sovereign, panted eagerly for an opportunity of striking a decisive blow against the enemies of Spain; tired at length by unavailing remonstrances to the Captain General Cienfugas, and feeling ashamed that M'Gregor's trifling force should so long profane the province under his command, ordered the small detachment of black troops in garrison, and the militia of the province, to advance against Amelia Island, supported by a few boats with light artillery, through the narrow channels which separate the islands of Talbot, Nassau, and Amelia from the main land. The whole consisting of about three hundred, including one hundred and fifty of the militia. This force, ample for its object, was confided to the command of an officer of the garrison who held the rank of major in the royal regiment of Cuba. The laws of Spain unfortunately did not permit the governor to command in person absent from the confines of his garrison; had it been otherwise, this expedition would have closed the career of the pseudo patriots of Amelia Island. These forces advanced apparently unobserved to within the range of the guns of the fort of Fernandina, and were screened by an elevation called M'Clure's hill. It had been preconcerted between the naval and military commanders of the expedition, that a rocket from the former should direct their mutual advance, and the troops were anxiously waiting for the signal, when the guns of Amelia, and those of the Morgiana Buenos Ayres gun brig, and other privateers, opened their fire upon the boats, and threw their shot over the hill among the troops; two of whom were killed and several wounded. The commander, panic struck at this unexpected salutation, instead of advancing under cover of the night, and through the obscurity of the woods in the rear of the town, where the insurgents had made no preparation for resistance, and where he would have been out of the range of the fire from the ships, immediately sounded a retreat, in spite of the remonstrances and entreaties of the officers about him, who were maddened by his pusillanimity, and who relied with confidence upon the courage and devotion of the troops.

The militia of East Florida, a brave and active race, had determined to convince those Buccaneers that they would not be compromised by their assumed title of patriots.

The black troops it is well known may be perfectly relied upon for steadiness and courage. The orders of the commander were however imperative, and were reluctantly obeyed, and this expedition, the success of which had never been doubted, returned ingloriously across the river St. John. The governor of St. Augustine received the report with the utmost indignation, and with those feelings of mortification, a brave man must endure on seeing his plans deranged, and his best hopes crushed by the cowardice of those to whom their execution was entrusted. The commander was immediately put under arrest, and a court martial, too favourable to the individual, acquitted him of cowardice, but decided him incompetent, by returning it as the result of an error in judgment.

The situation of M'Gregor's government had become extremely critical, and the want of unanimity among the parties threatened with political suicide this ill-arranged oligarchy, when the arrival of Commodore Aury, under the united flags of the republics of Mexico and Venezuela, in the brig " *Mexico-libre*," accompanied by several prizes, gave a new character to the occupiers of Amelia Island. This adventurer had for some time committed depredations upon the Spanish trade in the Gulph of Mexico, and when unable to meet with prizes of that nation, felt no repugnance at levying contributions upon those of other flags; hearing of the settlement of M'Gregor at Amelia, and aware of the superiority of the situation as a naval depot, entered with his prizes the harbour of Fernandina, amounting to the value of sixty thousand dollars. This arrival resuscitated the torpid faculties of the intruders, and animated their exhausted credit.

M'Gregor sick of the scenes, and fatigued by the vaccilating character of those around him, determined to withdraw from his conquest, proposed an arrangement for that purpose with Aury, who undertook to pay off the debts of the Amelian treasury, amounting to near fifty thousand dollars. A Mr. Hubbard, formerly sheriff of New York, an American citizen, had divided with M'Gregor the empire of Amelia; holding the office of civil governor, while the latter possessed the supreme military command. This latter capacity was in consequence of the arrangement, assigned to Commodore Aury, who was recognised by the authorities of the Island, and landed his followers, the refuse of all nations, and all colours, collected from the mass of iniquity spread over the islands of the West Indies, and the Spanish Americas.

M'Gregor, upon the completion of his agreement with Aury, retired to the Bahamas, and many of his followers (the most respectable) abandoned the cause of the Insurgents.

Aury, who had acquired his ideas of liberty in the French revolutionary school, soon disgusted by his arbitrary measures the Americans who remained upon the island. The people of the United States accustomed to do every thing by popular representation, are the least qualified by previous habits to become the instruments of military despots, and particularly under an authority, emanating from such a source, and unpossessed of either the confidence of those around, or the means of coercing their obedience. Many and frequent were the disputes and quarrels between them, and the mass of foreign adventurers.

The English (few of whom remained after the

departure of M'Gregor) felt a predilection for those of a common origin speaking the same language and similar in habits.

Governor Hubbard, whose health had been considerably impaired by the constant agitation produced from the difficulties of his situation, and the frequent occurrence of disputes among the soldiers and others of the garrison, suddenly died; and before any other appointment could take place, Aury seized upon his office, and consolidated it with his military supremacy. This arbitrary usurpation gave rise to two or three attempts to overturn the French party of Aury, but they were unsuccessful, from a want of proper intelligence and co-operation.—These ebullitions of feeling had subsided into comparative quiescence on our arrival at Amelia.

CHAP. VII.

M'Donald's dishonourable conduct—meditated revolution in Amelia —proposed coalition of English and Americans against the French party of Aury—Colonel Irvin refuses to co-operate—determine to quit Amelia—arrive at St. Mary's in Georgia—sickness at St. Mary's and the dreadful endemic at Charlston—receive a request to defend a British officer on trial at Amelia for high treason—arbitrary proceedings of the court-martial—prisoner ordered for transportation—sent off to the Morgiana brig—quarrel and personal contest with M'Donald—arrested by the adjutant-general—garrison in a state of alarm—confined under a corporal's guard—unpleasant situation of one of my friends—embarked for St. Mary's and banished the republic of the Floridas—arrive at St. Mary's—a party of Americans at St. Mary's waiting an opportunity to revolutionize Amelia—offered ample encouragement to join them—invited by the governor of East Florida to visit St. Augustine—engage a passage for St. A.— oblige Colonel Irvin to apologise to my friend the Lieutenant—embark for St. A.

M'DONALD's conduct since our arrival at Amelia had been extremely suspicious, and was now the subject of investigation to those who were heretofore professedly his supporters. He had sedulously endeavoured to cultivate the good opinion of Aury, and had been detected in practising a system of *espionage* particularly on the conduct of those I have denominated the moderate party. Disgusted with the character and conduct of this weak man, all deserted him but the few boys who were confided to his protection by their friends, and two or three of our party, who had no alternative but to follow their original destination.

The inhabitants of Fernandina, disaffected to the government of Aury, anxious to overthrow the French party, supposing we coincided in their views, soon conveyed to us their inclinations, and invited our co-operation in the meditated revolution.

Aury, however, by the defection of some of our party, particularly M'Donald, was well informed of our disposition towards him, and that we were stimulated to hostility by the inhabitants; but aware that our strength was too formidable for him to encounter with a certainty of success, and apprised that the crews of two privateers had offered us their aid, he dissembled his feelings, and with the view of counteracting our plans hastened the sailing of those vessels.

In the mean time our plot acquired strength and consistence, and many were the private meetings to arrange the system of attack. Colonel Irvin continued to hold the appointment of adjutant-general, under Aury; it was believed that he was favourable to the spirit of revolt: to gain him decidedly, was an important consideration, and for this I was authorised to seek an interview. The overture required some caution, for although he had expressed his disapprobation of the measures of Aury, he was deemed a man of too little nerve to excite our confidence in his discretion. Accident brought us together, and the subject of my mission was gradually introduced :—at length the important query was hazarded, whether he would co-operate, and could command the assistance of the Americans still in garrison. Evidently surprised at this conclusion to our interview, he evinced a degree of irresolution not to be pardoned in one who had previously expressed his favourable feelings. Pressed however to be explicit in his determination, he with much hesitation and reluctance declined to become an accessary, intimating that too much blood would be spilled in procuring a favourable issue to our enterprise.

Irritated by this result, I could not conceal my contempt for this *bloodless* soldier. To argue with such a man was impossible, and to attempt influencing the Americans without his concurrence was quite hopeless, and we had not then learnt that the people of the United States possess all those feelings of hostility, so conspicuous in the conduct of the American Government to every thing British.

Thus foiled in our only hope of rendering Amelia Island worthy of our attention, I determined with a few friends to retire from a cause so unpromising, and an association so discreditable ; and the following morning embarked for the town of St. Mary's, upon the river of that name, on the confines of Georgia, distant about seven miles.

Tired and disgusted with the scenes I had witnessed at Amelia, and cured of my expectation of finding patriotism in the Western Hemisphere, I arrived at St. Mary's, to avail myself of the first opportunity that might present itself to proceed to Charlston, distant about 250 miles.

The town of St. Mary's stands upon the eastern branch of that river, on a flat sandy soil, surrounded with extensive marshes, rendering it extremely unhealthy during the severe heats of summer : several cases of fever had occurred, but the misery of our situations and disappointments, excluded every other reflection, and rendered us insensible to the dangerous influence of the climate. We learnt that at Charlston the ravages of the yellow fever were cruelly extensive, and that hundreds were swept off by that malignant disease.

Three days after my arrival at St. Mary's, I received a request from some of the respectable inhabitants of Amelia Island, to attend as counsel on behalf of a British naval officer, who had been long on the island, about to be tried by a court martial, summoned by Aury, for alleged treasonable practices. Having nothing to occupy my time, and having made the bar my pursuit, I was ready to give the unfortunate individual all the assistance in my power, and with that view immediately proceeded for Amelia. The tempestuous state of the weather and the want of regular communication between that island and St. Mary's, considerably retarded our progress, and it was not until after the close of the examination of witnesses that I reached the court-martial. The mock gravity of this assembly might at any other time, and under other circumstances, have excited my risible faculties, but the knowledge of their feelings towards the prisoner and the blood-thirsty character of his judges, convinced me that nothing but the most determined opposition to their oppression could insure his safety, for they yet wished to give to their proceedings the colour of justice.

Aury, while the crews of the privateers of whose mutinous disposition I have already spoken, remained in port, dissembled his feelings towards the prisoner, (who was implicated in some revolutionary movements during, and subsequent to the existence of Governor Hubbard,) having sent them to sea, felt sufficiently strong to punish the temerity of one who had dared to question his sovereignty. The court, composed principally of the creatures of his will, ready for any purpose however villainous, their commander might commit to them, were determined to inflict the severest penalty upon the prisoner, to strike terror into the remaining disaffected by the vigour of their measures, and no one ventured to hope that the arm of vengeance would be restrained.

Having applied for a copy of the charges and proceedings, with minutes of evidence, I desired to know the code of laws by which the prisoner was tried? The president replied, by the code of the United States. Upon perusal of the proceedings, it was evident the prisoner's case had been predetermined, and that the formality of a court-martial was a mere colouring to their injustice : for finding the naval code of the United States more favourable than the military to their purposes, they had adopted it. Against this I strenuously urged my objections, and demanded a revisal of their proceedings. Captain Liers, the president, appeared disposed to admit my objections, but Aury, apprised of his want of devotion to his purposes, counteracted his influence by sending him immediate orders to embark, directing the judge advocate to swear in other members in the room of the president and two of his officers, who were thus removed by the arbitrary dictum of Aury. Against this admission of new members, who were to determine a cause, the evidence upon which they had not received, I unavailingly protested, borne down by the clamour of the judge advocate, (well known as the organ of the commander-in-chief,) I was obliged to submit. The judge advocate then addressed the court, expatiating upon the horrors that would have ensued, had the civil war, contemplated by the treasonable practices of the prisoner and his party, taken place, calling upon the court to protect the peaceable and respectable citizens of the republic, from the recurrence of such scenes, by inflicting upon the instigator of those atrocities, the vengeance due to his criminality, dwelling with much importance upon the dawning consequence and lustre of their republic, which had been threatened with destruction by the machinations of this traitor. This address, calculated to rouse the passions of his auditors, and to alarm their fears, was intended, not merely for the Court, of whose disposition he was well assured, but to operate as an apology to the inhabitants for the tragic scene about to be exhibited.

The situation of the prisoner was now extremely critical, and I felt that nothing less than an extraordinary effort could save him from the impending fate. Nerved by a sense of duty, and resolved upon the hazard, I advanced to the table, round which were seated those Buccaneers; and addressed the president, protesting against the entire proceedings of the court, stating my conviction, that the unfortunate prisoner was not likely to escape their vengeance, from the evident partiality of their conduct, that it only remained for me to state my sentiments, and to assure the individual members of the court, that I would forward their names to the different governments to which they were still subjects, and that I had no doubt, but their conduct would draw upon them the punishment their contempt of justice deserved. Rising simultaneously from their seats, and seizing their swords, I should have fallen the victim of my temerity, had not the bye standers murmured their approbation, and awed those daring ruffians. The president, who had more coolness than his fellows, and was perhaps aware of the dangerous experiment they were about to make, checked the ebullition of feeling, by commanding the members of the court to resume their seats, then turning to me, requested that I would recollect I was in the presence of a competent and independent tribunal, that I had hazarded too much by the freedom of my animadversions, at the same time assuring me that the prisoner should have the benefit of every legal objection contained in my protest, when respectfully presented. This temperate remonstrance was evidently produced by the impression made on the mind of the president by the murmur of disapprobation, well aware that the enemies of Aury were sufficiently powerful and ready to hazard the issue of a contest. The court was then cleared, and continued several hours in deliberation ; the following morning a copy of their sentence was handed to me, finding the prisoner guilty of two of the three charges, and sentencing him to perpetual banishment from the limits of the Republic!!! At noon on the same day, the prisoner was embarked on board a row boat, attended by a file of soldiers and two officers, and conveyed on board the "*Morgiana*" gun-brig, belonging to Buenos Ayres, bound on a cruize, then lying off the bar of the harbour:—she immediately got under weigh and cleared the Island of Amelia *

Scarcely had I reached my quarters to prepare for leaving the island, when one of my companions, formerly influenced by the speciousness of M'Donald, came attended by several others, with the information that M'Donald was loudly declaiming against me as a deserter from the cause of patriotism, and of having endeavoured to detach his followers. Had this charge been temperately made, it would not have excited my resentment, as I had certainly endeavoured to dissuade his partisans from following the wretched fortunes that awaited him; but having coupled with his complaints some insulting observations, I determined to demand an apology, or atonement for his insolence. I immediately sought and found him near my quarters, and on demanding an explanation, he replied with an insulting and supercilious frown, that " he did na want aught to say to me," and was preparing to retire. His dastardly conduct provoked me to tell him, that I conceived him to be a compound of the bully and the coward, and that I was ready to give him satisfaction if he had the courage to demand it. Roused by those epithets, and the mockery

---

* See Note E.

of the spectators, this doughty colonel aimed a blow at me, which I avoided, and repaid his intentions with interest. A personal contest ensued, in which it was probable he would have had the advantage from his superior strength, had not the bye-standers interfered, and seperated us, he then sneaked off to his friend Aury, demanding his protection; this hastened an order (under consideration,) for my arrest, and in a short time the adjutant-general, with two officers completely armed, arrived at my quarters, with directions to put me under arrest, and to attend me as a guard; in the evening I was marched under their escort to the house of the adjutant-general, where every attention was paid to my accomodation, consistent with my situation as a prisoner.

My commitment to the custody of the adjutant-general, created throughout the town of Fernandina, a considerable sensation, and much feverish agitation, particularly among those who had authorised me to attempt to gain Irvin to our proposed measures, they had no doubt but that my arrest was a prelude to the seizure of themselves. They were seen running up and down, in every direction, seeking to ascertain the views and motives of Aury, who unaware of their feelings, readily listened to his fears, which prompted him to believe they meditated a revolution. The guards of the fort were in consequence doubled, a strong patrole paraded the streets, and a large piece of artillery, an eighteen pounder, placed, well manned, in Washington-square, commanding the principle avenue, charged with grape shot; every thing denoted a state of alarming anxiety. Aury, with his aids and a guard, were every where on the alert, and in the course of the evening repeatedly visited the room in which I was detained.

Several of my comrades called, and some were refused admission, one, a lieutenant in the navy, was accosted as usual by Irvin, who took him on his entrance by the hand, and made some trifling observations respecting the weather, then suddenly turning to the captain of the guard, he ordered my friend to be conveyed to the fort. This unexpected proceeding astonished the lieutenant, who in vain demanded the motive of his conduct. The fiat of this doughty hero had gone forth, and was not to be questioned, my poor friend was carried off by the guard, and lodged in the fort, uncertain of what might be his fate on the morrow.

On retiring to rest, a corporal's guard was placed outside my bed-room door, and two officers slept completely equipped, on rugs near the fire, to secure my person. During the night, the corporal, (an Irishman,) several times came and whispered to me, that he could command the guard, if I was inclined to escape, but apprehensive that I should hazard too much by trusting to his overtures, and believing that it was a decoy, for the purpose of sacrificing me, I declined his offers, and endeavoured to prepare against the worst.

Early the ensuing morning, I received a visit from the adjutant-general, with orders to banish me from the Floridas, and at ten o'clock I was directed to be in readiness for embarkation, I then demanded from Irvin the place of my destination, but upon this he was inflexibly silent. The boat which had conveyed to the " *Morgiana*" the prisoner on the preceding day, was in attendance, the same signal was flying at her mast head, and she was manned by several ill looking fellows, when the guard marched me down to the beach for embarkation. I had now but little doubt that I was about to be conveyed to sea, and put on board one of the privateers still hovering near the coast ; my situation was by no means agreeable, and my nerves were considerably agitated by the prospect before me, but I derived consolation from observing that those in the boat were unarmed. I had accidently a brace of loaded pistols in my pocket, which had escaped the scrutiny of my gaolers, each having a small dagger; with these I could at least make some impression and resistance; with this view I placed myself near the steersman, on his right hand, upon the gunwhale of the boat, he was an old man, and there was little doubt of my ability to throw him overboard, and get possession of the tiller; in that situation, with my pistols, I had a chance of directing the boat up St. Mary's river, before I could be overpowered, and as the tide was favourable my escape might be thus ensured.

Waiting with anxiety the critical moment, the boat still making for the bar of the river, with a pistol ready to draw from my pocket, and just on the point of seizing the man at the helm, a boat from the shore of Tiger island, (a flat island dividing the American from the Spanish waters,) approached us, containing a Captain E. of the United States navy, with whom I was well acquainted; he hailed us, and as his boat closed with ours, I sprang into her, and turning to the one I had quitted, with my pistols cocked and pointed, I threatened to shoot the first man that should dare to follow me. Captain E. ignorant of my situation, and surprised at this conduct, requested an explanation. I briefly informed him how I had been treated by Aury, and that I apprehended they were about to convey me on board one of the privateers; he, however, dissipated those apprehensions, by assuring me that the boat was a regular packet between Amelia island and St. Mary's, and was bound to the latter place. The people in the boat, more alarmed than myself, began to recover from their consternation, and assured me that I was perfectly safe, and that they were conveying me to St. Mary's, but that the state of the tide had obliged them to keep so low down towards the bar, but that they should alter their course almost immediately. Tranquilised by the joint assurance of Cap. E. and the people in the boat, I returned on board, resuming my former situation, that I might be ready for any treasonable attempt. In the course of a few minutes, those fears were entirely dissipated, by our turning up the river St. Mary's, and I once more congratulated myself upon an escape from the Buccaneers. In about half an hour, my friend the lieutenant followed, he had been banished in the same summary way, after passing the night under the surveillance of his negro guards, and their Italian captain, in less comfortable quarters than myself, we mutually congratulated ourselves on an escape so unexpected.

From that moment I abjured the cause of the Insurgents, convinced from the specimen they had furnished, that neither honour nor honesty was to be gained, or found among them.

The people of St. Mary's, heartily tired of the proximity of Aury and his myrmidons, desired a change more favourable to the Americans. Several officers from different parts of the union had concentrated there with the view of counter-revolutionising the island: supposing my sense of injury, and feelings of revenge inclined me to promote their objects, they made me an overture to join their party, assuring ample encouragement, in case of success; but sick of this mock patriotism, I declined altogether association, resolved to embark the earliest opportunity that might occur for Charlston. While waiting for a passage, the surveyor-general of East Florida called upon me, expressing himself pleased with the resistance I had offered to the Buccaneers on the court-martial, which he conceived favourable to the Spanish cause. A few days after an invitation, arrived through that gentleman from the governor of the province of East Florida, who felt desirous of seeing me at St. Augustine.

Reflecting that I had never borne arms against Spain, and that it is only in *foræ conscientiæ* that we are responsible for our intentions, I availed myself of the opportunity thus afforded me, to visit a celebrated fortress, and to become acquainted with the governor, who was highly esteemed even by the enemies of his monarch. A small schooner was about to sail on that destination, and in her I engaged a passage.

In the mean time several of my comrades deserted the cause at Amelia, and had arrived at St. Mary's, to proceed to England by the way of Charlston. They were already embarked for that destination when Irvin and several of his officers came up to St. Mary's. My friend the lieutenant was on board very ill, exhausted with anxiety and disappointment. Anxious that he should have satisfaction, I addressed Irvin in the midst of his officers, taxing him with duplicity, and unmanly conduct towards my friend. Several of those who had sought my co-operation in their meditated counter-revolution at Amelia, supported my charges against Irvin, who appeared much disconcerted, and confessed his regret at the measures he had been obliged to sanction, but laid claim upon my gratitude, asserting that my liberty, and perhaps life, had been secured by his interference. I then demanded that he should go on board to the lieutenant, and express to him his contrition for those acts of severity he had directed. This he did, in the presence of a great concourse, who were not a little gratified at the humiliation of this mock hero.

On the following day I embarked for St. Augustine, but did not feel secure until the Island of Amelia was left far behind.

CHAP. VIII.

Sail for St. Augustine—friendly reception of the governor and inhabitants—description of St. Augustine—the fort of St. Mark's—Catholic the established religion—Protestants admitted to citizenship—climate—former state of the province of East Florida—Americans excluded from holding lands—Society of St. A.—beauty of the women—attempt of the Americans against St. A.—their defeat and dispersion—obtain a grant of land—treatment of negroes superior to other slave states—offer to retake Amelia.

THE wind favoured our departure, though light, the second morning we were off the bar of the harbour of St. Augustine. With the rise of the tide we reached the anchorage ground, abreast of the town of St. A. and the fort of St. Mark's. After receiving the visit of the town-major and physician, we were paraded before the governor, who received us with the most friendly marks of attention, expressing his pleasure at seeing us under the protection of the Spanish flag.

The arrival of a vessel was to this little community quite an event; the proximity of their enemies induced a high degree of interest, and numerous were the inquiries we had to answer.

The town of St. Augustine is the capital and seat of government of the province of East Florida, in

latitude 29. 30. on a tongue of land, bounded by
the waters of the harbour. The Island of St. Anastasia in front of the town, protects it and the anchorage ground from the violence of the sea, and extends
a distance of twenty-one miles, to the bar of Matanza, a flat and sandy soil, covered with scrub oak
and marine plants; its greatest breadth about
three miles. The bar of the harbour of St.
Augustine, owing to the weight of the waters
of the Atlantic ocean, and the rapid current
of the Gulph stream, is subject to frequent changes,
and is seldom capable of receiving vessels drawing
more than seven or eight feet water. This variation
of the bar, and the dangerous character of the coast,
will ever prevent St. Augustine's rising into commercial eminence. The scite of the town runs parallel with the coast, fronting the Atlantic, in the form
of a parallelogram, the streets cutting each other at
right angles. The houses, which are commodious,
are built of a marine cob, dug from the neighbouring island of St. Anastasia; by exposure to the air,
it acquires the solidity of stone, and is equally durable. On the northern end of the town upon a
gentle elevation stands the fort of St. Mark's, a regular well built square fortress, with four bastions,
two *en barbette*, and the others with embrasures—

the whole mounting sixty-four pieces of cannon, and from its interior being bomb proof, capable of sustaining a vigorous siege. From this fort to the extreme breadth of the tongue of land, extends a long range of wet ditch, and turf line, defended by three salient angles. The fort and bastions are built of the same materials as the houses of the town. This marine substance is superior to stone, not being liable to splinter from the effects of bombardment; it receives and embeds the shot, which adds, rather than detracts from its strength and security. The garrison is composed of a detachment from the royal regiment of Cuba, with some black troops, who together form a respectable force.

The houses and the rear of the town are intersected and covered with orange groves; their golden fruit and deep green foliage, not only render the air agreeable, but beautify the appearance of this interesting little town, in the centre of which (the square) rises a large structure dedicated to the Catholic religion. At the upper end are the remains of a very considerable house, the former residence of the governor of this settlement, but now in a state of dilapidation and decay, from age and inattention. The Catholic is the established religion, but the quiet observance of every other is so far tolerated, that no interruption is offered to their professors—indeed this is the only colony of Spain in which Protestants are admitted to the privileges of Spanish citizenship.

At the southern extremity of the town stands a large building, formerly a monastry of Carthusian Friars, but now occupied as a barrack for the troops of the garrison; at a little distance are four stacks of chimnies, the sole remains of a beautiful range of barracks, built during the occupancy of the British from 1763 to 1783: for three years the 29th regiment was stationed there, and in that time they did not lose a single man. The proverbial salubrity of the climate, has obtained for St. Augustine the designation of the Montpelier of North America; indeed such is the general character of the province of East Florida.

The few families that remain of the ancient settlers in the time of the British, remember with regret the contrast, the province, and the people then presented. Our nation, with a zeal highly laudable and considerate, encouraged the agricultural spirit of the early settlers by parliamentary aids; but the Spaniards, who consider themselves degraded by every act in which personal labour is concerned, and averse to all bodily exertion, suffer the various advantages of soil and climate, to pass unheeded; the province is consequently an extensive desert, the face of which industry would soon turn into smiling and luxuriant fields. Great encouragement is given to people willing to cultivate the soil, but a law of exclusion, which deprives the American citizens of a right of entry, retards the progress of population, and rejects the benefits that would otherwise result to the province. The distance of this settlement from Europe, together with the general ignorance of Europeans respecting its advantages, prevents them from availing of the encouraging terms offered to their enterprise.

The governor, of whom I have already spoken, is about forty-five years of age, of active and vigorous mind, anxious to promote by every means in his power the prosperity of the province confided to his command; his urbanity and other amiable qualities render him accessible to the meanest individual, and justice is sure to follow an appeal to his decision. His military talents are well known and appreciated by his sovereign, and he now holds, in addition to the government of East Florida, the rank of colonel in the royal regiment of Cuba. The clergy consist of the *padre*, (priest of the parish,)

a native of Wexford in Ireland; a Franciscan friar,
the chaplain to the garrison, and an inferior or *curé*
The social qualities of the *padre*, and the general
tolerance of his feelings, render him an acceptable
visitant to all his flock: for many hours of agreeable
relaxation I was indebted to the good man, whose
friendly offices are always ready to be bestowed.—
The judge, treasurer, collector and notary are the
principal officers of the establishment, besides a
number of those devoted solely to the military occupations of the garrison. The whole of this society
is extremely courteous to strangers: they form one
family, and those little jealousies, animosities and
bickerings, so disgraceful to our small English communities, do not sully their meetings of friendly
chit chat, called as in Spain *turtulias*. The women
are deservedly celebrated for their charms;
their lovely black eyes have a vast deal of expression, their complexions a clear brunette: much attention is paid to the arrangement of their hair; at
mass they are always well dressed in black silk
basquinas (petticoats) with the little *mantilla* (black
lace veil) over their heads; the men in their military
costumes: good order and temperance are their
characteristic virtues, but the vice of gambling too
often profanes their social haunts, from which even

the fair sex are not excluded: indolence is however one of the notorious foibles of the sex, and that neatness and cleanliness, so exquisitely captivating in our fair countrywomen, does not occupy much of their care and attention.

Two days following our arrival, a ball was given by some of the inhabitants, to which I was invited. The elder couples opened it with minuets, succeeded by the younger couples displaying their handsome light figures in Spanish dances.

The governor declined attending their assemblies until they should wipe off the stain fixed upon the province by the polluted presence of the Buccaneers.

The law excluding the people of the United States from settlement in the province of East Florida, was passed in consequence of their repeated attempts to wrest the province from the dominion of Spain.— About six years since, a number of adventurers in Georgia, collected together a force of near eight hundred men, commanded by a general M. and a colonel S. This expedition was supported by some gun-boats, &c. under commodore C. The Island of Amelia soon submitted to the intruders; they then directed their march against St. Augustine: the Americans unaccustomed to the resistance of regular fortifications, miscalculated their operations, and advanced too near the range of the guns. The Spaniards opened upon them an unexpected fire, and obliged them to retire in great disorder, they however rallied their disordered numbers, and took up a more distant position, where they remained several months, destroying and burning the plantations of those near their line of march and occupation. The garrison of St. A. were not inactive spectators of their enemies, several *sorties* were made particularly by a non-commissioned black officer called Prince, who in one of his *rencontres* carried off the whole of the enemy's forage, killed the commanding officer and three of his men, and wounded many of the remainder of the foraging party. These desultory attacks considerably weakened the confidence of the Americans, and induced them to think of retiring from the unavailing contest. In the mean time a gun-boat was fitted out at St. Augustine, and sent with a long gun in her bow up the north river, in a creek of which she commanded the American encampment; this she approached under cover of the night, and her fire from a quarter so little anticipated, and against which no preparation had been made, completely discomfitted and put to the rout, this band of intruders, who abandoned with rapidity and in disorder, every inch of ground they had occupied.

The Spanish government loudly complained to the executive of the United States, against this unwarrantable invasion, at a time the two countries were in a state of profound peace. To this remonstrance the president replied, that it was an unauthorised violation of individuals, unconnected with, and unsanctioned by the government. These he proposed to call to account, but the death of General M., and the critical situation of Spain lulled those feelings of resentment, and lessened the influence of her appeal for justice, and the whole affair seems buried in oblivion, except in the memories of those who have suffered by the violence of the invaders.

The levy of this number of troops, their equipment and organization, within the territory of the United States, either proves that the members of that government were not uninterested observers, or the insufficiency of their power to restrain the licentiousness of the people; in either case, it is fair to conclude, that those territories in the neighbourhood of the United States have little to hope from their justice, unless they possess the means of commanding respect.

This I have always considered one of the greatest defects of the federal government; the executive created and supported by popular suffrage, is seldom sufficiently strong and independent, to controul the violences of the people. To punish this infraction of neutrality, the court of Spain passed a law of exclusion to the people of the union, and they sigh in vain for admission to the advantages of the rich soil, and luxuriant pasturage of that province; some however steal in, and acquire possession as *squatters*, a term applied to vagrant and untitled settlers in the wilds of North America. To foreigners, grants of land are very liberal; a considerable tract was assigned me upon the borders of Lake St. George, one of the finest parts of the province, on the river St. John's, abounding with live oak, cedar, and cypress; the soil genial to the cultivation of cotton, rice, sugar, and other important products.

To the honour of the Spanish character in this and in all other of their colonies, their treatment of the negroes presents a striking contrast to the disgraceful and morbid selfishness of the possessors of this unfortunate race in other countries. Here the Negro is at least considered as a social animal, susceptible of the pains and joys of existence, who has a soul admissible into the presence of the deity, for his religious duties and moral conduct they feel bound to provide. The attachments of this degraded class of human beings to their owners, are, in this province generally strong, the sensibilities of our nature are not outraged by those continual and disgusting scenes of severity, which have marked our character as colonists next in barbarity to the Dutch, who are notoriously cruel to the African race. Here they continue long in one family, grow up with the rising generation, partake of their sports, sympathise in their griefs, and become identified with every member of their families. Manumission to them brings no alleviation of misery, for they have never known other than kind treatment, the lash is seldom heard on their plantations, the cry of their sufferings is rarely borne upon the winds of heaven. This general fact has been proved beyond a doubt; in the Island of St. Domingo, that extensive part occupied by the Spaniards, has hitherto resisted every effort to revolutionise the negroes. This does not arise from the power of the Spaniards, for they have scarcely sufficient force to protect their garrisons, but from the attachment of the negroes to their present condition. On the extensive continent of Spanish America, the Indians and negroes are amalgamated with the creole population, and it is not as in our colonies, and in the States of North America, an insurmountable barrier of exclusion from society, that the individual has a taint of African origin. Recently, one of the richest heiresses of the nobility of Mexico, at whose marriage, the streets leading to the cathedral were covered with bars of gold, and ingots of silver, strongly partook of the colour and blood of that people. The laws oblige the proprietor to feed his negroes, and clothe them with two suits annually; whether the crops are good or bad, whether success or misfortune attend the master, the slave may demand compliance with the laws, an infraction of which incurs the penalty of release of service.

The proximity of the banditti of Aury was a constant theme of feverish anxiety to the governor of St. Augustine, his brave and loyal feelings were ever alive to the disgraceful situation in which the remissness and culpable negligence of the Spanish authorities of Havanna, and the incapacity of the commander, and failure of the expedition sent against Amelia Island had placed him and his friends. The constant subject of conversation, he dwelt with no common regret upon the laws of Spain, which confined him to the command of his garrison, and restrained him from personally wiping off the pollution of the invaders. In one of our animated conversations upon this subject, I proposed to surprise and carry the fort of Fernandina, provided he would place under my command, one hundred and fifty men; every part of the garrison at Amelia was well known to me, not a particle of its weakness had escaped my observation, and I calculated with a certainty of success, my meditated enterprise: my plans met with the entire approbation of the governor, and several officers present volunteered their services, but a recent and renewed promise of naval co-operation from the Havanna, and the importance of a combined naval and military force, in order to secure the ships of the enemy which would have the means of escape, unless opposed by a marine expedition, obliged the governor reluctantly to decline my offer; thus were dissipated my hopes of being able to repay those Buccaneers the obligations they had conferred.

CHAP. IX.

Depart for St. Mary's—pass through the Royal Road—overtaken by a storm—sleep at a grazier's—suspicious character of our host—murder committed by his two sons—arrive at the village of Cowford—description of that part of the river St. John's—party of back woodmen—they remain with us as guards against the apprehended attack from Aury's gang—illness of one of my companions—his recovery—kidnapping of Negroes—character of the people on the back frontier of Georgia—pursue our route across the St. John's—disappointment of a breakfast—waylaid and fired at—one of the assailants wounded—proves to be the guide—arrive at a grazier's, good fare—proceed on our journey, and arrive on the confines of Okeyfenokey—badness of the roads—arrive at St. Mary's—find my fellow passengers from England windbound—death of one of the party—embark for Charlston.

HAVING concluded the object of my visit to St. Augustine, and being desirous of returning to St. Mary's, for the purpose of embarking for Charlston. I prepared for my journey: in the mean time intelligence was brought to the garrison, that Aury, apprised of my visit to St. A., and of my proposals to the governor, had determined to intercept my return to St. Mary's. For that purpose he had stationed three row boats, fully manned and armed, on the river St. John's, expecting to arrest me on passing it; these boats had been seen for three days lurking about the narrows.

Two officers who were to be the companions of my journey, were equally averse with myself, to fall into the power of the pirates; our course was consequently changed, and we prepared by a circuitous and extended route to avoid our enemies.

Taking leave of our good friend the governor, and the agreeable society of St. Augustine, we quitted the fortress, mounted upon Indian ponies, attended by a guide, who agreed to convoy us to the Cowford, a village forty miles above the mouth of the river St. John's, each armed with a rifle, a brace of pistols, and a sabre.

Our route lay through what is denominated the Royal road, along extensive pine woods. This road was formed during the sovereignty of Great Britain, and intersects several divisions of the province: the Spaniards have however neglected to keep it open, and in many places it is scarcely passable.

Soon after our departure from St. Augustine, the rain descended in torrents, but as it was important to proceed, and as our return to the garrison would be equally unpleasant, we continued our route, consoled by the reflection that the violence of the storm would confine our enemies to the shelter of their boats, or to some covertion shore.

About ten o'clock, wet with the pitiless storm, we were saluted by the barking of dogs at a grazier's house, on the right of the road, the storm still continued with but little promise of abatement. Digressing from the road, about a quarter of a mile, we reached the welcome shelter, where seated round a good fire, with comfortable fare, we heeded not the howling tempest.

Our guide had informed us when approaching this shelter, that the character of the host and his family was justly suspicious; one of his sons had, a few days previous to our quitting St. Augustine, been brought in, charged with a most cruel murder, in company with his brother, upon one of their neighbours. The unfortunate victim having incurred the displeasure of the brothers, they proceeded to inflict summary vengeance upon him; entering his hut one night, at a time he was both unprepared for, and incapable of resistance, they seized and carried him into the woods, and binding him to a tree, deliberately shot him, in spite of the poor man's tears and prayers for mercy. For some time they evaded the penalty of their crime, but a detachment of dragoons sent in pursuit, had the good fortune to meet with one of them; he was a man of singular appearance, at least seven feet high, large

but not strongly formed, pale and cadaverous, though
by no means possessing the ferocious aspect I anticipated from his criminality. The other brother
was supposed to be lurking in the woods, and it was
believed that he made frequent visits to his father.
Being well armed, we had little to fear from assault
while awake, but sleep, that friend to robbery and
murder, might deprive us of the power of resistance;
we, therefore, concerted to watch alternately, to
avoid being taken by surprise; our conversation was
carried on in French, unintelligible to our host, who
eyed us from our entrance with evident curiosity and
attention. The wife had acquired from her neighbours the character of a witch, but we were proof
against such idle opinions, and feared nothing
beyond the power of the human form from her influence. She was tall, brawny, and dark, with a wild
and scowling expression in her eye, her natural defects she, however, endeavoured to conceal, and
ministered to our wants with apparent alacrity.
Alone, I confess, I should not have felt so confident
of security; the door of our room was frequently
opened during the night, and the dogs were growl-
ing round the house. Overcome by fatigue, nature
was not to be cheated of her accustomed repose,
towards morning during my watch, I could not re-

sist the influence of sleep, and would almost have become a willing victim, rather than forego its enjoyment.

We rose early in the morning, and taking a good breakfast, proceeded on our journey to the Cowford, the rain had ceased, and the character of the woods had lost much of their gloom, we travelled on, relieving the tedium and monotony of the way with a variety of anecdotes. We had all been considerable travellers on the continent of Europe, except our negro guide, who compensated for that deficiency of information, by giving us accounts of his repeated visits to the Indian nations, between whom and the Spaniards he acted as interpreter.

About sun-set we reached the village of the Cowford, and learnt with much satisfaction that the pirates had not so far ascended the river. This village was once considerable, and is admirably situated, but the want of enterprise, and the small number of the inhabitants in the province, have not found sufficient encouragement to concentrate there. The houses are in a dismantled and ruinous condition. The river St. John's is here extremely beautiful, at least a mile and a half in breadth, a little higher up it opens into an extensive basin, from which are several branches called creeks, but which in England would acquire the dignity of rivers; their banks are covered with immense woods of live oak, cedar, cypress, and pine, and their waters filled with an infinite variety of fish. The magnitude of the St. John's entitles it to a respectable consequence, even when compared with the other and great rivers of North America. The banks of the Hudson are certainly bolder, but I do not think that the St. John's would suffer by a comparison with its beauty, with respect to the soil of its banks, and salubrity of climate, it far surpasses the former. During the American revolutionary war, our twenty-gun ships and small frigates, frequently entered this river, which is navigable two hundred miles above its mouth, to vessels capable of passing the bar; this must inevitably render the province of East Florida, at no remote distance of time, the finest, and most valuable section of North America. One of the greatest evils, and most difficult, as well as unprofitable labour of the settlers of North America, is the necessity of cutting down the forests, in order to cultivate the soil. The want of water carriage, and the distance from a place of sale, renders this natural and abundant production, an inconvenience, and expence to the cultivator; but in this province, the facilities of water carriage, the numerous mill streams, and the readily obtained value of the timber, instead of being a heavy loss, yield a considerable profit, while the settler in the back woods of North America has no other alternative than to fire his woods and consume them.

Entering the village of Cowford, we dismounted at a grog shop, where we met several graziers and woodmen gambling and drinking. This rencontre was rather agreeable than otherwise, they were all opposed to Aury's system, and would willingly have rewarded him with a halter for the liberty he proffered. Learning our critical situation, they readily engaged to become our defenders, if attacked during the night. These men always travel armed with a rifle, both for defence and the destruction of game. The night was passed in noisy mirth, drinking, and gambling, vices too prevalent. One of my fellow travellers, an officer of the provincial regiment of East Florida, was seized with a fever and ague, we were therefore under the necessity of making a large fire, which we did in an empty house, and wrapping him up in all the blankets we could muster, the other and myself prepared a mat before the fire, with our boat cloaks over us, and our heads supported by the baggage, obtained the rest we so much needed, previously appeasing the cravings of appetite with a slight repast of dried beef and yomine.* My friend still lay shivering under the blankets, and our fears increased, lest he should be unabled to go forward the next day.— This apprehension was indeed alarming, the proximity of our enemies, and our defenceless situation, when our friendly guards should depart, considerably increased our perplexities. At this moment I recollected that sweet spirits of nitre readily procures perspiration, my velisse contained a small bottle of this spirit, and I administered a plentiful dose: it had the desired effect, and he rose materially refreshed and relieved.

At day-break our guide took his leave to return to St. Augustine with our horses, afraid to venture across the river St. John's, least he might be carried off by the negro stealers, who are frequently found endeavouring to kidnap the slaves across the confines of Georgia. The people on the back frontiers of that province are the refuse of American society, driven by their crimes to seek an asylum on the limits of the union; they commit depredations indiscriminately upon every neighbour, whether friend or foe.

At sun-rise our friendly guards, after shaking us

---

* Bruised Indian corn, deprived of the husk, and boiled to a pulp.

cordially by the hand (the prevailing salutation in North America), took their leaves, wishing us safe to St. Mary's. Taking with us some assistants to carry our baggage, we directed our course higher up the river, for the purpose of passing over to an unfrequented part, where it was not likely we should be pursued. The planter, at whose house we halted, readily lent his assistance, and directed two of his slaves to ferry us across the St. John's.

On our reaching the opposite bank of the river, we made for the nearest settlement, where we expected to obtain a breakfast, in this however our hopes were disappointed, the idleness of the proprietor had suffered the greater part of his stores to be consumed, without providing for the demands of casual visitors. At the distance of a quarter of a mile we were assured of better success, and with the best disposition for this necessary meal, we hastened forward. Here again our evil fortune saluted us, the surly boor absolutely refused every entreaty to relieve our wants, his denial did not arise from a want of the means to relieve our pressing necessities, but from a species of devilism which forbad his ministring to our comfort. Neither money nor civility could urge this worse than corinthian boor to relax his obstinacy, and we reluctantly withdrew from the unavailing solicitation, but for the superior prudence of my fellow travellers, I had left him some memorable evidence of our sentiments and visit.

Constrained to return to the house we had quitted previous to this unavailing visit, we again implored of the owner relief to our craving appetites, he yielded, yet reluctantly; but in this case there was some excuse, it was not the want of inclination, but the want of means to satisfy our wants, without depriving his children of their expected dinner. This poverty is extraordinary, in a country abounding with plenty of every thing; the rivers are filled with fish, the woods with deer wild turkies and pigeons in abundance, the root *mandihoca,* from which the *cassava* flour is made, is found in every direction; in fact, there is no country in which the industry of man is less necessary to his existence; but in vain are the treasures of nature lavished upon this people, their habits of idleness and procrastination, destroy every germ of industry and regularity, the sources of national and individual importance, in other countries. Here however we obtained three horses and a guide, but as we were four in number, including our guide, one was obliged to walk in turn; this arrangement was extremely annoying, but there was no alternative, owing to the state of the guide's health, who on other conditions could not attend us.

Our route now lay through the most unfrequented part of the province, and in a track little known to travellers. The day was nearly closing, the sun beams still lingered upon the foliage of the tall cedars, when we emerged from the forest into an extensive plain, along the borders of which lay our course, its distance from the St. John's had lulled our apprehensions of the banditti to repose, and we had nearly banished from our memories the existence of danger, when a noise from the adjoining swamp checked our confidence, claiming all our attention; at the same moment two shots were fired from the wood, but fortunately passed harmlessly by. Our rifles were immediately directed to the spot from whence the shots were fired, and spurring our horses into the thick underwood, we returned their salute : here we discovered the tracks of three persons. The impression of shoes relieved us from the apprehension of Indians, and we followed, as well as the obscurity of the track and the retiring twilight would permit, the traces they had left, the groans of a person in pain led us to the spot, where one of the miscreants lay wounded. On demanding the motives of the attack, and who were his companions, we learnt that he had been pressed as a guide by an armed boat's crew, who had come up the river, in consequence of the information they had received of our route, from a canoe laden with oranges, which we remembered to have seen while at the Cowford, bound to Amelia; he had been obliged to act as a guide to a detachment, but some having separated from the party, were supposed to be bewildered in the intricacies of the forest.— Those who were with him seeing the failure of their attack, and feeling insufficient in numbers to cope with us, fled precipitately, leaving this wretch weltering in his blood. On examining his wound we found it merely a slight perforation of the fleshy part of the arm; having bound it up, we ordered him to precede us under the very muzzles of our rifles, which we determined to fire if we were not safely conducted.

The darkness of the evening and the obscurity of the way favoured our escape. The night had far advanced ere the welcome sound of watch-dogs assured us that some human habitation was near at hand. Our guide was just before us, and had cautioned us in passing a deep bog, over which several pine logs had been laid to form a pathway; scarcely had his warning reached me ere my horse plunged up to his withers, and threw me over his head into the mud. A portmanteau which I had borne before me on the saddle, and for the security and support, of which I had passed a string over my shoulders and through the handles, threw me from my balance, and precipitated me into the mire, from which I with difficulty extricated myself, covered with a plentiful sample of the soil, in a miserable plight: fortunately we were near a human habitation, and the approach of the dogs satisfied us of its proximity. We entered the enclosure of a grazier's farm. The house, as is usual with this migratory class, was built of pine logs, through the interstices of which the winds of heaven had free ingress. The family had retired to rest, but the alacrity of a black woman, whose domestic occupations were I apprehend *miscellaneous*, soon indemnified us for the misery of our journey, and the want of sustenance through the day. A plentiful supply of dried beef, venison, and *yomini* soon garnished the table, while a large fire dried our wet and soiled garments: bowls of rum and milk assuaged our thirst, and disposed us to seek in the arms of Morpheus before the fire, the renovation of our exhausted faculties.

Our prisoner was well known to our host, who pledged himself to the fact of his having been an unwilling guide to our enemies, and undertook to keep him at his house until the close of the following day, when we should be too far to fear his interruption. His wound was slight; some herbs, the sovereign remedy for every sore among the negroes, were put on by our good negress, who assured him of speedy recovery.

In the morning, after repeating our excellent repast and paying the moderate charges, we renewed our journey. The day was wet and comfortless: our route lay along the confines of the extensive and impervious swamp of Okeyfenokey: this impenetrable forest covers upwards of one hundred thousand acres, stretching along the boundary line of Georgia and East Florida fifty miles; the river of St. Mary's is supposed to take its rise in the bosom of this vast solitude, as yet untrodden by the foot of man. The warlike Indians of the Creeks and Seminoles have a religious veneration for this immense desert; they say it is inhabited by ærial beings, who interdict the intrusion of man. They have a number of legends connected with its history; that the centre is composed of high land, on which are erected their wigwams: many aver that they have seen those ærial beings on the confines of their enchanted habitation. Not even one of their warriors would venture amid the gloom of its shade, after sun-set, for the best American scalp. Thus we find the savages of North America are not without their supernatural creation and their superstitious veneration for their haunts.

The day was fast declining, and the intricacies of our way rather increased than diminished, when our guide declared his ignorance of the further continuance of the road, but depended upon the information he had received, to conduct us the residue of the journey; by his calculation, we were at least ten miles from the banks of the St. Mary's river, when I dismounted to take my turn of walking. We were advancing with as much rapidity as the nature, and our ignorance of the road permitted; here and there a blazed pine tree, (by which they designate the paths of the forest,) assured us that we were approaching some one of its outlets. The silence of the woods was at times relieved by the noisy flight of the turkey buzzard, and the screeching of the hooping crane, while our footsteps roused from their coverts, flights of wood pigeons; these were our only relief to the monotonous character of the way, and the ten miles had long since been traversed by our calculation of time and distance. A drizzling rain succeeded the retirement of twilight, and added to the misery of our tedious journey. After plunging in bogs, wading through creeks, and all the variety of a desert, we observed some distant lights, and the roaring of the waves on the bar of the St. Mary's River, was distinctly heard, and assured us, we were not far from human habitations; but whether the object we desired to attain, was a matter of uncertainty, the circuity of our path, which we did not notice, and the obscurity of the way, owing to the prevailing darkness, caused the cheering rays of light frequently to disappear, and we began to suspect we were the victims of the *ignis fatuus*, when suddenly emerging into an open country, we again discerned our beacon, and two hours after night fall brought us to the desired goal. The distance had been eighteen, instead of ten miles; here we were obliged to pass the night, the roughness of the tide in the river, and the darkness, were hostile to all attempts to cross it. In the morning the rain continued violent, but in spite of this impediment we passed over, through a narrow channel, cut through the marshes, at the back of Tiger Island, which divides the Spanish waters of the St. Mary's from those of the American. Through this communication was conveyed, the produce of the southern of the United States, (during the existence of the impolitic non-intercourse Act,) for shipment at Amelia; so great was the trade of that island during the operation of that act, that three hundred sail of square rigged vessels were seen at one time in the Spanish waters waiting for cargoes.

To my great surprise, at St. Mary's I found seven of the eight companions of my voyage, who had embarked for Charlston, and had already passed the bar, when I got under weigh for St. Augustine. The gale which had favoured me was adverse to their progress, and they were obliged to return, and here they had remained wind bound and ill; three were confined with agues and fevers, a fourth with a sore throat, three only were convalescent, the eighth poor fellow had been consigned to " the narrow house." When we parted, he expressed a melancholy presentiment of his approaching dissolution; I rallied him upon his failing spirits, but in vain; death had already seized his victim. He had been the soul of our society, of most florid conception and happy illustration; it was he who divided the empire in the shrouds with *Christophe*, on board the *Two Friends*. At the melancholy recital of his sufferings and death, the tears intruded in my eyes, I dashed them from me, reflecting that our loss was his gain; we had known enough of misery to poison our enjoyments, to his had been added that of ill health during the passage, and to this complication of evils he had fallen a victim.

My companions hailed my return as the dawn of better fortune, and the following day we embarked for Charlston, glad to escape from a place where they had been literally spell-bound.

A favourable gale carried us from the bar of the St. Mary's to Charlston, in less than twenty hours, and I once more congratulated myself upon an escape from the *virtuous* patriots.

CHAP. X.

The Americans take possession of Amelia—embark for that Island—fallen fortunes of the patriots—ball given by the officers of the United States navy—proceed for St. Augustine—pass the St. John's River to the plantation of a friend—the scite of the town of St. John's—account of Rolles Town—the object of the founder—proceed to another plantation—method of cultivating cotton and rice—agreeable life of a planter—set forward for St. Augustine—the carnival—the Seminole Indians—their habits—anecdotes respecting them, illustrative of their manners and feelings—the barbarous character of the war carried on by the Americans against them—General Jackson—anecdotes respecting him—depart for Charlston.

TOWARDS the end of November, 1817, the American government issued orders for the assembling of several detatchments of troops, at Point Peter, on the St. Mary's River, under the command of Colonel Bankhead, of the United States army, and a naval force, consisting of the *John Adams,* frigate, the *Lynx, Saranac,* and *Enterprize,* gun brigs, with some smaller vessels of war, were directed to co-operate under the controul and direction of Commodore Henley, in the reduction of the piratical establishment of Aury, at the island of Amelia. To the summons of the American commanders, a reply and remonstrance was returned by the Insur-

L 2

gents, breathing a tone of dignity, and claiming a higher distinction than can be accorded to their cause, or to the miserable association of adventurers.*

It happened unhappily for the government of the United States, that Aury's reasonings demonstrated their injustice, and the accommodating character of their principles, (which were rendered subservient to their interest,) though they by no means combatted the policy of their measures; and while this dislodgement of Aury evinces the wisdom and watchful character of the American government, it manifests their adoption of the reprobated European apology for every act of violence; namely, political expediency.

The American government availing of the unguarded expressions of M'Gregor in his proclamations, in which that officer avowed his project to conquer the *two* Floridas, not excepting that part of the western province claimed by the United States, menacing, agreeable to their political construction, the territory of the union, and perceiving that the establishment at Amelia was a mere nest of buccaneers, productive of the most serious injury

---

* See note F.

to their revenue, by introducing considerable quantities of contraband goods, and avoiding their statutory enactments, prohibiting the importation of slaves, (numbers of whom were daily smuggled across the borders of the state of Georgia,) resolved to remove their daring and demoralising neighbours.*

When sir Gregor M'Gregor took possession of Amelia Island, it was anticipated by the people of the United States, that the reduction, and independence of the Floridas, would have followed the invasion. Their anxiety to annex this important territory to the union, from its political as well as natural advantages, impelled this belief, and induced them to anticipate the success of the invaders with the most sanguine confidence; but the narrow policy of those buccaneers, true to the spirit of piracy, confined the range of their ambition to the present acquisition of wealth, neglecting those measures which alone obtained for them a tolerated existence on the borders of the union. It may not be hazarding too much to assert, that the government of the United States, entered fully into the views of their citizens, and were not uninterested observers, of the progress of this meditated

---

* See Note G.

revolution, the success of which, would have enabled the congress to recognise their independance, and to become the easy purchasers, and possessors, of this long desired peninsula, anticipating by this course of intriguing policy, every objection that might be urged, against the spoliation of the provinces while under the dominion of Spain.

About the middle of the following month of January, I was desirous of returning to East Florida, for the purpose of completing some arrangements I had proposed to the governor on my former visit. To the politeness of Captain Kearney, of the United States brig of war *Enterprize*, I was indebted for a passage to Amelia Island, to which she was bound with military and naval stores, then lying in the harbour of Charlston. The unfavourable state of wind and weather, kept us at sea five days, during which I received the kindest attention from Captain Kearney, (nephew to the late brave, but unfortunate Captain Lawrence, killed in the Chesapeake frigate) and his officers.

My letters of introduction to the American commander, Colonel Bankhead, procured from that gentleman all the attention in his power to bestow; and to the politeness of the officers of both naval and military service, I was much indebted.

My *quondam friends,* the *patriots,* were entirely crest fallen, they had lost those daring characteristics of the corsair, evident on my former visit. They appeared mortified at my witnessing their fallen and degraded consequence, which they rightly conjectured, would be a subject of triumph to one, against whom they had directed their ineffectual malice.

The troops of this *pseudo* republic were confined unarmed to the strict *surveillance* of the guard, and their officers permitted at large upon parole. Colonel Irvin, the adjutant general of Aury, appeared one of the most dispirited of the gang; and I could not avoid, what may be deemed an ungenerous triumph, asking him, while pointing at the American ensign waving on the fort, whether the stars and stripes of bunting, did not form a better flag than the mottled and chequered colours of the united republics of Mexico and Venezuela.

Proceeding from Amelia Island to the town of St. Mary's, I was detained at the latter place two days from the want of the means of conveyance to St. Augustine, the communication with which was both unfrequent and irregular. In the mean time, a ball was given by the officers of the navy at St. Mary's, to those of the United States army at Amelia and

Point Peter; invitations were also issued to Aury and his myrmidons, and a similar compliment paid to me; but suffering from a slight indisposition, and feeling no inclination to a further association with the brigands, I declined the civility.

The following morning an opportunity presented itself for my going forward to St. Augustine, of which I willingly availed, in company with a planter of Amelia, in his canoe, rowed by negroes; we passed the first night at his plantation, and the succeeding morning he sent me forward in his canoe, to the river St. John's, through the narrow channels seperating the islands of Amelia, Nassau, and Talbot, from the continent; passing in our route the fortified private plantation of Mr. Kingsley, at Fort George, a very eligible position at the entrance of the Nassau River.

It was about the close of day we prepared to cross the river St. John's, at a part about five miles above the bar. The sun still lingered upon the extensive forests of its banks, and undulated upon the trembling surface of its waters; the evening was pure and serene, and presented every object in the most alluring character. The noise of the oars, as they cut their liquid way, rousing the echoes of its banks, were answered by the noisy cadence of the negroes' boat-song, amusing and beguiling our way. As we entered upon the waters of the St. John's, we saw several canoes returning from fishing, their rowers were also chaunting their canoe-song, emulating at the same time the rapidity of our progress; we really flew along the glassy surface, such was the celerity of our movements.

Upon a high cliff or bluff, on the southern side of the river, I was shewn the scite, on which formerly stood the town of St. John's, built during the occupancy of the British, and promising at that time to become an important settlement, and admirably situated for that purpose; little now remains but the remembrance of its promise. Higher up the river, at the distance of seventy miles from its mouth, are a few vestiges of a town, formed by a Mr. Dennis Rolle, formerly member of parliament for Barnstaple, a near relative of the present Lord Rolle, bearing the name of its founder, who formed it for the singular and romantic purpose of affording an asylum to the penitent prostitutes of our country; hither numbers were brought, but whether the zeal of the founder subsided, or the penitence of his magdalen's ceased, I know not; but certain it is, they have left no other remembrance than the story of their settlement. We cannot but believe that the intentions of Mr. Dennis Rolle were formed and executed in the spirit of philanthrophy; but that there was a species of folly and infatuation in the choice of the objects of his bounty, daily observation demonstrates. We are also at a loss to conceive the motives of their seclusion, in a remote and thinly populated country; did he propose to found a colony of amazons? surely he chose the worst materials for such an object. The most probable conjecture is, that he intended to promote their intermarriage with the Seminole Indians, agreeable to the humane policy recommended to the Americans by Washington, in his plans for amalgamating the North American Indians with the people of the United States.

On reaching the southern bank of the river St. John's, we entered and landed on a small inlet, called Pablo Creek, at the settlement of a planter with whom I was previously acquainted; there I passed the night, and the following morning went over to another plantation, about four miles distant, from which I expected immediate means of conveyance to St. Augustine; in this, however, I was disappointed, and obliged to remain two days for the arrival of a boat expected up the north river, (in the harbour of St. A.) at a place about sixteen miles

distant, to which a cart would convey my baggage.
These two days were spent very agreeably in noticing the mode of culture of cotton and rice. The former is cultivated upon the high dry ground of the plantation, while the latter is uniformly sown on the low land, on the margins of their rivers and creeks; five acres are generally allotted for the work of a single negro, from which he rears his provisions of Indian corn and potatoes, and cultivates the cotton for his master. A hoe is used here in preference to the plough, in consequence of the lightness of the soil, and the thinness of the strata; having prepared the ground, a hand drill is employed for making the holes, into which the seed is put and covered; after this, little is necessary for the labour of the negro, who has merely to attend occasionally with his hoe, to remove the weeds, which would otherwise obstruct the growth of the plants. The sowing time is generally from December to March, though sometimes later, and the gathering of the crop about September and October. There are two sorts of cotton, the sea island, and the upland, or the long and short staple: the former, as its name implies, requires to be cultivated close upon the borders of the sea, or on the islands, to avail of the marine particles with which the air in those situations is impreg-

nated; the other, on the contrary, may be produced in the interior. It is said, from the narrow character of the province, and the extension of sea air over the surface of East Florida, that every part is capable of producing the sea island cotton, which is of material consequence to the planter, as I have known it sell in the market of Charlston and Savannah at sixty-five cents, while the upland could not obtain more than thirty-seven per pound. The texture of the former is finer, and the staple considerably longer; on this account in great demand for the manufacture of Scotch muslins and the high-priced cottons of Manchester and London. The sea-island plant blows irregularly, and requires more attention than the upland, which is usually gathered at, and within a certain time.

The rice swamps, or fields, are (as I have already stated,) on the margin of rivers or creeks, to have the convenience of water necessary to its cultivation. When the young plant begins to shoot, the field is inundated frequently for the purpose of destroying the weeds, which would otherwise obstruct the growth. The action of the sun upon these decayed vegetable substances produces putridity, creating the miasmata so fatally and widely destructive to the white inhabitants of the states of the

Carolinas and Georgia, who are in consequence obliged to quit their plantations, and even the towns on the coast, from the month of June to that of October, while the negroes remain insensible to its influence. This destructive vapour does not exist in the province of East Florida, or is dissipated by the constant currents of air from the Gulph of Mexico and the Atlantic ocean, sweeping over its surface, bearing health and exhilaration. The planters remain upon their estates with their families, uninjured by the climate, throughout the year.

The plantation at which I was detained was within two miles of the Atlantic: the fine white sand of the beach furnished me with a very agreeable ride, the recent fall of the tide had given to it a firm consistence. Here and there, were scattered numerous and various vestiges of wrecks, and the reflection that many unhappy beings had perished upon that fatal coast, alone embittered my enjoyment.

On the third morning I mounted my horse, having sent forward my baggage in a cart belonging to my friend the planter, to whose kindness during my short stay I was much indebted. To those who are fond of a country residence, and its consequent seclusion, I imagine the life of a planter must have peculiar charms, particularly in a country where they are not distressed by the visits of tax-gatherers or parish wardens. Not a single cent is paid here to either the government or the local institutions, the only income derived by Spain is the duties levied upon the importation of goods, amounting to six per cent. *ad valorem*, upon a very liberal estimate of value. The planter has a sure vent for his produce, and an immediate return. In Carolina and Georgia the income of the planter is estimated at twenty-five per cent. upon his principal, independent of the maintenance of his family. In the province of East Florida the profits of the planter are still higher, in consequence of his exemption from every species of taxation, and the price of his negroes, which is considerably lower. A good field hand in the Carolinas and Georgia is worth, on the average, from eight to nine hundred dollars, while those of Florida may be purchased at an average price of four to five hundred, consequently little more than one half of the capital is necessary. The quantity of deer and turkies in the woods, the turtle, tarapins (the fresh water turtle) and the abundance and variety of fish, furnish the table requiring merely the labour of hunting and catching them, with what we Europeans would esteem luxuries. The fields yield two crops of Indian corn annually, and the groves are filled with the fox-grape and the finest oranges I have ever seen. The climate is salubrious; the heats of summer relieved by the diurnal breezes from the sea, as certain in their visits as those of the West Indies, and the frost of winter never exceeds the eighth of an inch in thickness. The residence of the planter is large and commodious, formed from the timber on the plantations, with virandas in front, offering an agreeable lounge during the heat of the day. If he is fond of hunting, he has game in profusion; does he shoot, the woods abound with wild fowl of various descriptions, and the aligators, which are numerous in the creeks, and are sometimes twenty feet in length, afford the finest amusement for his adroitness with the rifle. These animals never attack the inhabitants, unless during the rutting season, when it is prudent to avoid them; at other times they would rather avoid than meet you.

The day was extremely fine, as I quitted the plantation of my friend, to follow the track of the cart to the head of the north river, where I anticipated meeting the boat from St. Augustine, the road tolerably regular and open. I wandered at the discretional pace of my horse, enjoying the woody scenery, broken at intervals by views of the

Atlantic ocean, across whose waves my imagination painted those beloved friends, for whose happiness my heart constantly and fervently aspirated. There is a melancholy pleasure in recreating the scenes of happier days, and in visiting in idea, those haunts endeared by circumstances of early and tender attachment. The mind that cannot sympathise in these feelings, and conceive their influence, must be without sensibility, and consequently without passion. I remember with gratitude those ideal enjoyments, which have snatched from the existence of misery, the sense of suffering. In four hours I reached the head of the north river, the cart had arrived before me, owing to my frequent halts, and digressions from the road, to observe some striking appearance, or to admire the beauty of the woodland scenery, relieved by the views of the white waves of the ocean. We had passed in our route three plantations, but they were by no means important settlements. The boat had not arrived, and the tide still continued to flow, I therefore threw myself upon the grass to await its arrival, ordering the negroes to hobble my horse, and turn him to graze. It was now near two o'clock, and I began to feel hungry; I had neglected to provide against the claims of appetite, but the negroes were dining upon sweet potatoes, with which I contrived to satisfy my wants; a few glasses of Madeira, with which I was well stored, gave a zest to this otherwise humble fare. To the negroes, I distributed some whiskey, a rare but acceptable present to this degraded race. The tide had by this time receded from the landing place, and all idea of seeing the boat that day, was consequently abandoned. Under these circumstances I determined to go forward on horseback to St. Augustine, a distance of twenty-three miles, but my ignorance of the road, rendered a guide absolutely necessary; leaving my baggage in the care of the negroes, I retrogaded about two miles, to the house of a planter, where, with some difficulty and delay, I obtained another horse and a guide. The sun was fast declining, my host endeavoured to dissuade me from continuing my journey that night, assuring me I should arrive too late for admission to the town of St. Augustine, the gates of which are regularly shut at sun-set. But being the bearer of some dispatches from the Spanish minister at Washington, and relying upon the personal favour of the governor, I determined to hazard the experiment, rather than sacrifice another day on the journey. I accordingly set forward, preceded by my guide, over an extensive plain of marshes.

The sun had long since sunk in the west, and the shades of evening, which in all southern latitudes quickly follow the retirement of his beams, were fast crowding around us, when we entered upon the woodlands, increasing the obscurity of our tract with their shade; a drizzling rain now descended, and added to the difficulties of our progress; my guide was frequently obliged to precede me, to explore the road, rendered almost imperceptible by the darkness that screened it; these circumstances considerably retarded our advance. As we entered farther into the woods, fires were perceptible in several directions, and I began to suspect they proceeded from some Indian camp, or were kindled by some benighted traveller. As we approached nearer, we discerned they arose from the woods, recently fired, through some of whose burning alleys we were obliged to pass. Emerging from these solitudes and shades, we espied the distant, yet distinct lights of the watch towers of the fortress of St. Augustine, delightful beacons to my weary pilgrimage. The clock was striking ten as I reached the foot of the draw-bridge; the sentinels were passing the *alerto*, as I demanded entrance; having answered the preliminary questions, the draw-bridge was slowly lowered. The officer of

the guard, having received my name and wishes,
sent a communication to the governor, who issued
orders for my immediate admission. On opening
the gate, the guard was ready to receive me, and a
file of men with their officer, escorted me to his
Excellency, who expressed his satisfaction at my
revisit to Florida. I soon retired to the luxury of
repose, rendered necessary from my severe fatigue,
and the following morning was greeted as an old
acquaintance by the members of this little community. I had arrived at a season of general relaxation, on the eve of the Carnival, which is celebrated
with much gaiety in all Catholic countries. Masks,
dominoes, Harlequin's, Punchinelloes, and a great
variety of grotesque disguises, on horseback, in
cars, gigs, and on foot, paraded the streets with
guitars, violins, and other instruments; and in
the evenings, the houses were open to receive masks,
and balls were given in every direction. I was
told that in their better days, when their pay was
regularly remitted from the Havanna, these amuse-
ments were admirably conducted, and the rich
dresses exhibited on these occasions, were not
eclipsed by their more fashionable friends in Cuba,
but poverty had lessened their spirit for enjoyment,
as well as the means of procuring it; enough how-

ever remained to amuse an idle spectator, and I entered with alacrity into their diversions.

On my former visit to St. Augustine, I had been disappointed in my desire to see some of the aborigines of this part of the Continent of North America. This curiosity was now gratified; about thirty of the hunting warriors of the Seminoles, with their squaws, had arrived, for the purpose of selling the produce of the chace, consisting of bear, deer, tiger, and other skins, bears' grease, and other trifling articles. This savage race, once the lords of the ascendant, are the most formidable border enemies of the United States; existing, like all other North American Indian tribes, upon the produce of the chace, despising the more limited, though not less independant pursuits of agriculture. This party had arrived after a range of six months for the purposes of sale, and barter. After trafficking for their commodities, they were seen at various parts of the town, assembled in small groups, seated upon their haunches, like monkeys, passing round their bottles of *aqua dente*, (the rum of Cuba) their repeated draughts upon which, soon exhausted their contents; they then slept off the effects of intoxication under the walls, exposed to the influence of the sun. Their appearance was extremely wretched, their skins of a dark, dirty, chocolate colour, with long, strait, black hair, over which they had spread a quantity of bears' grease. In their ears, and the cartilages of the nose, were inserted, rings of silver and brass, with pendants of various shapes, their features prominent and harsh, and their eyes, had a wild, and ferocious expression. As I approached, their regards were those of resentment, but those feelings were dissipated on a closer examination, I had been mistaken for an American, an object of their natural antipathy; but the thickness of the lips, soon convinced them of that error, and disposed them to the courtesy they always feel towards an Englishman. I have since observed, that this is not a fancied distinction, the lips of the natives of North America, are much thinner than those of Europeans, a person accustomed to an intercourse with both, readily distinguishes the natives of each hemisphere, from that, and other evidences; and I have little doubt, but that our future generations will have a much stronger distinctive evidence, than the present, as the degrees of consanguinity are removed. I do not mean to adopt the opinion of Mr. Buffon, who asserts, that the whole of the animal creation, degenerates on the American Continent; certain, however, it is, that the carnivorous animals are far less savage in the Western hemisphere; man may not (I allude to the European settlers) yet, have felt the full influence of climate.

A torn blanket, or an ill-fashioned dirty linen jacket, is the general costume of those Indians, a triangular piece of cloth, passes round the loins, and between their legs; the women vary in their apparel, by merely wearing short petticoats, the original colours of which were not distinguishable, from the various incrustations of dirt. Some of the young squaws, were tolerably agreeable, and if well washed and dressed, would not have been uninteresting; but the elder squaws, wore the air of misery and debasement. They are, as in other uncivilised communities, the beasts of burthen, our fair countrywomen would derive, a high degree of consequence and satisfaction, by contrasting the wretchedness of their transatlantic sex, with their own happiness, and the species of adoration with which they are encircled. A gentleman of the province, long acquainted with the habits and peculiarities of this intractable race, gave me some interesting anecdotes respecting them.

The Seminoles, as it has been already observed, like the other nations of North American Indians, depend principally upon their hunting excursions,

for the restraints of civilised life, are to them
intolerable; some, however, possess extensive herds
of cattle; and negroes, to whom the culture of
rice, Indian corn, and potatoes, is confided; with
these cattle they occasionally trade with the graziers, and planters of Florida, and those on the
confines of Georgia. Their towns, or wigwams,
are built of pine logs, rudely shaped, with little
attention to cleanliness, and none to comfort. In
the centre of their wigwams, they form a square,
on the sides of which are buildings occupied by the
chief and warriors, and one house is appropriated to
the rights of hospitality. Before a stranger commu-
nicates the object of his visit, he must partake of
their liberality, and there arises a spirit of emulation
to minister to his necessities; from every hut, its
occupier sends to the stranger, something to allay his
hunger, or assuage his thirst. When the repast is
finished, the chief demands the motive of his visit;
if it be to require satisfaction for the injuries of an
individual, summary punishment is inflicted in the
open square, and on the instant. Such is their peculiar sense of honour, that a culprit never denies the
charges made against him, if true; but the experiment of making a false accusation, would be attended with fatal consequences, to the person who

should have the malevolence, to hazard the attempt. The accuser is then asked if he is satisfied with the extent of punishment, and is dismissed with presents. They despise the delays and formalities with which civilised communities have disgraced, and disguised the administration of justice; averring that the prompt revenge of injuries, and the certainty of punishment, operates as a check to the commission of crime.

They have no fixed ideas of the form and attributes of the deity, they believe in the existence of a great spirit, to whose approbation or anger, they ascribe the success or failure of their schemes, but have no defined mode of adoration. The sun and moon are also objects of veneration, as the sources from which they derive the benefits of light and heat, and therefore entitled to their respect.

Their government is a species of oligarchy, composed of the council of chiefs and warriors, to whom is confided the direction of their interests, both in war and peace; and as courage among savage tribes, is considered the highest and most important species of virtue, the possessors are sure to obtain respect, for their opinions and advice.

The laws of marriage are relaxed, poligamy being permitted to their chiefs, and they are restricted to the number of three wives. These reside in three distinct huts, opposite the dwelling of the chief, to each of which there is but one way of egress, and the methods they adopt to protect their honour, and detect their infidelity, might furnish an amusing experiment, and useful hint, to European husbands. The doors of the huts being in front of the buildings, and opposite to the residence of the chief, they have but few opportunities during the day, of eluding his vigilance, but the night, friendly to lovers' intrigues and disguise, requires more certain methods of precaution; to effect these, the fronts of the huts, occupied by the less fortunate pair of wives, being inclosures of light sand, are swept parallel with the houses at night fall; if the print of a foot, either in egress or ingress, is discovered in the morning, the unfortunate woman is subjected to the penalties of adultery; a crime visited by them with exemplary punishment; for the first offence they cut off the ears of both parties, for the second, the loss of part, and a slit through the remainder of the nose, compensates; but the third procures a further disfiguration; they are then consigned to their unfortunate paramours, permitted after these penalties, to indulge uninterruptedly their guilty passions. This punishment is by no means the peculiar privilege of their chieftains, but extends to the meanest of the tribe; yet notwithstanding a punishment so severe awaits their criminality, such is the propensity of mankind to this crime against society, that I saw several, who bore evidences of their turpitude, and detection.

They look with contempt upon the whites, as beings of an inferior order, but the negroes are still lower in their estimation; the scalp of the latter is no more desirable than that of a dog, while the brutus fronts of our pericraniums, exalt the young Indian to the council of the nation, and enable him to assume the distinctive dress of its warriors.

They are habituated in early life, to view unmoved every thing connected with our manners and our habits; this was strikingly illustrated in the conduct of two young Indians, one about nine, and the other fourteen years of age; the latter held in his hand a tube, through which he blew, with considerable adroitness, a small arrow; my friend offered him a piece of money to shoot a bird, he essayed, and missed his object, turning round he replaced the money, refusing, as he had not compleated his part of the contract, to receive the purchase, and it was only upon condition that my friend should take the tube and try himself, that he could be prevailed upon to accept it. My friend having placed his hat upon the ground, as a mark, lodged an arrow in the crown;

this produced the strongest evidence of gratification, in the little fellow, who jumped about with the most extravagant expressions of joy, at the supposed misfortune, while the elder remained unmoved, not a single muscle relaxed the wonted gravity of his face, but he looked with an eye of anger and rebuke upon his joyous brother, who would not restrain the expression of his feelings.

Revenge is considered an imperative obligation, neither time, nor distance, lessens their appetite for its indulgence; whether by accident or intention, one of a tribe is killed, it becomes the duty of his nearest relative to revenge his fall upon the homicide, and in rotation the task of vengeance descends to the remotest degree of consanguinity. For this purpose the Seminole Indian will encounter hunger, thirst, the burning heat of summer, and the chilling frosts of winter, neither distance, nor difficulty, detains him from his object, nor lessens his thirst for vengeance; indefatigable in the pursuit, they have been known to traverse the most distant regions of their continent, in search of the homicide, who, aware of the unremitted pursuit, either meets his adversary resigned to his fate, or adds another victim to his criminality.

During the American revolutionary war, Colonel Thomas Brown, an American royalist, well-known in the annals of Georgia, for the vigour and decision of his measures, whose services were highly important to the British interests during that unhappy contest, raised a regiment of Rangers, in which, as superintendant of the Indians, he incorporated a number of the Seminole warriors, among others, two young men of some distinction in their nation, and most intimate friends. By some misfortune, one fell by the hand of the other, whose poignant sorrow and regret was increased by the knowledge of the forfeit he had incurred. The humanity of the commander induced him to seek the means of averting the fate that menaced him : fourteen years saw him distant from his country and connections. The death of his father, and the weariness of absence, induced him to return to his home, where he possessed both negroes and herds of cattle. Scarcely had he reached his paternal settlement, indulging the hope that time had softened the resentment of his enemies, when one day he was called to the door of his hut to receive a stranger, as he passed the threshhold, a well directed shot from a rifle, laid him dead: it was inflicted by the uncle of his unfortunate friend, who thus healed the wound of his family. In this case, revenge was uncalled for, and its indulgence cruel; but if the operation of this passion could be confined within the bounds of just retribution, its exercise might be rendered beneficial to the community, and the certainty of punishment, might deter those insidious villains, who destroy the peace of individuals and society, by blasting characters with the pestilential breath of scandal, sheltered by irresponsible situations from that punishment, their crimes deserve, but which their cowardice would have withheld them from committing, had they been otherwise circumstanced. These injuries are frequently more seriously destructive to the individual than the loss of health and property—

———— Invitat culpam qui peccatum præterit.———Syrus.

Nature has implanted in us a spirit of resentment for injuries sustained, but we are instructed and directed by education and the precepts of Christianity, to resist the indulgence of those feelings. Thus countenancing, by silent sufferance, the extension of those crimes, and their consequences, which prompt and commensurate retaliation might punish and avert. I would not be understood to sanction that spirit of vengeance, which would only minister to the gratification of malignant feelings; this I abhor, while I acknowledge and lament the depravity of human nature, which forbids us to intrust to individuals, the task of vengeance. The press is perhaps, the best engine for the correction of those evils, but that wholesome monitor is deprived of its rational influence, by the doctrine, that the truth of a statement cannot be admitted to repel the charge of libel, a doctrine at once monstrous and absurd, abhorrent to every sentiment, and repugnant to the dispensation of justice.

The Seminole savages have a vague idea of the creation of man: they believe that he was originally formed from the clay, that the Great Spirit submitted his creation to the influence of fire, but that his ignorance of the degree of heat, necessary to give consistence, caused the first batch to be over baked, black and crusty: these were the aborigines of the negro race. Again, the Creator essayed, but endeavouring to avoid the error of the former attempt, he plunged into another, that of applying too little fuel, they were in consequence but half baked, of a pale ash colour, these were our first parents: but in the third and last effort, the great master, created perfect models, both in shape and colour, producing to the world the founders of the Indian tribes. Such is their traditionary tale of the creation, certainly entitled to as much respect as our belief, that Eve was formed from the rib of Adam.

The frequent incursions of the Georgia back woodmen, in the Floridas, to steal cattle, and negroes, from the Indians, obliges them to keep scouts constantly on the alert, to detect and punish the maurauders; these are generally the young men, who have not obtained the rank of warriors. The avidity with which they hunt after the scalps of the predatory Americans, often betrays them to the power of those free booters, who, equally expert as themselves, to the wood warfare, and not less savage in character; devote to slaughter the Indian, with as little compunction, as they feel in the destruction of the wild animals of the forest.*

On the eve of battle, the Seminole warriors paint their bodies in the most fantastic manner, with vermilion and ochre, in order to terrify and discourage their enemies.

When the hunters bring to town the produce of the chace, they come in small parties of from twenty to forty; the major part of the women are left at some distance, to protect the cattle, as well as to preserve them from the violation of the whites. After completing their sales and barter, they return with the latter to their encampment, the principal

---

* See Note H.

part of which is rum or whisky; one cask is set apart for the women. The following day is devoted to the enjoyment of the men; this is passed in excessive intoxication, and they generally exhaust the whole of their purchase, the produce of many months indefatigable labour in the chace, excepting the women's share, which they religiously preserve. The want of nourishment, for they seldom think of eating, during this debauch, produces the most destructive inebrity, and they frequently become the victims of this vice. On the following day, the orgies of the women commence, and no interference, or intrusion is offered, or permitted by the men; they show themselves no mean imitators of their husbands, in this beastly indulgence, and their cask of spirits, fails, from their repeated draught upon its contents. The liquor, as usual, gives fluency to their tongues, for even among savages, the daughters of Eve, claim the use of this female weapon, and the vocabulary of Billingsgate would derive considerable augmentation from their abusive phraseology. The war of words usually terminates in blows, tearing of hair, cloathes, &c. and all the variety of attack and defence, a broil in St. Giles's might furnish. All this time the men are cool spectators of the animated scene before them; but on the morrow, ill or well, bruised, lame or blind, these unfortunate beings must endure the misery of their situations, and follow, unrepining their obdurate husbands, unpitied, and unnoticed. This intemperate indulgence in ardent spirits, has been extensively instrumental in the destruction of the savage tribes of North America, many of whom have entirely disappeared, or been reduced to a few miserable remnants. This fact, the evidence of which is unquestioned, at length occupied the attention of the American legislature, who, impelled by a spirit of humanity, and christian consideration, for the existence and welfare of their red brethren, fast verging to annihilation from this fatal intemperance, passed a law, prohibiting private trade with the Indian nations, establishing depots for that commerce, on the Indian borders, subject to the supervision of the executive, and confided to agents of approved fidelity and discretion, who receive a liberal compensation for the devotion of their time and services. The cupidity of private traders had induced them to sell to those unfortunate beings, the most deleterious compounds under the denomination of spirits, for those savages were not satisfied, unless they were ardent and intoxicating.

I was very anxious to visit the Indian nation, to become more intimately acquainted with their

General Jackson, against them, rendered the attempt extremely hazardous, some of their straggling parties might have mistaken me for an American, and without waiting to ascertain the fact, I might have paid the forfeit of their error, withe xistence.

Of the people of the United States, they have a most contemptible opinion, believing them incapable either of honour, or honesty. Bowlegs, the principal chieftain of the Seminoles, and Monakatapa, the second in command, are men of strong minds, and determined courage, yet shrewed, and suspicious. In a conference with the governor of East Florida, on the subject of American spoliations, that gentleman assured them, that the government of the United States, discountenanced the aggression, and would observe with fidelity, their pledges to Spain, not to molest them, or their property. Bowlegs, enraged by an assurance, so oft repeated and dishonoured, by the executive and people of the union, told the governor that he was a fool to believe them ; for himself, he would never trust an American beyond the range of his rifle.

The war against the Seminole Indians was conducted in a spirit of barbarous cruelty, but little habits ; but the war conducted by the American honourable to the American people, who appear determined on the extirpation of this unfortunate race. That the people of Kentucky, Tennessee, and other of the Western states, feel a fixed hatred towards the Indians; being accustomed from infancy to the details of their horrid enormities, when their forefathers were obliged to hold the sword with one hand, while the other conducted the plough; whose wives, whose children, and whose aged parents, were often butchered in their presence, with the accustomed barbarity of savages, cannot be a matter of surprise; but that their government, existing with as much security, as any on the older Continent of Europe, and cannot therefore plead the reprobated apology of political expediency, should enter into those feelings of resentment, and countenance the destruction of the unfortunate Indians, excites our suspicion, that their liberality of sentiment, and respect for public rights, exists only in sound, or is confined in its operation to the limits of their union. But I am willing to hope, and to believe, that the enormities committed by the army of General Jackson, and under the orders of that commander, proceeded altogether from his intemperate passions, and will be discountenanced

by that government, who are peculiarly interested
in proving to the world, the superiority of their
political experiment, in morality, and good faith,
over those governments they effect to despise.*

This *celebrated* General Jackson, possesses an
extensive influence over the people of Kentucky
and Tennessee, who believe him to be invincible
in arms, and unequalled in courage. His defence
of New Orleans against our ill conducted attack
upon that city, has fixed in their opinions, his
immoveable, and imperishable fame. His con-
quests over the Creek Indians, and his notable
exploit, in enticing ten of those unfortunates from
their hiding place, under a promise of protection,
and then delivering them up to be butchered by
his followers, is another wreath in the chaplet of
this hero.

The passions of this man are of the most violent
and barbarous character, despising, under every
circumstance, the forms, and restraints of society,
outraging decency on every occasion. During the
defence of New Orleans, Judge Hall had directed
the service of some process, which did not please
this leader, who, forgetting the respect due to

---

*See Note I.

the judgment seat, and the character of the individual who presided, ordered a file of soldiers to remove him, saying he would arrest the president of the United States, if he should dare to interfere with his command. After the restoration of peace, the judge summoned the general to answer for a contempt of court, and fined him one thousand dollars, which was immediately paid by public subscription. He is much addicted to gambling, particularly in horses; if he loses his money, and requires a further supply, he sends a cart to his plantation, for a load of negroes, who are thus exposed to the chance of changing masters, upon the hazard of the race. He has been known to challenge the owner becaue he asserted his horse had greater speed than the general's, in fine his extravagant follies, and his crimes, are without number, and disgusting in the recital.

The object for which this second visit to Florida, was undertaken, having been satisfactorily arranged, I once more bid adieu to the Province, embarked in a small schooner of forty-five tons burthen. Soon after quitting the bar of St. Augustine, a storm arose, which continued with violence through the succeeding night, carrying away our foresail and fore-top-mast, which alone saved us from being engulphed in the ocean : in thirty hours we reached the harbour of Charlston ; a distance of near three hundred and fifty miles.

From Charlston I proceeded through the United States, receiving, in every part, the warmest hospitality from that people. But while I offer this testimony of my grateful remembrance of kindnesses, I shall ever be proud, and pleased to confess; I cannot repress the expression of my regret, that their hatred to the English, as a nation, is the most fixed, and rooted of their resentments : leading them into the indulgence of feelings, upon political subjects, ungenerous, and unjust. To conciliate, to sooth, and avert their hostility, will be vain and fruitless. Our policy must be conducted with the sword in one hand and the olive branch in the other. While they are sensible we have the power of resorting to the *ultima ratio*, they will respect, though they will not cease to hate us.

" Oderint dum metuant."

CONCLUDING CHAPTER.

Arrival of the *Two Friends*, at Margaretta—the reception by the Commander, General Aresmendez—the captain of the *Two Friends*, proceeds up the Oronoco—the ship quits Margaretta, and escapes to Aux Cayes—four of her passengers ascending the Oronoco, are taken by the Spaniards—the unemployed passengers, at Margaretta, sent off the Island—M'Donald proceeding up the Oronoco, is shot by the Indians, with one of his companions—meet in the United States officers, who had quitted the Insurgent cause—Foreigners omitted in the accounts of their battles, and the jealousy that opposes their progress—Sir Gregor M'Gregor's policy—his present plan to join Aury—their probable objects—The importance of Venezuela to the Spaniards—the danger of the climate, and its influence upon Europeans—the declining state of the Insurgents—titles of nobility, their influence on the Creoles—Morillo recruits from among the Creole population—treatment of French officers, at Buenos Ayres—the general ignorance in England respecting the state of the contest in Venezuela—the Morning Chronicle, the sole channel of information—the independance of South America, desirable to the British—favourable disposition of the United States to South American independance—their probable motives.

THE ship, *Two Friends*, on quitting St. Thomas's in the clandestine way, already described, proceeded to the Island of Margaretta, at which general Aresmendez commanded. That general received them in a manner little according with the interest of the Insurgents, and extremely ungenerous, to those who had arrived from Europe, ready to shed their blood in their battles to achieve their independance. The first salutation of this imperious, and ungrateful leader was, that they wanted men to fight in their ranks, not officers to command. A few only were admitted to the *honour* of the republican service.

Aresmendez aware that the *Two Friends*, had on board four pieces of cannon, sent a requisition, at the same time directing the people of the ship to assist in the constructions of a battery, to receive them.

In the mean time the captain of the *Two Friends*, quitted Margaretta, and proceeded up the Oronoco, to demand from Bolivar, the payment of the two hundred dollars, for each passenger, promised by Mendez, and to obtain a commission for his ship, to cruize under the Venezuelan flag, leaving instructions with those, to whose care the vessel was confided during his absence, to await his arrival one month; if he failed to return in that time, they were to depart with the ship from Margaretta.

No sooner had the people succeeded in the erection of the battery, and landed, and mounted the guns, than Aresmendez, in the plenitude of his authority, and the characteristic honesty of his partisans, demanded that the provisions on board the *Two Friends,* should be delivered for the use of his garrison. This requisition being resisted, he directed the guns of the battery, which they had so recently constructed, should be turned against the ship, to enforce his orders; with difficulty the crew succeeded in getting under weigh, but not until after they had received considerable injury, and were in danger of being entirely destroyed. On clearing the island, they made sail for Aux Cayes, in the Island of St. Domingo, and entering that harbour struck upon a rock. Such is the account of one of the party.

The situation of those unfortunates, left on the Island of Margaretta, may be easily imagined, but cannot be readily described, they were literally starving, being refused every sort of assistance by the Insurgent authorities. In the midst of this distress and desolation, four of them determined to ascend the Oronoco; for this purpose they carried off a canoe from the island, and were, in their attempt to reach Angostura, taken by the Spaniards, and hung as rebels. Those who remained behind, were now forced on board the schooner, *Gladwin,* and sent off to the Island of Trinidad, almost in a state of nudity. Such was the treatment of the remnant of the *Two Friends*, from those champions of liberty, and advocates for independance.

M'Donald, with his party, safely reached the Oronoco, and was ascending that river, when his incorrigible vanity induced him, in some boat excursion to the shore, to assume his uniform. The Indians, who were lurking on the banks of the river, supposing, from the superiority of his dress and equipments, that they belonged to the royal army, (for they well knew the Insurgents could not boast such splendour,) poured upon him and his companions, a shower of arrows; one pierced the heart of M'Donald, another, that of one of his companions. Thus fell a victim to his vanity this unfortunate man, involving in his fate his misguided adherent. The remainder arrived at Angostura, and were received into the army of the Insurgents, where they are now wearing out existence, amid the complicated evils of famine and disease.

During my tour through the United States of America, I met several officers, both American and English, who had quitted, in secrecy and disgust, the armies of the Insurgents. Many had been wounded in their battles, but were abandoned, without pensions, and without pay, to the misery of want, since they had ceased to be useful.

I have frequently noticed in the details of the Insurgent successes, a profusion of their own names, but no record of the bravery of foreigners. We cannot doubt but that Englishmen are ever forward to deserve the mead of praise, yet they are altogether omitted, or but slightly and vaguely noticed. This jealousy of the merits of their supporters, the most illiberal and disgraceful, extends to exclude them from the higher ranks of the service; and so far this spirit influences the Republican leaders, that they receive with suspicion, and treat with contemptuous neglect, every effort to improve their discipline and resources, when recommended by foreigners.

Sir Gregor M'Gregor, with the natural and judicious policy of a Scotchman, saw his only chance of success with this ungenerous people, depended upon his becoming identified with them, and their interests; on that account he married the neice of Bolivar, acquiring, through that channel, the influence which for a time attended his progress. But recurring to their prejudices in favour of their own people, to the illiberal exclusion of foreigners; he fell in favour as rapidly as he had risen by his successes.

M'Gregor, it is said, is now gone to co-operate with Aury, the itinerant patriot, who, finding his assumption of the flags of Mexico, and Venezuela, ceased to be respected, has dubbed himself a knight errant of the Republics of Buenos Ayres, and Chili, forming a depot for his prizes, &c. at the Spanish Island of Santa Catherina, from which he has issued a pompous, and inflated address, and invitation, to the enterprising and homeless adventurers of all nations; thither M'Gregor is reported to have proceeded with a very considerable number of British recruits, to unite with his quondam friend, dividing with him the military and naval command.* It is far from improbable, that with these accessions of strength, they will offer their services to those who will pay them best, whether Spaniards or Insurgents, and like the Elector of Hesse, charge so much per head for their pugnacious subjects.

---

* It is suspected that M'Gregor and Aury, meditate renewing their attempts upon Florida—in the Bay of Tampa; this will furnish another excuse for American intrusion.

The conclusion of the struggle in South America, particularly in Venezuela, appears very remote and uncertain. The Spaniards, aware of the importance of obstructing this communication with Mexico, have abandoned nearly the whole of the interior to the progress of the Insurgents, concentrating their strength and resources, at those points, and fortresses of importance on the coast.

To dislodge the royalists from their strong holds, the armies of the Insurgents must descend, in order to invest them, to the sandy and burning plains of Venezuela, stretching along the coast, unsheltered from the fervid beams of the sun, in the latitude of ten degrees.

European soldiers exposed to the intense heats of that climate, ill fed, and worse cloathed, will perish by hundreds, while those who escape immediate destruction, will be too much enfeebled by disease to render assistance. One hundred of those soldiers in Europe, would be more effective than five hundred on the plains of Venezuela. Those who never felt the enervating influence of warm latitudes, cannot estimate their effects upon the animal spirits. The Spaniards are well aware of this evil, and will not fail to give their enemies the full benefit of it.

The royal forces will get supplied with provisions,

either by the Americans or the English, while they have the means of payment, and the Insurgent declarations of blockade will be treated as mere waste paper. That the Spaniards are excellent defenders of fortresses, is generally admitted, even by their enemies; there is an obstinate adherence to their objects in the character of this people, not easily shaken, and the magnitude of the take, will render them more tenacious. It is vain to expect that a contest, which has continued nine years, will be terminated by a campaign, when we reflect that the Insurgents have retrogaded, rather than advanced in success.

However vain and ridiculous titles of nobility may be to the minds of philosophers, we know they have surprising influence upon the feelings and motives of those, who seldom examine below the surface. The vulgar, accustomed to look upon those distinctions with respect and deference, will, in their loss, lose their confidence in, and devotion to, the former possessors. This has been felt by that class of society in Venezuela, who foresaw in the admission of the constitution of the United States, (a measure proposed by some of their speculative chieftains) the overthrow of all their fancied distinctions, they have withdrawn from the Insurgent cause, and many have recruited, the army of Morillo, who has lately received considerable augmentations from the Creole population.

If, however, in spite of all these impediments, the cause of the Insurgents shall succeed, can we suppose that the Insurgents of Venezuela will treat foreign officers better than their countrymen at Buenos Ayres, the government of which has directed all the French officers to quit their service. They have had their courage, their talents, and their best blood, and now that they cease to be necessary, they are abandoned to the world.

I know there exists a favourite idea among those who have lately gone out in this miserable cause, that from the number and materials of their force, they will be permitted to act in distinct bodies, but they will find these hopes and expectations, vanish into air; Bolivar will amalgamate them with his motley troops, in spite of the paper contracts of his friend Mendez.

The people of England are deceived in, and kept ignorant of the real state of affairs in Venezuela: listening only to the generous sympathy of their characters, they are led away by the specious sophistry of those who profit by the delusion. How does it happen that the Morning Chronicle has the exclusive possession of all the important and favourable proceedings of the Insurgents? Are their successes of so little interest, or their scale of operations so limited, that a single paper has been able to monopolize the intelligence? It comes in a very questionable shape, and I am inclined to believe is home made, though it may be of *foreign manufacture.*

That the independance of South America is greatly to be desired, the interest of my country assures me: in its emancipation from the tyranny of superstition, and the exactions of the local authorities, I shall heartily rejoice; but I lament to see the cause of freedom and rational liberty, abandoned to the controul, and made the foot balls of mock patriots, and disguised despots, sacrificing the generous enterprise of my countrymen, to their unfeeling and inordinate ambition.

The trade of Great Britain, would doubtless materially benefit by the opening of the ports on the Spanish main, to its commercial enterprise; but if the war of the Insurgents proceeds, with their present success, and is much longer protracted, the inhabitants will have neither produce for sale, nor dollars for purchase. England is peculiarly situated with regard to this contest, and her claims are of

such a nature on Spain, that she might interfere for
the S. Americans, and endeavour to procure for them
a liberally constituted government, though still under
the sovereignty of that nation, and thus stop the exhaustion of treasure, and the deplorable and extensive sacrifice of human life.

The North Americans are decidedly favourable
to South American independence; I do not assert
that this feeling arises from motives of philanthropy.
The intercourse would be highly beneficial to the
Atlantic commercial States of the Union, but perhaps there is another and more important influence,
namely, their hatred to all monarchical and European governments, which may lead them to expect,
that the South Americans, some time hence, will
become their allies, in effecting their overthrow and
destruction. These vindictive feelings, blind and
obscure, the otherwise wary policy of that giant republic, and excite our regret, that a power so prosperous, should admit the indulgence of resentment,
by no means honourable to their national character.
In the opening of the trade of the Spanish Americas,
the union will find a material decrease in the demand
for the produce of their southern and western states,
and the planters of those states will be thrown out
of competition in the European markets, by the

cheaper and more abundant productions of the fruitful soil of the southern continent.

That the agents of the Insurgents are able in this country to raise numerous recruits to their standard, cannot be a matter of surprise, when we reflect upon the peculiar circumstances favouring their objects, and the greedy credulity of our countrymen.

The recent reduction of the army has thrown numbers of privates upon the country, and it is well known, that those individuals who have been engaged in military occupations, are, by such habits, unfitted for a season, for the sober pursuits of laborious industry. The prospect of employment, in a way of life suited to their feelings, their ignorance of the actual state of the service in which they are to be engaged, and that *esprit du corps,* natural to military men, all concur to render them willing victims to those, who although they have proved personally, the wretchedness of the cause of the Insurgents, have, however, found their resources sufficient to bribe their individual cupidity and villainy, to become the seducers and sacrificers of their unguarded countrymen.

Let us not therefore mistake the cause and circumstances, which have given success to their deceptions, by reasoning only from effects.

Time will, unhappily, manifest to those unfortunate victims, the miserable certainty which awaits their progress, and expose to the world, the fabric of falsehood and deception, by which they have been betrayed.

APPENDIX.

The Seminole war—Execution of Arbuthnot and Ambrister, &c.

THE barbarous conduct of the war against the Indian nation of the Seminoles, by the American General Jackson on the confines of Georgia, and also within the Spanish territory of the Floridas, has already been a subject of remark and reprobation, in the preceding part of this narration; but the course of that hostility, heretofore confined in its operation to the savage tribes of Indians, has, in the latter part of this war of extermination of that unhappy race, assumed a new character of policy, in which the American executive, and commanders, obliquely charge, and endeavour to implicate the British people and government, accusing them of exciting and fomenting the hostile incursions of the Indians, into the territories of the United States.

The judicial murder of the unfortunate Arbuthnot and Ambrister, British subjects, within the Spanish territory, while under the protection of that nation, by the judgment of a court-martial, and the arbitrary dictum of General Jackson, is an unequivocal evidence of the political feelings and prejudices entertained towards the British nation by a portion of the American people, and evince the most ungenerous suspicion. The approbation of General Jackson's proceedings, not only in his violent occupation of the Spanish fortresses of St. Mark's and Pensacola, but also in the atrocious murder of our unhappy countrymen, expressed in the recent correspondence of Mr. Quincy Adams, (the American secretary for foreign affairs,) with Mr. Erving, the minister of the union, at the court of Madrid, under date the 28th of November past, laid among other papers (connected with the Seminole war) before Congress, betrays a spirit of hostility to this country, inconsistent with the cautious policy, hitherto pursued by that wary government in their official correspondence, which must be met by us with dignity, or be submitted to with disgrace.

This subject, so highly important to the honour and interest of every Briton, will doubtless meet with that grave and solemn investigation, so essentially necessary to our national character, from which the spirit of party will retire, leaving the discussion untrammelled with politicald istinctions and prejudices. Under these impressions, the narrator abstains from the indulgence of irritated feeling, and by a brief statement of unquestionable facts, places the subject before the public, for their sober judgment. To arrive, however, at the point important to the enquiry, the narrator is under the necessity of slightly tracing the origin and progress of the Seminole war, which led to this unhappy catastrophe.

The frequent and violent acts of spoliation, committed by the frontier settlers of the United States, upon the property and lives of their Indian neighbours, naturally called forth the vindictive resentments of the savages, who listen only to the claims of vengeance, and who, in the progress of retaliation, sacrifice with indiscriminating barbarity, the innocent and the guilty, the aged and the young.

Repeated aggressions of the American borderers, accompanied with the most barbarous violence, stimulated a party of the Seminoles to make an incursion into the United States, for the purpose of vengeance and reprisal upon their predatory enemies; they accordingly crossed the river Santilla in Georgia, surprising an American settlement, fourteen of whose inhabitants were inhumanly put to death and scalped. Complaints of this savage intrusion, were immediately forwarded to the executive of the United States government, conveyed in all the pathetic and plaintive language of affliction, of which this barbarous atrocity was capable, but the relation of the previous wrongs of the Indians, which had led to this act of vengeance, was withheld from the American government, concealed in the bosoms of those, whose turpitude had produced this violent re-action. The American executive, listening with too credulous confidence to the detail of facts, at which humanity shudders and recoils, incapable of investigating them, and perhaps unwilling seriously to question the justice of the demand for punishment, directed Generals Gaines and Scott, with detachments of the United States army, Georgia militia and volunteers, to march against the Seminole Indians. These troops having destroyed the Indian settlements in Georgia, and driven the fugitives across the boundary line, which separates the Spanish and American territory, were preparing to follow them into the former, in consequence of an unsuccessful requisition made by General Gaines to the Indians, for the delivery of those concerned in the murders upon the Santilla River, when Lieutenant Scott, of the United States army, with about forty persons, (men, women and children,) ascending the river Appalachicola, with military stores, &c. destined for the provision of a fort on that river, was surprised by a party of Indians, and, with the exception of six men who escaped, and one woman preserved, put to death with the accustomed barbarity of savages.

Intelligence of this fresh act of atrocity having reached the American executive, they resolved to direct a vigorous warfare against the Seminoles, and by exterminating their warriors, have the certainty of punishing the real delinquents. With this view, General Jackson, already noticed for his notable exploits, fitted by nature, habits, and feelings, for this indiscriminate butchery, was selected to conduct this object, and ordered to take the chief command of the American detachments, augmented by several troops and companies of volunteers from Kentucky and Tennessee, who entered into the Indian warfare with savage enjoyment.

General Jackson having taken up his line of march, advanced against the Indians, penetrating the Spanish territory, driving before him, and devoting to destruction, the intractable enemy. The fort of St. Mark's, situated upon the river of that name, near the Appalachicola, was the first Spanish post at which the American troops arrived. The incompetency of the Spanish force to oppose a successful resistance to the summons to surrender, after an ineffectual remonstrance on the part of the governor with the American general, upon the gross violation intended, placed that fortress in the possession of the intruders. It was in this fort that our unfortunate countrymen were tried by a court-martial, and executed by the orders of General Jackson.

Having garrisoned fort St. Mark's, the remainder of the American army crossed the river Appalachicola, penetrating into the interior of West Florida. In the mean time, an American gun boat, by hoisting the British ensign in one of the creeks of the Appalachicola, decoyed on board two Indian chiefs, Hemattlemico, and Hidlis Hadjo, the latter the chief who accompanied Major Nichols to England, and who also bore the name of Francis the Prophet. Hidlis Hadjo, on discovering the deception of his enemy, shed some tears, but presently resuming the characteristic fortitude of his race, he awaited with firmness the advance of General Jackson. The general, having in vain endeavoured to draw from his prisoners, some information respecting the state of their nation, ordered them to immediate execution; they were instantly suspended on a temporary gallows, to which they advanced with stoical indifference.*

The Spanish governor of Pensacola, learning the advance of the American army, after vainly protesting against the progress of the invaders, retired to the fort of Barrancas, three miles below the city of Pensacola, the city being untenable against the attacks of a considerable force on the land side. In the fort of Barrancas, with one hundred and fifty men, he defended himself against the enemy for three days; but a mutiny among his troops, obliged him

---

* This is an example of the generosity and gratitude of General Jackson: a short time previous to the capture of those Indians, a straggler from the militia of Georgia, named M'Krimmon, was captured by the Indians, and was about to be sacrificed to Indian vengeance, tied to the stake, the tomahawk raised to terminate his existence, no chance appeared of escape; at that moment Milly Francis, the daughter of Hidlis Hadjo, placed herself between the executioner and his victim, and arrested his uplifted arm, then throwing herself at the feet of her father, she implored the life of his prisoner, it was granted, and he was liberated. To the honour of M'Krimmon, it must be added, that some time after, learning that Milly Francis had given herself up, with others of her unfortunate race, in a state of wretched destitution, to the commander at Fort Clairborne, he immediately set forward to render her assistance, determined to make her his wife, and thus in some sort, repay the noble and disinterested generosity of his saviour.

Milly, upon learning the intentions of M'Krimmon, declared she was not influenced by any personal motive, that she should have acted in the same way for any other unfortunate victim; she therefore declined his offer.

reluctantly to abandon the ineffectual protraction of resistance. These troops, with the governor, were in compliance with the terms of capitulation, embarked for the Havanna.

General Jackson, upon the occupation of Pensacola, appears to have been well aware of, and alive to, the wishes of his government respecting the entire possession of the Floridas: with these views, he removed the Spanish authorities, treating the territory, as one lawfully acquired, in the progress of sanctioned hostility. Numerous speculators, in the same spirit, from Kentucky, Tennessee, Georgia, and Alabama, poured down, purchasing land, in every direction, on very high terms.

While the troops under General Jackson were marching in one direction, the governor of Georgia, in the spirit of opposition, directed a party of the Georgia militia, under the command of Capt. Obed Wright, to march against the Indians in another quarter.

Capt. Obed Wright, with his detachment, penetrated the Indian territory, and surprised the village of Chehaw, putting to death the old men, the women and children, left in possession by their warriors, who were then fighting in the American ranks under Jackson.

The destruction of this friendly village, called forth the strongest expressions of abhorrence at this barbarous transaction, and the government of the United States hastened to appease the angry feelings of the Chehaw warriors, by offering them the only compensation in their power, pecuniary indemnity for the spoliation. Orders were issued from the seat of government, directing the arrest of Capt. Wright, who was in consequence placed in confinement, upon the charge of murder, but his immediate flight from prison, under very suspicious circumstances, suspended an enquiry, not likely to result honourably to the character of those concerned in the transaction, who were supposed to have made Capt. Wright the scape goat of their criminality. The imbecile, and naturally savage character of this man, rendered him the ready agent of those, who knew how to use his services to their own advantage, and it has been more than hinted, that their desire to possess the valuable lands, occupied by the Chehaw Indians, was the motive which induced this violent and wanton aggression.

With the occupation of Pensacola, the Indian warfare appears to have terminated; the volunteers from Kentucky and Tennessee, returned to their homes, and the Georgia militia were immediately disbanded. Several troops of volunteer mounted rangers were, however, embodied, and directed to scour the country, and to put to death *all* the hostile Indians.*

Upon the arrival of the dispatches of General Jackson at Washington, announcing the progress and termination of the Seminole war, together with the occupation of the Spanish territory, the members of the American executive assembled in council, upon those extraordinary proceedings, and were occupied in close deliberation several days: many, and serious difficulties presented themselves, and the members of the executive were much divided in opinion, respecting the course they ought to pursue. General Jackson's conduct, they felt, had not merely involved them in responsibility to the Spanish government, (for whose rights they had shewn but little delicacy) but the execution of two British subjects, they were well aware, would call forth the spirit of a nation, of whose power and inclination to resent an insult, they were too well convinced to doubt. To meet this difficulty, and by way of expiation, some proposed the immediate dismissal of General Jackson, and a public disavowal

---

* See Note I.

of the course pursued by that officer; but the equivocal character of their instructions to that general, plunged them in a difficulty from which they saw no immediate extrication. It was at length determined to keep the whole of the proceedings from the public, until the meeting of Congress should demand their publicity, and in the mean time, to answer the complaints of Spain, by offering the restoration of Pensacola and St. Mark's; the former unconditionally, the latter under certain stipulations to Spanish authority.

Soon after the meeting of Congress, the papers connected with the Seminole war, were anxiously called for by the House of Representatives. These documents, upon being laid before Congress, excited an expression of feeling, honourable to many members of the legislative body, and leads us to hope that they will do strict justice in a cause so materially interesting to our feelings, and their own honour, and convince the world that no situation, however high, no services, however meritorious, shall screen a delinquent in the American Union from punishment for offences, nor operate as a controul upon the arm of the law.

In the occupation of the Spanish territory, it appears, however, that General Jackson was not wholly unauthorised by the American government. The following extracts from the instructions given to that officer, and his coadjutor, General Gaines, unquestionably proves, that the American executive, was fully prepared for that event; it is true, that the army was not imperatively directed to take possession of the Spanish fortresses, but the commanders were authorised to *enter* the territory of Spain in *case of necessity*, and it was beyond the calculations of probability to suppose, that with this permission to violate the boundary, that the generals would respect the neutrality of the garrisons, and permit them to remain uninvested in their rear. The American Government doubtless foresaw that this interpretation would be given to their instructions: the character of General Jackson was well known to them; the violences which had previously marked the career of that intemperate man, did not permit any other conclusion. In the letter of Mr. Quincy Adams to Mr. Erving, minister from the United States at Madrid, dated 28th of November, 1818, it appears that so far from censuring the aggressions of General Jackson, or palliating his offences for this conduct, he claims the meed of praise, and though in possession of the proceedings on the court-martial upon the unfortunate Arbuthnot and Ambrister, which do not offer a single evidence of the criminality of the former, or the legal responsibility of either, the American minister pronounces that they were acts of retributive justice!!!

Instructions from the Secretary at War, to Generals Gaines and Jackson, and the Governor of the Alabama Territory.

Extract of a Letter to General Gaines, from the Secretary at War, dated 30th October, 1817.

" After adverting to the reply of the Seminole Indians to the demand of General Gaines, for the delivery of the murderers on the Santille River, the secretary assures General Gaines of the president's approbation of his measures, and the advance of the troops; and continues, " should they," the Seminoles, "however, persevere in their refusal to make such reparation, it is the wish of the president, that you should not, *on that account*, pass the line, and make an attack upon them, within the limits of Florida, until you shall have received further instructions from this department."

From the same to the same, dated 2d December, 1817.

" The state of our negociations with Spain, and the temper manifested by the principal European powers, makes it impolitic, in the opinion of the president, to move a force at this time into the Spanish possessions, for the mere purpose of chastising the Seminoles, for depredations which have heretofore been committed by them."

From the same to the same, dated 9th December, 1817.

" Referring to the letters addressed to you from this department, on the 30th of October, and 2d of December, as manifesting the views of the president, I have to request that you conform to the instructions therein given; should the Indians, however, assemble in force on the Spanish side of the line, and persevere in committing hostilities within the limits of the United States, you will, in that event, exercise a sound discretion as to the propriety of crossing the line, for the purpose of attacking them, and breaking up their towns."

From the same to the same, 16th December, 1817.

" On the receipt of this letter, should the Seminole Indians still refuse to make reparation, for their outrages and depredations on the citizens of the United States, it is the wish of the president, that you consider yourself at liberty to march across the Florida line, and to attack them within its limits, should it be found necessary, unless they should shelter themselves under a Spanish fort. In the last event you will immediately notify this department."

From the same to General Jackson, dated December 26.

"If, however, the general," (General Gaines,) "should have progressed to Florida before the subsequent orders may have reached him, he was instructed to penetrate to the Seminole towns, through the Floridas, provided the strength of his command at Amelia would justify his engaging in offensive operations."

From the same to General Gaines, 26th December.

" Before this will reach you it is hoped that the views of the president, in relation to the settlement on Amelia Island, will have been effected; should that be the case, it is his wish that you should immediately repair to fort Scott, and resume the command, till General Jackson's arrival, to whom orders have this day been sent, to command there; or, if you should think the force under your command sufficient, and other circumstances will admit, to penetrate through Florida, and co-operate in the attack on the Seminoles. I am not sufficiently acquainted with the topography of the country between Amelia and their town, to say whether it is practicable, or what would be the best route; but it is not improbable that some advantage might be taken of the St. John's River, to effect the object."

From the same to the same, January 16, 1818.

" The honour of the United States requires that the war with the Seminoles should be terminated speedily, and with exemplary punishment for hostilities so unprovoked. Orders were issued soon after my arrival here, directing the war to be carried on within the limits of Florida, should it be necessary to its speedy and effectual termination."

From the same to W. W. Webb, Esq. Governor of the Alabama Territory, dated 13th May, 1818.

" Enclosed is a copy of the order, authorising General Gaines to carry the war into Florida, and you will consider it as furnishing authority to the troops of the territory, to pass the Florida line, should it be necessary. I send also a copy of a message of the president, communicating information in relation to the Seminole war. General Jackson is vested with full powers to conduct the war in the manner which he may judge best."

General Jackson in his dispatches to the seat of government, states, that Arbuthnot was found an inmate of the family of the governor of Fort St. Mark's, concealing the treacherous means, by which that unfortunate individual was decoyed from under the Spanish flag.

Upon the advance of the American army, Arbuthnot, who was a trader with the Indians, under the sanction of a licence from the Spanish authorities, retired to Fort St. Mark's, to avoid the dangers inseparable from Indian warfare; General Jackson informed of his retreat, sent his aid-du-camp to that fort, with a message to Mr. Arbuthnot, requesting to see him in the American encampment; his unsuspecting victim, feeling that no act of his life had rendered him amenable to the laws of the United States, that towards him no hostility could be intended, at the same time relying upon the good faith of the American commander, unhesitatingly accepted the invitation, and accompanied the aid to the American camp, upon a horse borrowed from the governor of Fort St. Mark's. On reaching the tent of General Jackson, Arbuthnot was treacherously seized and ironed, and ordered to await the decision of a court-martial,* formed upon the following charges:—

April 26, 1818.

Charge I.—Exciting and stirring up the Creek Indians to war against the United States, and her citizens, he (Arbuthnot) being a subject of Great Britain, with whom the United States are at peace.

Specification—That the said A. Arbuthnot, between the months of April and July, or some time in June, 1817, wrote a letter to the little prince, exhorting and advising him not to comply with the

---

* This fact was communicated by the governor of Fort St. Mark's, in his dispatches to the Spanish minister at Washington, from whom the narrator received it.

treaty of Fort Jackson, stating that the citizens of the United States were infringing on the treaty of Ghent, and, as he believed, without the knowledge of the chief magistrate of the United States ; and advising the Upper and Lower Creeks to unite and be friendly, stating that Mr. Hambly was the cause of their disputes; also advising the little prince to write to the governor of New Providence, who would write to his Royal Highness the Prince Regent, through whom the United States would be called to a compliance with the treaty of Ghent, and advising them not to give up their lands under the treaty of Fort Jackson ; for that the American citizens would be compelled to give up to them all their lands under the treaty of Ghent.

Charge II. Acting as a spy, aiding, abetting, and comforting the enemy, and supplying them with the means of war.

Specification I.—In writing a letter from the Fort of St. Mark's, dated April 2, 1818, to his son John, at Suwany, (marked A.) detailing the advance of the army under General Jackson, stating their force, probable movements, and intentions, to be communicated to Bowlegs, the chief of the Suwany towns, for his government.

Specification II.—In writing the letters marked B. without date, and C. with inclosures, 27th of

January, 1818, and D. called " a note of Indian talks," and E. without date, applying to the British government, through Governor Cameron, for munitions of war, and assistance for our enemies;—making false representations, and also applying to Mr. Bagot, British ambassador, for his interference, with a statement, on the back of one of the letters, of munitions of war for the enemy.

Charge III.—Exciting the Indians to murder and destroy William Hambly and Edmund Doyle, and causing their arrest, with a view to their condemnation to death and the seizure of their property, on account of their active and zealous exertions to maintain peace between Spain, the United States, and the Indians, they being citizens of the Spanish government.

Specification.—In writing the letters marked F. dated 26th August, 1817; G. dated 13th May, 1817; and H. threatening them with death—alleging against them false and infamous charges, and using every means in his power to procure their arrest. All which writings and sayings excited, and had a tendency to excite, the negroes and Indians to acts of hostility against the United States.

By order of the Court,
J. M. GLASSEL, Recorder.

The following are the names of the officers who composed the court-martial for this extraordinary trial.

April 26th, 1818.

President.

Major-General E. P. Gaines.

Members.

Colonel King, 4th Infantry.
Colonel Williams, Tennessee Volunteers.
Lieutenant-Colonel Gibson, Ditto.
Major Muhlenburg, 4th Infantry.
Major Montgomery, 7th Infantry.
Captain Vashon, 7th Infantry.
Colonel Dyer, Tennessee Volunteers.
Lieu-Col. Lindsay, Corps of Artillery.
Lieu-Col. Elliott, Tenesee Volunteers.
Major Fanning, Corps of Artillery.
Major Minton, Georgia Militia.
Captain Crittenden, Kentucky Volunteers.

Recorder.

Lieutenant I. M. Glassel, 7th Infantry.

To these charges the prisoner pleaded generally, *Not Guilty*.

John Winslett, a witness on the part of the prosecution, deposed to the specification of the first charge, charging the prisoner with sending a letter to the little prince, advising the union of the Creeks, &c.

In the course of cross-examination by the prisoner, it appeared that the witness swore from memory, without other evidence of the existance of the letter; he also identified the signature of letter A.

John Lewis Phenix, the next witness, deposed to the first specification of the second charge, stating, that the letter was received by Ambrister, that though he saw it, he did not hear it read; that Ambrister stated it came from the prisoner.

The court was about to continue the examination, when, a member questioned the jurisdiction of the court on the third charge, and its specification. After considerable deliberation, it was determined, that the court could not take cognizance of the offences therein stated.

Peter Cook, formerly a clerk with the prisoner, a witness for the prosecution, was next examined,[*]

---

[*] The character of this witness, and the credibility of his evidence, may be estimated from the opinion entertained of him by those to whom he was well known.

Extract from the New Providence Gazette.

"Cook, who is said to have been the only evidence against Mr. Arbuthnot, lived here as a collector of vendue accounts, with a gen-

and deposed, that about December or January last, the prisoner received a large quantity of powder, at Suwany, and sold it to the Indians and Negroes, and that subsequently, the prisoner had received a further quantity of nine kegs, and a large quantity of lead, brought by Arbuthnot in the prisoner's vessels, and taken possesion of by the negroes. The witness identified the following letters, referred to in the charges and specifications, marked A. B. C. D. E. F. G. and H. as being the prisoner's hand writing; also the power of attorney granted by the Indians to Arbuthnot. No. 1.

A.

From A. Arbuthnot to his Son, John Arbuthnot, dated Fort St. Mark, 2d April, 1818, 9 o'clock in the morning.

Dear Son;

As I am ill able to write a long letter, it is necessary to be brief. Before my arrival here, the commandant had received

---

tleman in that line of business; converted to his own use a considerable sum which he had collected, and was in consequence discharged. Mr. A. being in want of a young man, to assist in his store in Florida, conceiving that as this was his first offence, he might be reclaimed, took Cook into his employ; but, finding soon after his arrival that he recommenced his former tricks, he delivered him over to the Spanish commandant at St. Mark's, to be dealt with according to law. Such is the witness which General Jackson produced at the trial, as it is called.

an express from the governor of Pensacola, informing him of a arge embarkation of troops, &c. under the immediate command of General Jackson; and the boat that brought the dispatch reckoned eighteen sail of vessels off Appalachicola. By a deserter that was brought here by the Indians, the commandant was informed that 3000 men, under the orders of General Jackson, 1000 foot, and 1,600 horse, under General Gaines, 500 under another general, were at Prospect Bluff, where they are rebuilding the burnt fort; that 1000 Indians, of different nations, were at Spanish Bluff, building another fort, under the direction of American officers; that as soon as these forts were built, they intended to march. They have commenced. Yesterday morning advice was received that they had appeared near ——, and taken two of the sons of M'Queen, and an Indian. Late in the afternoon three schooners came to anchor at the mouth of the river, and this morning the American flag is seen flying on the largest.

I am blockaded here; no Indian will come with me, and I am now suffering from the fatigue of coming here alone.

The main drift of the Americans is to destroy the black population of Suwany. Tell my friend Bowlegs, that it is throwing away his people to attempt to resist such a powerful force as will be down on Sahwahnee; and as the troops advance by land, so will the vessels by sea. Endeavour to get all the goods over the river in a place of security; as also the skins of all sorts; the corn must be left to its fate. So soon as the Sahwahnee is destroyed, I expect the Americans will be satisfied and retire; this is only my opinion, but I think it is conformable to the demand made by General Gaines to the King Hachy some months since; in fact, do all you can to save all you can save, the books particularly. It is probable the commandant will receive some communication from the vessels to day, when he will know more certainly what are their motives in coming off the fort. I think it is only to shut up the passage to the Indians. Twenty canoes went down yesterday, and were forced to return. The road between this and Mickasucky is said to be stopped. Hillisajo and Himathlo Mico were here last night, to hear what vessels; they will remove all their cattle and effects across St. Mark's River this morning, and, perhaps, wait near thereto for the event.

I have been as brief as I can, to give you the substance of what appear facts, that cannot be doubted; to enter into details in the present moment is useless. If the schooner is returned, get all the goods on board of her, and let her start off for Mounater Creek, in the bottom of Cedar Key Bay. You will there only have the skins to hide away. But no delay must take place, as the vessels will, no doubt, follow the land army, and, perhaps, even now some have gone round. I pray your strictest attention; for the more that is saved will be eventually more to your interest. Let the bearer have as much calico as will make him two shirts, for his trouble; he has promised to deliver this in three, but I will give him four days.

I am yours, affectionately,

A. ARBUTHNOT.

B.

From A. Arbuthnot, to Charles Cameron, Governor of Bahamas.

Sir;

Being empowered by the chiefs of the Lower Creek nation, to represent the state of their nation to your excellency, that you may be pleased to forward the same for the information of his Majesty's government, to whom alone they look for protection against the aggressions and encroachments of the Americans, I beg leave to submit to your excellency the enclosed representations, humbly praying that your excellency will be pleased to take an early opportunity of forwarding the same to Great Britain.

I am instructed by Bowlegs, chief of the Sahwahnee, to make the demand herein inclosed, he never having had any share of the presents distributed at Prospect Bluff, though he rendered equally essential services as any of the other chiefs to the British cause, while at war with America, and was at New Orleans with a part of his warriors. His frontiers being more exposed to the predatory incursions of the back Georgians, who enter his territory, and drive off his cattle, he is obliged to have large parties out to watch their motions, and prevent their plundering; and being now deficient in ammunition, he prays your excellency will grant his small demand, humbly submitting the same.

I have the honour to be, &c.

A. A.

The Humble Representation of the Chiefs of the Creek Nation, to his Excellency Governor Cameron.

We beg leave to represent, that Edmund Doyle and William Hambly, late clerks at Prospect Bluff, to Messrs. Forbes, &c., and who still reside on the Appalachicola River, we consider as the principal cause of our present troubles and uneasiness. Hambly was the instrumental cause of the fort at Prospect Bluff being destroyed by the Americans, by which we lost the supplies intended for our future wars. Since then, both these men have kept their emissaries among us, tending to harrass and disturb our repose, and that of our brethren of the middle and upper nation; they spread among us reports that the Cowetas, aided by the Americans, are descending to drive us off our land; they equally propagate other falsehoods.

C.

From A. Arbuthnot to Benjamin Moodie, Esq. inclosing Letters to Charles Bagot, Esq. British Minister at Washington.

Sahwahnee, in the Creek Nation, 7th Jan. 1812.

SIR;

The enclosed containing matter of serious moment, and demanding the immediate attention of his excellency the British ambassador, I trust he will for this time forgive the trifling expence of postage, which I have endeavoured to prevent as much as possible, by compressing *much matter* in one sheet of paper. Should you, Sir, be put to any trouble or expence, by this *trouble* I give you, by being made acquainted with the same, I will instruct Bain, Dunshee, and Co. to order payment of the same.

I have the honour to be, Sir,

Your most obedient humble Servant,

A. ARBUTHNOT.

From A. Arbuthnot to the Honourable Charles Bagot.

Sir;

It is with pain I again obtrude myself upon your excellency's notice; but the pressing solicitations of the chiefs of the Creek nation, and the deplorable situation in which they are placed, by the wanton aggressions of the Americans, I trust your excellency will take as a sufficient apology for the present intrusion.

In August last, the head chief of the Seminole Indians, received a letter from General Gaines, of which I have taken the liberty of annexing your excellency the contents, as delivered me by the chief's head English interpreter, with king Hachy's reply thereto.

This letter appears to have been intended to sound the disposition of the chief, and ascertain the force necessary to overrun the nation; for, from then until the actual attack was made on Fowl Town, the same general, with General Jackson, seem to have been collecting troops and settling in various quarters.

If your excellency desires to have farther information respecting the situation of this country and its inhabitants, I can, from time to time, inform your excellency of such facts and circumstances as are stated to me by chiefs of known veracity, or which may come under my own observation; and your excellency's order, addressed to me at New Providence, will either find me there, or be forwarded me to this country.

With great respect, I have the honour to be
Your excellency's most obedient Servant,
A. A.

The following memorandum was on the back of the foregoing letter:

King Hachy 1,000, Bowlegs 1,500, Oso Hatjo Choctawhacy 500, Himasby Miso Chattchichy 600, at present with Hillisajo. At present under arms, 1,000 and more; and attacking those Americans who have made inroads on their territory.

A quantity of gunpowder, lead, muskets, and flints, sufficient to arm 1,000 or 2,000 men; muskets 1,000, arms smaller if possible;

10,000 flints, a proportion for rifle, put up separate; 50 casks of gunpowder, a proportion for rifle; 2,000 knives, six to nine inch blade, good quality; 1,000 tomahawks; 100lb. vermillion; 2,000lb. lead, independent of ball for musket.

(Signed) King HACHY.
(Signed) BOWLEGS.

From General Gaines to the Seminoly Chief.

To the Seminoly Chief,
Your Seminolys are very bad people; I don't say whom. You have murdered many of my people, and stolen my cattle, and many good horses, that cost me money; and many good houses, that cost me money, you have burnt for me; and now that you see my writing, you'll think I have spoken right. I know it is so; you know it is so; for now you may say, I will go upon you at random; but just give me the murderers, and I will show them my law, and when that is finished and past, if you will come about any of my people, you will see your friends, and if you see me you will see your friend. But there is something out in the sea, a bird, with a forked tongue: whip him back before he lands, for he will be the ruin of you yet. Perhaps you do not know who or what I mean—I mean the name of Englishman.

I tell you this, that if you do not give me up the murderers who have murdered my people, I say I have got good strong warriors, with scalping knives and tomahawks. You harbour a great many of my black people among you, at Sahwahnee. If you give me leave to go by you against them, I shall not hurt any thing belonging to you.

(Signed) GENERAL GAINES.

From King Hachy to General Gaines, in answer to the foregoing.

To General Gaines,
You charge me with killing your people, stealing your cattle, and burning your houses. It is I that have cause to complain of the Americans. While one American has been justly killed, while in the act of stealing cattle, more than four Indians

have been murdered, while hunting, by these lawless freebooters. I harbour no negroes. When the Englishmen were at war with America, some took shelter among them, and it is for you, white people, to settle those things among yourselves, and not trouble us with what we know nothing about. I shall use force to stop any armed Americans from passing my towns or my lands.

(Signed) King HACHY.

D.
Note of Indian Talks.

In August, Capp had a letter from General Gaines, in substance as annexed, No. I. and returned the answer as by No. II. Nothing farther was said on either side. The end of October, a party of Americans, from a fort on Flint river, surrounded Fowl Town during the night, and began burning it. The Indians then in it, fled to the swamps, and in their flight had three persons killed by fire from the Americans: they rallied their people, and forced the Americans to retire some distance, but not before they had two more persons killed. The Americans built a block-house or fort, where they had fallen back to, and immediately sent to the fort up the country for assistance, stating the Indians were the aggressors; and also settled with Inhemocklo, for the loss his people had suffered; at the same time sending a talk to King Hachy, by a head man, (Apiny,) that he would put things in such a train as to prevent farther encroachments, and get those Americans to leave the fort. But no sooner was the good talk given, and before the bearer of it returned home, than hundreds of the Americans came pouring down on the Indians: roused them to a sense of their own danger: they flew to arms, and have been compelled to support them ever since. It is not alone from the country, but by vessels entering Appalachicola River, in vessels with troops; and settlers are pouring into the Indian territory. These proceedings are not countenanced by the American government, but originate with men devoid of principle, who set laws and instructions at defiance, and stick at no cruelty and oppressions to obtain their ends. Against such oppressions, the American government must use not only all their influence, but, if necessary, force; or their names will be handed down to posterity, as a nation more cruel and savage to the unfortunate aborigines of this country, than ever were the Spaniards, in more dark ages, to the nations of South America.

The English government, as the special protectors of the Indian nations, and on whom alone they rely for assistance, ought to step forward and save those unfortunate people from ruin; and, as you, Sir, are appointed to watch over their interests, it is my duty, as an Englishman, and the only one in this part of the Indian nation, to instruct you of the talks the chiefs bring me for your information: and I sincerely trust, Sir, you will use the powers you are vested with, for the service and protection of the unfortunate people, who look up to you as their saviour. I have written to General Mitchell, who, I hear, is an excellent man; and, as he acts as Indian agent, I hope his influence will stop the torrent of innovation, and give peace and quietness to the Creek nation.

I pray your excellency will pardon this intrusion, which nothing but the urgency of the case would have induced me to make.

I have the honour to be
Your excellency's most obedient Servant,
A. A.

E.
From Cappiahimicco and Bowlegs to Governor Cameron.

To his Excellency Governor Cameron,

It is with pain we are again obliged to obtrude ourselves on your excellency's notice, in consequence of the cruel war we have been forced into, by the irruptions of the Americans into the heart of our lands. It will be first necessary to state to your excellency, that one head chief (Kinhijah) received a letter from General Gaines, in August last, a copy of which is enclosed, with the answer returned thereto. This letter only appears to have been a prelude to plans, determined on by the said General and General Jackson, to bring on troops and settlers, to drive us from our lands, and take possession of them; for, in the end of October, a party of Americans surrounded Fowl Town during the night, and in the morning began setting fire to it; making the unfortunate inhabitants fly to the swamps, and who, in their flight, had three persons killed by the fire of the Americans. Our Indians, rallying, drove the Americans from the town, but in their exertions, had two more of their people killed. The Americans retired some distance, and built a fort or block house to protect themselves, until the assistance they had sent for to the fort up the country should arrive. A letter falling into the hands of General Mitchell, the Indian agent, which states the Indians to have been the aggressors, he suspected its truth, and on inquiry, found it was the reverse; in consequence, he made satisfaction to Inhermocklo, the chief of the Fowl Town, and his people, for the injuries they had sustained; at the same time desired a talk to be sent to our head chief, stating his wish to see all the Indian friends, and that in twenty days he would send and get the Americans to retire from the forts. But this had no effect on the lawless invaders of our soil; for, before the bearer of our talks could return home, he met hundreds of Americans descending on us. Thus, seeing no end to those inroads, necessity compels us to have recourse to arms, and our brethren are now fighting for the lands they inherit from their forefathers, for their families and friends. But what will our nations do without assistance? Our sinews of war are almost spent: and harassed as we have been for years, we have not been able to lay by the means for our extraordinary wants; and to whom can we look up for protection and support, but to those friends, who have, at all former times, held forth their hands to uphold us, and who have sworn, in their late treaty with the Americans, to see our just rights and privileges respected and protected from insult and aggression? We now call on your excellency, as the representative of our good father King George, to send us such aid, in ammunition, as we are absolutely in want of; and as our brother chief Hillisajo was informed, when in England, that when ammunition was wanted, to enable us to protect our rights, your excellency would supply us with what was necessary. We have applied to the Spanish officer at the fort of St. Mark's, but his small supply prevented his being able to assist us, and we have only on your excellency to depend. We likewise pray your excellency would be pleased to send an officer or person to lead us right, and to apportion the supplies you may be pleased to send us, agreeably to our proper wants.

In praying your excellency will lend an ear to our demand, and dispatch it without delay, we remain your excellency's faithful and most obedient friends and Servants,

CAPPIAHIMICCO,
BOWLEGS,
For ourselves, and all the other Chiefs
of the Lower Creek Nation.

F.
Letter from A. Arbuthnot to Colonel Edward Nichols.

Nassau, N. P., 26th Aug. 1817.

Lieutenant Colonel Edward Nichols,

SIR; especially authorized by the chiefs of the Lower Creek nation, whose names I affix to the present, I am desired to address you, that you may lay their complaints before his majesty's government. They desire it to be made known, that they have implicitly followed your advice, in living friendly with the Americans, who are their neighbours, and nowise attempt to molest them, though they have seen the Americans encroach on their territory, burning their towns, and making fields where their houses stood. Rather than make resistance, they have retired lower in the Peninsula. The town Eachallaway, where Olis Micco was chief, is one instance of the encroachments of the Americans. This town is situated under the guns of fort Gaines, and Micco was desired to submit to the Americans, or his town would be blown to atoms; rather than do so, he retired, and is now living in the Lower Nation; and his fields, and even where the town stood, is ploughed up by the Americans. They complain of the English government neglecting them, after having drawn them into a war with America; that you, Sir, have not kept your promise in sending people to reside among them; and that if they have not some person or persons resident in the nation, to watch over their interest, they will soon be driven to the extremity of the Peninsula. You left Mr. Hambly to watch over the Creek nation; but you hardly left the nation, when he turned traitor, and was led by Forbes to take the part of the Americans. His letter to me, of which I annex you a copy, will show you what lengths he could go if he had the means. It is Hambly and Doyle who give the Indians all the trouble they experience. They send their emissaries among the Lower Creeks, and make them believe the Cowetas, aided by the Americans, are coming to destroy them; thus both are put in fear, and their fields are neglected, and hunting is not thought of. I have endeavoured to do away this fear, by writing to the chief of the Coweta towns, that they ought to live on friendly terms with their brethren of the Lower Nation, whose wishes were to be on good terms with them, and not listen to any bad talks, but to chase those that give them from among them. My letter was answered from them rather favourably; and I hope that the talk that was sent to the Big Warrior last June, will heal the difference between them.

Hillisajo arrived in my schooner, Ocklocknee Sound, last June, and was well received by all the chiefs and others, who came to welcome him home; in consequence of his arrival, a talk was held, the substance of which was put on paper for them, and it was sent, with a pipe of peace, to the other nations. Hillisajo wished to return to Nassau with me, but I prevailed on him to stay in the nation, and to keep them at peace. I regret, Sir, to notice this poor man's affairs, though by his desire. It appeared that he arrived at Nassau, a short time after I had left it in January, and Capt. W. being here, took charge of him, his goods, and money, prevailing on the governor to let him stay with him, until he went down to the nation, which was his intention to do. Of the money received of Governor Cameron, he had only given him eighty dollars, by Captain W., a barrel of sugar, a bag of coffee, and a small keg of rum; and the interpreter Thugart, informed me, that when Hillisajo asked for an account, Captain W. refused it, saying, it would be useless to a man who could not read. He also misses two cases, one of which, he thinks, contains crockery. I have made inquiry of his majesty's ordnance storekeeper, and he informs me, the whole were delivered to Captain W. They are therefore lost to Hillisajo.

I am desired to return Hillisajo's warmest acknowledgments, for the very handsome manner you treated him in England, and he begs his prayer may be laid at the foot of his Royal Highness the Prince Regent. I left him and all his family well, on the 20th June. Old Cappachimicco desires me to send his best respects, and requests that you will send out some people to live among them, and all the land they took from Forbes shall be theirs. At all events, they must have an agent among them, to see that the Americans adhere to the treaty, and permit them to live unmolested on their lands. This agent should be authorized by his Majesty's government, or he will not be attended to by the Americans. In the gazettes of Georgia, the Americans report the Seminoly Indians are continually committing murders on their borders, and making incursions into the state. These are fabrications tending to irritate the American government; for, during the time I was in the nation, there was only one American killed, and he, with two others, were in the act of driving off cattle belonging to Bowlegs, chief of Suwany; whereas three men and a boy were killed last June, by a party of American cattle-stealers, while in their hunting camps. The boy they scalped, and one of Bowlegs's head men was killed in St. John's river, in July. The back-wood Georgians, and those resident on the borders of the Indian nation, are continually entering it, and driving off cattle. They have in some instances made settlements, and particularly on the Choctohachy river, where a considerable number have descended.

By the treaty with Great Britain, the Americans were to give up to the Indians all the lands that may have been taken from them during the war, and place them on the same footing they were in 1811. It appears they have not done so; that Fort Gaines, on the Chatahoochy, and Camp Crawford on the Flint river, are both of Indian territory, that was not in possession of America in 1811. They are fearful that, before any aid is given by the English government, they will no longer be in possession of any territory.

I wrote last January to his excellency, the Honourable Charles Bagot, respecting the encroachments of the Americans; as I was informed by the copy of a letter from the Right Honourable Earl Bathurst, handed me by his excellency, Governor Cameron, that his Majesty's ambassador had received orders to watch over the interest of the Indians. Since my return here, I have received of Mr. Moodie, of Charleston, an extract of a letter from the Honourable Charles Bagot, that the expence of postage is so considerable, any farther communications of the same nature must be sent by private hands. Now, Sir, as no person goes from this direct to Washington, how am I to be able to comply with his desire? Thus, he will be kept ignorant of the situation of the poor Indians, and the encroachments daily made on their lands by American settlers; while he may be told by the American government, that no encroachments have been made, and that the forts they still hold are necessary to check the unruly Seminoles. Thus, the person appointed to watch over the interest of the Indians, having no other means of information, than from the parties interested in their destruction, and seeing, from time to time, in the American Gazettes, accounts of cruel murders, &c. committed by the Indians on the frontier settlements of the United States, he apprehends the Indians merit all the Americans do to them.

But let his Majesty's government appoint an agent, with full powers to correspond with his Majesty's ambassador at Washington, and his eyes will then be opened, as to the motives that influenced American individuals, as well as the government, in vilifying the Indians.

The power given me, and the instructions, were to memorialize his Majesty's government, as well as the Governor General of the Havanna; but, if you will be pleased to lay this letter before his Majesty's Secretary of State, it will save the necessity of the first, and I fear that a memorial to the governor general would be of no use.

Referring you to the answer, I am, most respectfully, your obedient servant,

A. ARBUTHNOT.

G.

From A. Arbuthnot to William Hambly.

Ocklocknee Sound, May 3, 1817.

Sir;

On my return home this day, I received a letter signed by you, and dated 23d March. As you therein take the liberty of advising me, *as you say*, by order of the chiefs of the Creek nation, I am glad of, and shall embrace this opening you give me, and reply to you at some length—and, Sir, let me premise, that when you lived at Prospect Bluff, a clerk to Messrs. Forbes and Co., you did not consider Cappachimiccho, M'Queen, or any other of the chiefs of the Lower Creek nation, as outlaws, nor have they been considered as such by the English government, who are the special protectors of the Indian nations; and it ill becomes Mr. Hambly, to call Cappachimicco an outlaw—that man who has ever been his friend, and by his authority has prolonged his life. Yes, Sir, the young chiefs and warriors of the Creek nation, considering you as the chief cause of all their troubles, would have, long ere this had possession of you, and, perhaps with your life, made you pay the forfeit for the injuries heaped on them, had not that man, who has been your friend from your early youth, stepped in as your protector. Yes, this is the man, whom Mr. Hambly presumes to call an outlaw. A pardoned villain, when going to the gallows, would bless the hand that saved his life; but Mr. Hambly blasphemes his saviour.

As Mr. Hambly's generous friend is the principal cause of my being in this country, as an honest man, I shall endeavour to fulfil my promise to him and the other chiefs. The guilty alone have fear—an honest and upright man dreads no dangers, fears no evil, as he commits no ill; and your arm of justice ought to be applied where it would rightly fall, on the heads of the really guilty. Your mean and vile insinuations, that I have been the cause of thefts and murders, come ill from him who has been the cause of the murder of hundreds. Though your usage was made villainous at the fort, yet your revenge was too savage and sanguinary.

If your conduct, Sir, to the Indians, were guided by as pure motives as mine, it would endeavour to influence them to respect each other as brothers, and live in harmony and friendship, cultivating their lands in summer, and taking their diversions of hunting in winter, respecting their neighbours, and making themselves respected by them. If thus, Sir, you would act (and by your knowledge of their language, you have much more in your power than any other man,) you would then be the true friend of the Indians. Were I an instigator of theft and murder, would I hold the language I have done to the chiefs and others who have called on me ? Ask the lieutenant commanding at Fort Gaines, if my letter to him breathed the strains of a murderer? Ask Opy Hatch, or Dany, his interpreter, if the recommendatory note I sent him by order of Apiny, could be written by an instigator of murder ? Ask Apiny himself, if my language to him was that of a murderer ? Ask Mappalitchy, a chief residing among the Americans on Oakmulgee, if my language and advice to him favoured that of a murderer ? All those, and every Indian who have heard my talks, will contradict your vile assertions.

But Mappalitchy has given me a clue, by which I can unravel whence the aspersion comes. Not from Apiny, Hatchy, or any of the chiefs of the upper towns, but from he who endeavours to lead them to mischief and quarrels with each other. Did not the chiefs hear my note read with respect, and perfectly according to my sentiments, of being all as brethren uniting with bonds of frendship and love? Did not they agree to smoke the pipe of peace with their brethren of the lower nation, and live in future as brothers ? What made some of them alter their minds afterwards? The interference of a humane man, who counsels them to write to me, demanding my removal from a band of outlaws, and which letter is signed *" William Hambly"*

I shall only make one more observation, and that will show from whence I came, and whether I came amongst the Indians as revenger, or as the friend of peace and harmony.

In the spring of 1816, W. Hambly sent Governor Cameron a letter, containing talks of the Chiefs of the Indian nations; they are forwarded to England, and his excellency handed me, on my leaving Providence, an answer thereto, from the Right Honourable Earl Bathurst, one of his majesty's chief secretaries of state, that I might make the same known to the chiefs on my arrival in the nation. What will Governor Cameron think of the man who, in 1816, could write against the encroachments of the Americans on the Indian nation, and in the spring of 1817, called the chiefs of that nation, for whom he more especially wrote, outlaws? Mr. Hambly may sell his services to America; but no man can expatriate himself from that allegiance due to his native conntry; and a government may call on a friendly nation to give up a subject that has seriously wronged her.

I recommend Mr. Hambly to be content with the *douceur* he may have received, and permit the unlettered Indian to live quietly and peaceably on his native and.

I shall send a copy of this letter, with the one from you, to be read by the chiefs of this nation, and shall, at the same time, take an opportunity of expressing myself, more fully than I did in the note sent by Apiny. Wishing you a speedy recantation of your errors, and a return to your former way of thinking, I am your obedient,

A. ARBUTHNOT.

H.

Letter from A. Arbuthnot to the Governor of Havannah.

To His Excellency Don, Governor General, &c.

The Chiefs of the Creek nation, whose names are hereunto annexed, beg leave to approach your excellency, and represent their complaints. Long imposed upon by the persons keeping stores in this country, in charging us exorbitant prices for their goods, while they only allow us a very trifling one for our peltry; we have found it necessary to look out for a person that will deal fairly with us, and we wish to establish a store for him on Appalachi River; we have made application to the commander of St. Mark's, and he refers us to your excellency. It is not alone the impositions that have been practised upon us that has made us presume to address your excellency; we have complaints of a more serious nature, against the persons employed by the only house that has been established among us. In the first place, some years back, under false pretences, they attempted to rob us of a very large portion of our best lands, and we the more readily acceded to it, from the faithful promise given us, that they would get English people to settle and live among us; but far from doing this, Mr. Forbes attempted to sell it to the American government, and settle it with Americans. Thus, finding ourselves deceived and imposed on, we withdrew our grant about three years since; which, from the stipulations contained therein not being fulfilled on the part of Mr. Forbes, we conceived we had a right to do. Secondly, Mr. Doyle and Mr. Hambly, the two persons left in the nation to carry on Mr. Forbes's business, have, for more than two years, been endeavouring to influence us to join the Americans; and finding that fair means would not sever us from our attachment to our ancient friends the English, they have recently had recourse to threats of bringing the Americans down upon us; and that people only want a pretext to attack us, which they said Doyle and Hambly attempt to give them, by spreading false reports of our murdering the Americans, stealing their cattle, and preparing for war against them; while, in fact, it is the Americans who murder our Red brethren, and steal our cattle by hundreds at a time, and are daily encroaching on our lands, and maintaining the settlers in their ill-gotten possessions by armed force.

On the Choctawhatchy river, there are a large body of Americans forming settlements, and more are joining them. As this river is far within that line marked out by your excellency's government and the Americans, some years since, (though that line was unknown to us until very lately, and we never gave our sanction, nor, in fact, knew of any sale of our lands made to the Americans,) we trust your excellency will give orders to displace them within the line, and send them back to their own country. Our delaying to address your excellency, to represent the forementioned grievances, has been owing to the want of a person to attend to our talks, and put them in writing for us. The commander of the fort of St. Mark's, has heard all of our talks and complaints. He approves of what we have done, and what we are doing; and it is by his recommendation we have thus presumed to address your excellency.

<blockquote>
We have the honour to be,

Your Excellency's Most Obedient,

And very Humble Servant,

A. ARBUTHNOT.
</blockquote>

No. 1.

Power of Attorney, for the Indian Chiefs to A. Arbuthnot.

Know all men by these presents, That we, Chiefs of the Creek nation, whose names are affixed to this power, having full faith and confidence in A. Arbuthnot, of New Providence, who, knowing all our talks, is fully acquainted with our intentions and wishes, do hereby, by these presents, constitute and appoint him, the said Alexander Arbuthnot, our attorney and agent, with full power and authority to act for us, and in our names, in all affairs relating to our nation, and also to write such letters and papers as to him may appear necessary and proper for our benefit, and that of the Creek nation.

Given at Ocklockee Sound, in the Creek nation, this 17th day of June, 1817.

1. CAPPACHIMACO, his ✕ mark.
2. INLEMOHTLO, his ✕ mark.
3. CHARLES TUCTONOKY, his ✕ mark.
4. OTUS MICO, his ✕ mark.
5. OCNACONE TUCTONOKY, his ✕ mark.
6. IMATCHLACLE, his ✕ mark.
7. INHIMATCCHUCLE, his ✕ mark.
8. LOHOE ITAMATCHLY, his ✕ mark.
9. HOWRATHLE, his ✕ mark.
10. HILLISAJO, his ✕ mark

11. Tamuches Haho, his ✕ mark.
12. Oparthlomico, his ✕ mark.

Certified explanation of names and towns to which the foregoing Chiefs belong, agreeably to the numbers set opposite thereto.

WILLIAM HAMBLY.

1. Kinhigee, Chief of Mickasuky.
2. Inhimarthlo, Chief of Fowl Town.
3. Charles Tustonoky, second Chief of Ockmalgee Town.
4. Chief of the Conholoway, below Fort Gaines:
5. Opony, Chief of Oakmulgee Towns.
6. Chief of the Atlapalgas.
7. Chief of Pallaichucoley.
8. Chief of the Chehaws.
9. Chief of the Red Sticks.
10. Francis, (the prophet.)
11. Peter M'Queen, Chief of the Tallahasses, (an old Red Stick.)
12. A Red Stick, created Chief by the Lower Towns.

The examination of Cook being resumed, he deposed, that he had heard the prisoner tell Bowlegs, (one of the Indian Chiefs,) that he had sent letters to the Prince Regent, and expected soon to have answers; that some of the negroes doubted this statement, when the prisoner assured them that he had done so; he further stated, that he saw a negro give the letter marked A. to Ambrister, saying, that he had received it from an Indian; that the Indians and negroes, in consequence of the contents of this letter, began to prepare for the enemy, removing their families and effects across the river; that the

Indians and negroes said they would fight together. To No. 2, a letter without signature, to the government of St. Augustine, and another, No. 3, without date, to Mr. Mitchell, the Indian agent—to No. 4, an unsigned petition of the chiefs of the lower Creek nation to Governor Cameron, praying his aid in men, and munitions of war, the witness deposed being the hand-writing of the prisoner.

No. II.
Supposed to be from Bowlegs to the Governor of St. Augustine.

To his Excellency Don Jose Coppinger.
To his Excellency James Green,
  Governor of St. Augustine.

Sir;

I had the honour of receiving your letter of September, but the impossibility of finding a person to write an answer to the same is the cause of this apparent neglect.

I shall be very happy to keep up a good understanding and correspondence with you, and hope you will, when occasion offers, advise me of such things as may be of service to myself and people. My warriors and others that go to St. Augustine return with false reports, tending to harass and distress my people, and preventing them from attending to their usual avocations. At one time the Americans and Upper Indians, supported by a force of about eight thousand men, were running lines far within the Indian territory;—another time, are collecting a force at Fort Mitchell, in the forks of Flint and Chatanoochy rivers, to fall on the towns below. Now, Sir, we know of no reason the Americans can have to attack us, an inoffensive and unoffending people. We have none of their slaves; we have taken none of their property since the Americans made peace with our good father King George. We have followed the orders of his officer, that was with us, Lieutenant-Colonel Edward Nichols, and in no wise molested the Americans, though we daily see them encroaching on our territory, stealing our cattle, and murdering and carrying off our people.

The same officer also told us, we, allies to the great king, our father, were included in the treaty of peace between our good father and the Americans, and that the latter were to give up all the territory that had been taken from us before and during the war.— Yet, so far from complying with the ninth article of that treaty, they are daily making encroachments on our land, getting persons, who are not known to the chiefs, and without any power or authority, to grant and sign over lands to them. Thus they deceive the world, and make our very friends believe we are in league with them.

The principal chiefs of the nation, with the head warriors, assembled at my town on the 8th instant, and came to the resolution of informing the British minister at Washington, of the conduct of the Americans, and the officers of their government, towards us ;— it has been done accordingly, and copies sent to England. We demand of the king, our father, to fix some of his people among us, who may inform him, from time to time, of what is passing, and see the Americans do not extend themselves on our lands. The Spanish subjects in Floridas are too much in the interest of the Americans to be our friends. For the governors I shall always entertain the greatest regard ; but, for the people, they do not act so as to merit any esteem and protection. You desire I would chase those marauders, who steal my cattle ; my people have lately driven some Americans from Lahheway, and I have no doubt the Americans will hold off this as a pretext to make war on us, as they have before done, in stating we harbour their runaway slaves.

No. III.

General Mitchell, Agent for Indian Affairs ;

King Hatchy, the head chief of the Lower Creek nation, has called on me to request I would represent to you the cruel and oppressive conduct of the American people, living on the borders of the Indian nation, and which, he was in hopes, from a talk you were pleased to send him some weeks since, would have put a stop to, and restored peace between the Indians and American people. But far from any stop being put to their inroads and encroachments, they are pouring in by hundreds at a time; not only from the land side, but ascending the Appalachicola in vessel loads:— thus the Indians have been compelled to take up arms to defend their homes from a set of lawless invaders. Your known philanthropy and good will to the Indians induces the head chiefs to hope, that you will lose no time in using your influence to put a stop to those invasions of their lands, and order that those, who have already presumed to seize our fields, may retire therefrom.

The Indians have seized two persons they think have been greatly instrumental in bringing the Americans upon them, and they are now in their possession as prisoners. It is even reported, they have made sales of Indian lands without the knowledge, consent, or approbation of the chiefs of the nation: and, from their long residence in the nation, and the great influence that one of those people formerly enjoyed among the chiefs as their chief, there is some reason to believe he has been guilty of improper conduct to the Indian nation.

No. IV.

Petition of the Chiefs of the Lower Creek Nation, to Governor Cameron.

We, the undersigned, are deputed by the Creek nation to wait on your excellency, and lay before you their heavy complaints. To the English we have always looked up as friends, as protectors, and on them we now call to aid us in repelling the approaches of the Americans, who, regardless of treaties, are daily seizing our lands and robbing our people; they have already built seven forts on our lands; they are making roads and running lines into the very heart of our country, and, without the interference of the English, we shall soon be driven from the land we inherited from our forefathers.

The Americans tell us the English will regard us no more, and we had better submit to them; but we cannot submit to their shackles, and will rather die in defence of our country.

When peace was made between the English and the Americans, we were told by Lieutenant-Colonel Nichols, that the Americans were to give up our lands they had taken, and we were desired to live quietly and peaceably, in no wise molesting the Americans.—We have strictly followed those orders; but the Americans have not complied with the treaty. Colonel Nichols left Mr. Hambly in charge of the fort at Prospect Bluff, with orders to hear us, if any cause of complaint, and represent the same to the British government; but he turned traitor, and brought the Americans down on the fort, which was blown up, and many of our Red brethren destroyed in it. The ammunition stores, intended for our use, were either destroyed or taken off by the Americans. We have sent several messengers to inform your excellency of the proceedings of the Americans, but they have never returned to us with an answer. Three of our Red brethren have lately been killed by the Americans, while hunting on our lands, and they threaten to attack the towns of Mickasuky and Sahwahnee, the only two large towns left us in the Creek nation, and, without aid from your excellency, we cannot repel their attack. We are, therefore, deputed to demand of your excellency the assistance of troops and ammunition, that we may be able effectually to repel the attack of the Americans, and prevent their farther encroachments; and, if we return without assistance, the Americans, who have their spies among us, will the more quickly come upon us.

We most humbly pray your excellency will send us such a force as will be respected and make us respectable.

(The following endorsed on the foregoing.)

Charles Cameron, Esq., Governor,
   Commander in Chief, &c. &c.

      I beg leave to represent to your excellency the necessity of my again returning to the Indian nation, with the deputies from the chiefs; and as my trouble and expense can only be defrayed by permission to take goods to dispose of amongst them, I pray your excellency will be pleased to grant me such a letter, or license, as will prevent me from being captured, in case of meeting any Spanish cruiser on the coast of Florida.

Cook further deposed, in answer to an inquiry from the prisoner, whether the powder and lead shipped would more than supply the Indian and negro hunters?—That he did not see the quantity of powder and lead, but that Bowlegs told him, he had a great quantity keeping to fight with. Upon being asked by the court, how he knew that the son of the prisoner had the letter A. in his possession?— replied, " I saw him with it, which he dropped, and a boy called John, picked up and gave to me." When asked whether the Indians and negroes, would have punished the prisoner had he not complied with their wishes, in sending letters to the Prince Regent? he replied, " I do not know." To the enquiry, whether the prisoner was compelled to write the Indian communications?—answered, " he was not compelled."

William Hambly, the next witness examined, commenced by stating what he had heard the chiefs say—to this hearsay evidence the prisoner objected; the court, however, over-ruled his objection, declaring it not valid!!! This witness deposed, that fifteen or twenty days after the arrival of the prisoner at Ochlocknee, the Seminole Indians began to steal horses from the United States settlements, and committed murders on the Satilla river, which he was informed by them were at the instigation of the prisoner.

That the chiefs of the little villages in witness's neighbourhood then desired him to write a few lines to the prisoner, stating those reports, and that he did not know that those Indians he was exciting had long been outlawed, and cautioned him against such proceedings, as he might be involved in their ruin. This the witness did, when the prisoner wrote him a long and insulting letter, which was lost, upbraiding the witness for calling those Indians outlaws, and accusing him of exciting the Indians to cruel war.

The witness was told by chiefs and Indians, who had seen the prisoner, that he advised them to go to war with the United States, if they did not surrender them the lands which had been taken from them, and that the British government would support them in it.

That the Indians, who took the witness, and a certain Mr. Doyle, prisoners, which happened on the 13th of December last, told them, that it was by the prisoner's order, and on their arrival at Michaseky, (as prisoners) King Huah and all his chiefs told them it was by the prisoner's orders they were taken and robbed. On their arrival at Suwaney, they were told by the Indians and negro chiefs, who sat in council over them, that the prisoner had advised that they should be given up to five or six Choctaw Indians, who were saved from the negro fort, who would revenge themselves for the loss of their friends at that place. On their return from Suwaney, the chief, King Hijah, told them that he had got the prisoner to write several letters for him; one to the governor of Providence, one to the British minister at Washington, one to the secretary of state in London, and one to the American agent for Indian affairs, protesting against the proceedings of the commanding officer at Fort Scott. While the witness was at Suwaney, the Indian chiefs told him that the prisoner had arrived at that place with ten kegs of powder on board his vessel; and whilst at Fort St. Mark's, some time in March, Hillisajo, or Francis, brought an order from the prisoner to the commandant for two kegs of powder, with other articles, which were in his possession.

Questioned by the Court—Were any murders or depredations committed on the white settlements, by the Indians, previous to the prisoner's arrival at Ochlocknee? *Ans.*—None, except one murder at Fort Gaines, which was before or about the time of the prisoner's arrival.—Q. How long have you resided among the Indians? State to the court, whether you are acquainted with the Indian language, and how long since you learned it?—A. I have resided among them fourteen years, and have understood their language twelve years.—Q. Do you believe the Seminoles would have commenced the business of murder and depredation on the white settlements, had it not been at the instigation of the prisoner, and a promise on his part of British protection?—A. I do not believe they would, without they had been assured of British protection.—Q. What was the light in which the prisoner was received by the hostile Seminoles; was it that of an authorised agent of the British government?—A. The different chiefs always represented him to me as such. The witness deposed to the copy of the letter marked G.—*Questioned by the prisoner*—Was the prisoner considered as the agent of the Seminoles at the time those murders were committed?—A. I had not seen the prisoner at that time; but the Indian chiefs told me the prisoner had reported himself to them as an English agent —

Q. Where did you understand the prisoner to be, when you were taken prisoner?—A. The Indians told us that he had gone over to Providence, but was expected back by the time we should arrive at Suwaney?—Q. Did you not request King Hijah to prevail upon the prisoner to give you a passage in his schooner to Providence?—A. Yes; but was told that the prisoner refused it, stating that if we were forced upon him, he would blindfold us and make us walk overboard.—Q. What were the reasons given by King Hijah for the prisoner's not granting your request?—A. King Hijah stated, that the prisoner was fearful of meeting with an American vessel, when we should be taken out, and he thereby lose his schooner.

William Fulton, the next witness examined—testified to the copy of a letter from the prisoner to General Mitchell, agent for Indian affairs, dated Suwaney, January 19, 1818, and marked No. 6—as acknowledged by the prisoner to be the same in substance, as one written by himself at that time. An extract from the letter was then read.

No. VI.

Extract of a letter written by A. Arbuthnot, to General Mitchell, American Agent for the Creek Nation of Indians, dated Sahwahnee, Jan. 19, 1818.

In taking the liberty of addressing you, Sir, in behalf of the unfortunate Indians, believe me, I have no wish but to see an end put to a war, which if persisted in, I foresee must eventually be their ruin; and as they were not the aggressors, if in the height of their rage they committed any excesses, that you will overlook them as the just ebullitions of an indignant spirit against an invading foe.

I have the honour to be, &c.

A. ARBUTHNOT.

By order of King Hijah and Bowlegs, acting for themselves and the other chiefs.

Questioned by the prisoner—Where did the prisoner acknowledge the letter just read to be a copy of the one written by himself?—A. In the encampment before this place, about the 6th or 7th instant.—Q. Was not the acknowledgment when he was a prisoner?—A. It was.—Q. Did you hear a gentleman say to the prisoner, whilst in custody, that those who recommended the scalping knife and tomahawk should feel their keenest edge?—A. I did hear a gentleman say, that those who excited the Indians to the murder of the unoffending, should feel the keenest edge of the scalping knife; but as well as I recollect, that observation was not made until after the repeated acknowledgments of the prisoner of having written the letter.—*Question by the Court*—Was not the confession of the prisoner to this letter made voluntarily, and without any constraint whatever?—A. I conceive it was.

The evidence on the part of the prosecution being closed, the prisoner requested as a witness Robert C. Ambrister, against whom criminal charges had been filed, and who was in custody on account thereof; to which the judge-advocate objecting, the court was cleared to take its sense: when it was decided, that Robert C. Ambrister, now in custody for similar offences with the prisoner, cannot be examined as evidence before the court.

John Lewis Phenix—*Questioned by the prisoner*—Was there any other vessel at the mouth of the Sahwahnee river, when Ambrister seized your vessel?—A. Yes.—Q. What vessel was it? Was it not the vessel which Ambrister came in?—A. It was a sloop, and I understood Ambrister came in her.—Q. Did Ambrister ever mention to you who recommended him to seize the prisoner's schooner, or who assisted him in stimulating the negroes to do so?—A. No; I understood he came on board of his own accord.—*Question by the Court*—Have you, since you commanded the prisoner's vessel, ever brought any arms to that part of the country? A. No; I brought a quantity of lead, and ten kegs of powder, in the last ship.

John Winslett—*Questioned by the Prisoner.*— Are you not of opinion, that the letter, which you say was written by the prisoner to the little prince, is now in the possession of the little prince? A. After reading it, I returned it to him, and believe it to be still in his possession, as Indians seldom destroy papers of that kind.

The prisoner having requested time to prepare his defence, it was granted, when he delivered the following:

May it please this honourable Court,

The prisoner arraigned before you, is sensible of the indulgence granted by this honourable court, in the examination of the case now before them. It is not the wish of the prisoner, in making his defence, to try the patience of the court, by a minute reference to the voluminous documents and papers, or to recapitulate the whole of the testimony which has come before the honourable court, in the course of this investigation. Nor is it the intention of the prisoner to waste the invaluable time of this court, by appeals to their feelings or sympathy, though I am persuaded that sympathy nowhere more abounds than in a generous American breast.

My only appeal is to the sound and impartial judgment of this honourable court, the purity and uprightness of their hearts, that they will, dispassionately and patiently, weigh the evidence they have before them, apply the law, and on these, and these alone pronounce their judgment.

If this honourable court please, I shall now proceed to examine the law and evidence that is relied on, by this honourable court, in support of the first charge and specification.

Winslett, a witness on the part of the prosecution, says, the little prince showed him a letter, written in June last, signed A. Arbuthnot, requesting his friendship with the lower nation of Indians. The same witness stated, that he believed the letter to be now in the possession of the little prince. Here, may it please this honourable court, I will call their attention to the law relating to evidence. First, presuming that the rules of evidence are the same, whether in civil or military tribunals—Mr. Comb, (96.) This point being conceded, the next enquiry is—what are the rules of evidence with respect to the admission of letters or papers of private correspondence, in a court of criminal jurisdiction? May it please this honourable court, must you not produce the original letters and papers, if they are not lost, or mislaid, so that they cannot be obtained; and in case they are lost, proof must be made of the hand writing being the same as that of the original, before they can be received as evidence?—M'Comb on Courts Martial; Peake's Evidence; Gilbert's Law of Evidence. No instance can be cited, where the copy of a letter was read as evidence, when the original could be obtained, much less the giving in evidence the contents of such letter from bare recollection. The only proof, that this honourable court has, of the existence of such letter being in the hands of any person, or its contents being known, is the vagrant memory of a vagrant individual. Make this rule of evidence, and I ask you, when would implication, construction, and invention stop? Whose property, whose reputation, and whose life would be safe? Here, I would beg leave to mention a remark made by the president of this court, in the course of this investigation, which was, that notwithstanding the letter was proved by the witness to be in the possession of the little prince, that this court could not notice that circumstance, because there was no means by which it could be obtained. I would ask the honourable court, what means they have adopted, or what exertions have they made to procure this letter? If the honourable court please, I shall here close the defence of the first charge and specification, believing that they are neither supported by law or evidence.

May it please the honourable court, I will now come to the second charge and specification of that charge. In support of this charge and specification, the evidence is a letter written to my son. If the court please, this letter was written in consequence of my property at Sahwahnee, and the large debts that were due to me from Bowlegs and his people. Nothing I believe, of an inflammatory nature can be found on reading the document marked A. authorising the opinion that I was prompting the Indians to war. On the contrary, if the honourable court will examine the document marked A. they will see that I wished to lull their fears, by informing them that it was the negroes, and not the Indians, the Americans were principally moving against. If the honourable court please, I will make a few remarks upon the second specification, and here close my defence. In proof of this charge, the court have before them the evidence of Hambly, Cook, and sundry letters, purporting to be written by myself to different individuals. May it please the court, what does Cook prove? Why, that I had ten kegs of powder at Sahwahnee; let me appeal to the experience of this court, if they think that this quantity of powder would supply one thousand Indians, and an equal number of blacks, more than two months for hunting? As to the letters named in this specification, may it please the court, the rules of evidence laid down in the first part of this defence will apply with equal force in the present case.

It remains now, may it please the court, to say something as to Hambly's testimony, and may it please this honourable court, the rule laid down in this case, as to hearsay evidence, will be found without a precedent. A strong case was stated by an intelligent member of this court, on the examination of this part of the evidence: that is, would you receive as testimony what a third had said, who, if present, you would reject as incompetent? Apply this principle to the present case. Could an Indian be examined on oath in our courts of judicature? If then, the testimony of savages is inadmissible, Hambly proves nothing.

Here, may it please this honourable court, I close my reply to the charges and specifications preferred against me, being fully persuaded, that, should there be cause of censure, my judges will, in the language of the law, lean to the side of mercy.

Fort St. Mark, April 28, 1818.

The court being closed, and the proceedings having had their mature deliberation, resolved as follows:—

The court find the prisoner, Alexander Arbuthnot, guilty of the first specification to the first charge, and guilty of the first charge.— Guilty of the second specification of the second charge, and guilty of the second charge, leaving out the words, " acting as a spy." They therefore do, on the most mature reflection, sentence the prisoner, Alexander Arbuthnot, to be suspended by the neck until he is dead, two thirds of the court concurring.

EDMUND P. GAINES,
Major-General by Brevet, President of the Court.

I. M. Glassel, Recorder.

TRIAL OF R. C. AMBRISTER.

Fort St. Mark's, April 27, 1818.

The court proceeded to the trial of Robert Christie Ambrister, a British subject, who, being asked if he had any objections to any one of the members of the court, replied in the negative, and was arraigned before the members of the court on the trial of A. Arbuthnot, with the addition of Captain Allison, of the seventh infantry, as a supernumerary member, upon the following charges.

Charge 1.—Aiding, abetting and comforting the enemy, supplying them with the means of war, he being a subject of Great-Britain, at peace with the United States, and lately an officer in the British Colonial Marines.

Specification.—1st. That the said Robert C. Ambrister, did give intelligence of the movements and operations of the American army, between the 1st and 20th of March, 1818, and did excite them (the negroes and Indians,) to war against the army of the United States, by sending their warriors to meet and fight the American army; whose government was at peace and friendship with the United States, and all her citizens.

Charge 2.—Leading and commanding the Lower Creeks, in carrying on a war against the United States.

Specification 1.—That the said Robert C. Ambrister, a subject of Great-Britain, which government was in peace and amity with the United States, and all her citizens, did, between the 1st of

February and 20th of March, 1818, levy war against the United States, by assuming a command of the Indians, in hostility and open war with the United States, and ordering a party of them to meet the army of the United States, and give them battle, as will appear by his letters to Governor Cameron, of New Providence, dated March the 20th, 1818, which are marked A. B. C. and D., and the testimony of Mr. Peter B. Cook, and Captain Lewis, of the schooner " *Chance.*"

By order of the court,
J. M. GLASSEL, Recorder.

To which charges and specifications, the prisoner pleaded as follows:

To the first charge and specification, *Not Guilty.*

To the second charge and specification, *Guilty, and Justification.*

John Lewis Phenix, a witness for the prosecution, deposed, that about the 5th or 6th of April, 1818, his vessel and himself, having been captured by the prisoner, and he brought to Suwaney as a prisoner, there was an alarm among the negroes and Indians, created by learning some news from Michasucky, at which time the prisoner appeared active in sending orders, and sending a detachment to meet the American army. The witness also stated, that the prisoner appeared to be a person vested with authority among the negro leaders, and gave orders for their preparation for war, providing ammunition, &c.; and that the leaders came to him for orders. The prisoner furnished them with powder and lead, and recommended to them the making of ball, &c. very quickly. The witness also states, that the prisoner occasionally dressed in uniform, with his sword; and, that on the first alarm, which he understood was from Michasucky, by a negro woman, he put on the uniform.

The witness further stated, that some time about the 20th of March, 1818, the prisoner, with an armed body of negroes, (twenty-four in number,) came on board his vessel, and ordered him to pilot them to fort St. Mark, which, he stated, he intended to capture before the Americans could get there, threatening to hang the witness if he did not obey. *Question by the Court.*—Did you ever understand by whose authority, and for what purpose, the accused came into the country?—A. I have frequently heard him say, he came to attend to Mr. Woodbine's business, at the bay of Tamper. *Question by the Prisoner.*—Did I not tell you when I came on board the schooner "*Chance*," I wished you to pilot me to St. Mark's, as I was informed that two Americans, of the name of Hambly and Doyle, were confined there, and I wished to have them relieved from their confinement?—A. You stated you wanted to get Hambly and Doyle from St. Marks, I do not know what was your intention in so doing.—Q. Did I not tell you that I expected the Indians would fire upon me, when arriving at St. Mark's?—A. You did not; you stated that you intended to take the fort in the night, by surprise.—Q. Did you see me give ammunition to the negroes and Indians? and, if so, how much, and at what time?—A. I saw you give powder and lead to the negroes, when you came on board, and advised them to make balls; and I saw you give liquor and paint to the Indians. —Q. Have you not often heard me say, between the 1st and 20th of April, that I would not have any thing to do with the negroes and Indians, in exciting them to war with the United States?—A. About the 15th of April, I heard you say you would not have any thing to do with the negroes and Indians; I heard nothing about exciting them to war.—Q. Can you read writing?—A. Not English writing. —Q. Did you not hear me say, when arriving at Suwaney, that I wished to be off immediately for Providence?—A. I did not; after the alarm you said you wished to be off for Tamper.—Q. Did you not say to the accused, you wished to visit Mr. Arbuthnot, at his store on Suwaney, and get provisions yourself?—A. I did not; I stated I wanted provisions.—Q. Did I send or command any Indians, to go and fight the Americans?—A. I did not exactly know that you sent them; the Indians and negroes were crowding before your door, and you were dividing the paint, &c. among them; and I understood a party was going to march.—Q. Did I not give up the schooner to you in charge, as captain?—A. After our return from Suwany town, you directed me to take charge of her to go to Tamper.

John J. Arbuthnot, (the son of the other prisoner,) a witness on the part of the prosecution, deposed, that some time about the 23d of March, the prisoner came with a body of negroes, partly armed, to his father's store, on Suwany River, and told the witness that he had come to do justice to the country, by taking the goods, and distributing them among the negroes and Indians; which the witness saw the prisoner do; and that the prisoner stated to him, that he had come to the country on Woodbine's business, to see the negroes righted. The witness has further known the prisoner to give orders to the negroes, and that, at his suggestion, a party was sent from Suwany to meet the Americans, to give them battle; which party returned on meeting the Mickasucky Indians in their flight. The witness testified to the following letter, marked A. referred to, in the specification of the second charge, as the writing of the prisoner.

———

A.

Robert C. Ambrister to Governor Cameron.

Sahwanhee, near St. Mark's Fort, March 20th, 1818.
Sir;

I am requested particularly, by all our Indian Chiefs, to acquaint your excellency, that the Americans have commenced hostilities with them two years ago; and have advanced some considerable distance in this country, and are now making daily progress. They say they sent a number of letters to your excellency, but have never received one answer, which makes them believe that he never delivered them, and will oblige them much if you will let me know whether he did or not. The purport of the letters were, begging your excellency to be kind enough to send them down some gunpowder, musket balls, lead, cannon, &c. as they are now completely out of those articles. The Americans may march through the whole territory in a month, and without arms, &c. they must surrender. Hillisajo, or Francis, the Indian Chief, the one that was in England, tells me to let your excellency know, that the Prince Regent told him, that whenever he wanted ammunition, your excellency would supply him with as much as he wanted. They beg me to press upon your excellency's mind to send the above-mentioned articles down by the vessel that brings this to you, as she will sail for this place immediately; and let the

S

Prince Regent know of their situation. Any letters that your excellency may send down, be good enough to direct to me, as they have great dependence in my writing. Any news that your excellency may have, respecting them and America, will be doing a great favour to let me know, that I may send among them.

There is now a very large body of Americans and Indians, who I expect will attack us every day, and God only knows how it will be decided. But I must only say, this will be the last effort with us. There has been a body of Indians gone to meet them, and I have sent another party. I hope your excellency will be pleased to grant the favour they request.

I have nothing further to add, but am, Sir, with due respect, your obedient humble servant,

ROBERT C. AMBRISTER.

Questioned by the Prisoner.—Did you hear me say, that I came on Woodbine's business?—A. I did.—Q. Were not the negroes, alluded to, at Arbuthnot's store before I arrived?—A. No, you came with them.

Peter B. Cook, a witness on the part of the prosecution, deposed, that he never heard the prisoner give any orders to negroes or Indians; that the prisoner distributed Arbuthnot's goods, and also paint, to the negroes and Indians; also, that some powder was brought from the vessel to Suwany, by the prisoner, and distributed among the negroes by Nero. Some time in March, the prisoner took Arbuthnot's schooner, and with an armed party of negroes, twenty-four in number, set out for St. Mark's, for the purpose of taking Arbuthnot's goods at that place, and stated, that he would compel the commandant to deliver them up. On hearing of the approach of the American army, the prisoner told the negroes it was useless to run, for if they ran any farther, they would be driven into the sea.

The prisoner told the witness, that he had been a lieutenant in the British army, under Colonel Nichols.

The prisoner was sent by Woodbine to Tamper, to see about those negroes he had left there. The prisoner told the witness, that he had written a letter to Governor Cameron, for ammunition for the Indians, some time in March; and also told the witness, that he had a commission in the patriot army, under M'Gregor, and that he expected a captaincy.

The witness testified to the preceding letter, marked A.; to the following, marked B. C. D. and E. referred to in the specification of the second charge, as being the hand writing of the prisoner.

B.

From Robert C. Ambrister, to Major Edward Nichols.

Suwany, near River Appalachicola.

Dear Sir;

Francis, and all the Indian Chiefs, have requested me particularly to acquaint you, that the Americans have commenced hostilities with them these two years past, and are making daily progress in their territory, and say they will proceed. That you are the only friend they have in that part of the world, and hope that you will exert yourself in their behalf, and ask for as much assistance as can be had. That the Americans are at the forks of the river Appalachicola. They have written a number of times to England and Providence, but have never received one answer; they expect the man never delivered the letters, but they have full hopes in my writing. They request that you would make the Prince Regent acquainted with their deplorable situation. The Americans have been very cruel since they commenced, and I hope you will lose not a single moment in forwarding their views. They say they will be extremely happy to see you; nothing would give them greater pleasure than to see you out at this time. If they should not see you, to send them out all news and directions, that they may be guided by it.

There are about three hundred blacks at this place, a few of our Bluff people. They beg me to say, they depend on your promises, and expect you are on the way out. They have stuck to the *cause*, and will always believe in the faith of you; and any directions you may give, send to me at this place, and I will do what I can.

And remain, my Dear Sir,
Most truly yours,
ROBERT C. AMBRISTER.

N. B. Francis says that you must bring the horses when you come out, that you promised, and that his house has been burnt down, and burnt his uniform clothes.

R. A.

C.

From Robert C. Ambrister to Governor Cameron.

March 20th, 1818.

Sir;

I am requested particularly by the Indian Chiefs, to acquaint your excellency, that the Americans have commenced hostilities with them a long time since, and have advanced some distance in their territory, and are still continuing to advance. That they, (the Chiefs of Florida,) have sent repeatedly to your excellency, and have never received one answer. They suspect Mr. Arbuthnot has never delivered the papers to your excellency. They wish me to state to you, that they are completely out of ammunition, muskets, &c. begging your excellency will be pleased to send them the articles above mentioned, with a few cannon; as the Americans build their boats so strong, that their rifle-balls cannot penetrate their sides. The captain of the vessel, who will come down again, I have given orders to make your excellency acquainted what time the vessel will sail for this place. Your excellency will, I hope, be good enough to make the Prince Regent acquainted with their situation, and ask for assistance; which they have pressed me very hard to press upon your excellency's mind, and likewise to send them down what news may be respecting them and the country, which will be a great satisfaction to them.

I have the honour to be, &c.

ROBERT C. AMBRISTER.

N. B. They beg your excellency will be as expeditious as possible. That your excellency is the only dependence they have, and who the Prince Regent told them would give them every assistance that laid in your power.

ROBERT C. AMBRISTER.

D.

From Robert C. Ambrister to Governor Cameron.

Sahwanee, 20th March, 1818, near Fort St. Mark's.

SIR;

I am requested by Francis, and all the Indian Chiefs, to acquaint your excellency, that they are at war with the Americans, and have been some time back. That they are in great distress, for want of ammunition, balls, arms, &c. and have wrote by Mr. Arbuthnot several times, but they suppose he never delivers them to your excellency. You will oblige them much to let them know whether he did or not.

I expect the Americans and Indians will attack us daily. I have sent a party of men to oppose them. They beg on me to press on your excellency's mind, to lay the situation of the country before the Prince Regent, and ask for assistance.

All news respecting them, your excellency will do a favour to let us know, by the first opportunity, that I may make them acquainted. I have given directions to the captain to let your excellency know when the vessel will sail for this place. I hope your excellency will be pleased to send them ammunition; I expect, if they do not procure some very shortly, that the Americans will march through the country. I have nothing farther to add.

I am, dear Sir,

Your most obedient humble servant,

ROBERT C. AMBRISTER.

E.

From Robert C. Ambrister, to Peter B. Cook.

Mouth of the River.

D'R COOK;

The boat arrived here about three o'clock on Thursday; the wind has been a-head ever since I have been down. The rudder of the vessel is in a bad condition, but I will manage to have it done to-night. The wind, I am in hopes, will be fair in the morning, when I will get under weigh, and make all possible despatch. I will make old Lewis pilot me safe. If those Indians don't conduct themselves straight, I would use rigorous means with them. Beware of Mr. Jerry; I found him on board when I came. Keep a good look out. I have sent two kegs of powder, and one bar of lead.

Your's, &c.

R. A.

Tuesday, 3 o'clock.

Questioned by the Prisoner.—Did you not frequently hear me say, that I would have nothing to do with the Indians, in exciting them to war with the United States?—A. I do not recollect.—Q. Are you acquainted with Lewis Phenix, and have you not heard him express ill will against me, in consequence of my wishing him to pilot me to St. Mark's?—A. I never did.—Q. Do you know of my sending troops at any time to fight against the United States? Have I not been constantly with you, so that you would have had an opportunity of knowing if there had been any sent by me?—A. I have not; they might have been sent without my knowledge.

Jacob Harrison, a witness for the prosecution, deposed, that some time in the latter end of March, or 1st of April, the prisoner took possession of the Schooner "*Chance*," with an armed party of negroes, and stated his intentions of taking St. Mark's. On his way thither, going ashore, he learned from some Indians that Arbuthnot had gone to St. Mark's, which induced him to return. The witness also stated, that while the prisoner was on board, he had complete command of the negroes, who considered him as their captain. The prisoner took the cargo of the vessel up towards Suwany, which consisted of, with other articles, nine kegs of powder, and 500lbs. of lead.

The proceedings here closed, and in the evening the prisoner delivered the following

DEFENCE.

To the first charge, the prisoner at the bar pleads *Not Guilty*;—and as to the second charge, *Guilty, and Justification.*

The prisoner at the bar, feels grateful to this honourable court, for their goodness in giving him a sufficient time to deliberate, and arrange his defence on the above charges.

The prisoner at the bar here avails himself of the opportunity of stating to this court, that inasmuch as the testimony which was introduced in this case, was very explicit, and went to every point the prisoner could wish, he has nothing further to offer in his defence, but puts himself upon the mercy of the honourable court.

BOBERT C. AMBRISTER.

The court having deliberated upon the proceedings and the defence, found the prisoner Robert C. Ambrister, *Guilty* of so much of the specification to the first charge, as follows, viz. " And did excite them to war with the United States, by sending their warriors to meet and fight the American army, he being a subject of Great-Britain, which government was at peace and friendship with the United States, and all her citizens;" but *Not Guilty* of the other part of the specification; *Guilty* of the first charge. *Guilty* of the specification of the second charge, and *Guilty* of the second charge; and do therefore sentence the prisoner, Robert C. Ambrister, to suffer death, by being shot, two-thirds of the court concurring therein.

One of the members of the court requesting a reconsideration of his vote on the sentence, the sense of the court was taken thereon, and decided in the affirmative, when the vote was again taken, and the court sentenced the prisoner to receive fifty stripes on his bare back, and be confined with a ball and chain to hard labour, for twelve calendar months.

EDMUND P. GAINES,

Major-General by brevet,

President of the court.

I. M. GLASSELL, Recorder.

Head Quarters, Division of the South.

Adjutant-General's Office, Camp four miles north of St. Mark's, April 29th, 1818.

GENERAL ORDERS.

After reciting the charges and specifications against the prisoners, A. Arbuthnot, and R. C. Ambrister, and their pleas thereto, the order continues:

" The commanding general approves the finding and sentence of the court, in the case of A. Arbuthnot; and approves the finding and first sentence of the court, in the case of Robert C. Ambrister, and disapproves the reconsideration of the sentence of the honourable court in this case.

It appears from the evidence and pleading of the prisoner, that he did lead and command, within the territory of Spain, (being a subject of Great-Britain,) the Indians, in war against the United States, these nations being at peace.

It is an established principle of the laws of nations, that any individual of a nation, making war against the citizens of any other nation, they being at peace, forfeits his allegiance, and becomes an outlaw and pirate. This is the case of Robert C. Ambrister, clearly shewn by the evidence adduced.

The commanding general orders, that brevet Major A. C. W. Fanning, of the corps of Artillery will have, between the hours of eight and nine o'clock, A. M. A. Arbuthnot *suspended by the neck with a rope, until he is dead;* and Robert C. Ambrister, to be *shot to death;* agreeable to the sentence of the court.

John James Arbuthnot will be furnished with a passage to Pensacola, by the first vessel.

The special court, of which brevet Major-General E. P. Gaines, is president, is dissolved.

By Order of Major-General Jackson,

ROBERT BUTLER,

Adjutant-General.

The sentence thus pronounced, was carried into effect, agreeable to the orders of General Jackson, and thus was consummated one of the most infamous murders, that ever stained the annals of a civilized country, conducted with all the formality of justice, but without one particle of its essence. The mind recoils with horror, at the narration of this systematic and cold blooded indulgence of vengeance, inflicted upon two victims, the one decoyed by the basest treachery into the power of his enemies, the other taken fighting in the ranks of those, who were advocating not only the law of nature, but the law of society, namely, the defence of property and country. We may endeavour, but in vain, to conceal from ourselves the fatal truth, that this sacrifice of our countrymen, was mixed up with political enmity to our nation. No sophistry, however specious, no declaration, however positive, can rase the damning record of that hostility, from the proceedings of the court-martial.

Arbuthnot, on being led to execution, shed tears of anguish, not that he feared to die, for he had been schooled in the lessons of affliction; not that he felt he had deserved the ignominy that awaited him; but because the exercise of those virtues, which ennoble human nature, and raise man above

the level of his species, had been arrayed against
him as offences, and cited as evidences of his criminality. Throughout the series of letters submitted to the court, he breathed a spirit of benevolence, coupled with a manly feeling of indignation
against the persecutors of the untutored savage.
Anxiously occupied in promoting the harmony of
the Indians, in endeavouring to protect their interests from the spoliations of a dastard and treacherous enemy, whose false representations to their
own government were industriously fabricated, to
destroy their defenceless neighbours; he was exposed to the inventive malice of those wretches,
(whose testimony, in the civil courts of their own
country, would neither have found admission nor
credit) before a tribunal, too evidently constituted,
for the purpose of ministring to the vindictive resentments of a military despot, who, vainly flattered
himself, his victims were without the pale of British
protection. Another, and a tenderer feeling, occupied in the moment of extremity, the mind of the
unfortunate Arbuthnot, against which his manly
fortitude but vainly combatted; he was about to
be torn for ever from his family, from those
dear dependents upon his exertions, who fondly
anticipated, a successful issue to his commercial

enterprise: yet, at the fatal moment, which was for ever to sever those endearments of life, while his spirit fluttered upon the verge of eternity, the remembrance of his country, her honour, and her glory, flashed as a bright vision upon his mental desolation, and soothed his agonized spirit, with the certainty that she would demand atonement; turning to his murderers, he pronounced with firmness, " England shall avenge her slaughtered son!"

Ambrister met his fate as became a soldier; he had staked his life upon the hazard, and bowed to destiny, confirming with his last breath, the warning prophetic voice of his fellow victim.

While I urge the necessity of vindicating the insulted honour of my country, of asserting rights thus shamefully violated, it is far from me to express, or to form a wish, which may destroy or infringe that political harmony, enjoyed relatively with the United States of America; but, while I should consider our silence and neglect of this momentous occurrence, a dereliction of principle, and a compromise of national honour, I would advocate that temperate investigation, that strict and punctilious enquiry which may comport with our own high character, and the honour of the United States sullied by the unauthorized act of some of its mem-

bers, and I trust with confidence in the integrity of
the American people, for ample reparation.

Englishmen and Americans derived from one
common ancestry, similar in habits, pursuits, and
feelings, speaking the same language, and bearing
the same names, are too nearly linked in the chain
of social beings, to permit those ties to be severed,
upon any other, than subjects of vital importance.
That generation, which suffered amid the horrors
of the convulsion, which tore, with violence, the
branches from the parent tree, have passed away,
or have outlived the stormy passions which animated
them, and usurped the place of better feelings, in
that war of desolation. The young and rising
generation are, on neither side, responsible for the
political errors of their ancestors; it is their duty,
as well as interest, rather to soothe than irritate,
and I will venture to hope, that the political independence of America, will generate and nourish, a
sentiment of honour, above the indulgence of the
mean spirit of jealous envy, of our superiority. The
lapse of time, and the progress of circumstances,
must give to the United States, the highest degree
of political importance in the western hemisphere,
and, while we on this side the Atlantic, view the
vigorous efforts of the infant republic, let us not

forget, that she is the imitator of our institutions, and the admiring copyist of our glorious constitution, and not deride, as puny and insignificant, the strenuous efforts of adolescence.

When the documents connected with the Seminole war, and the proceedings of the court-martial on our unfortunate countrymen, were laid before the Congress of the United States, it was naturally anticipated, that they would present, at least, a colourable pretence for the violation of the Spanish territory, and the summary executions of Arbuthnot and Ambrister; but to complete our astonishment, and to confirm our indignation, the parties concerned in those daring outrages, have had the temerity to avow and publish their criminality, without once attempting to offer, through the recital of crime and infamy, a single circumstance to palliate, or a single sentence to exculpate them from the charge of violence and murder.

The instructions from the secretary at war, to Generals Gaines and Jackson, during the progress of the Seminole campaign, instead of cautioning these officers against a violation of the territory of Spain, indirectly sanctioned, early in the correspondence, their desire to cross the boundary line, at the same time avowing, that the president is alone restrained by political considerations, from entering the provinces of the Floridas; in the subsequent letters it appears, that those political motives had ceased to operate, and the generals are instructed, with Jesuitical caution, to pass the boundary, *if necessary.*

By the 9th Article, 1st section of the Articles of Confederation, it is declared, " The United States " in Congress assembled, shall have the sole and " exclusive right and power of determining on " peace and war;" and by the 8th section of the 1st Article of the Constitution of the United States, declaratory of the power of the Congress, it is expressed, " To declare war; grant letters of marque " and reprisal; and make rules concerning captures " on land and water." Those instructions to the commanding generals, authorising the violation of the territory of a friendly power, amount, in general acceptation, to a declaration of war; and will, we may presume, be considered by the people of the American Union, as an assumption of the high and exclusive prerogative of Congress, by the executive; it behoves the people of the United States, to watch, with suspicious jealousy, every advance of their executive towards arbitrary power, least their boasted restrictions may vanish into air, and be remembered only, when they have ceased to exist.

The charges exhibited against Arbuthnot and Ambrister, so far from warranting the institution of a court-martial upon them, are so substantially defective, that they do not present a single apology for subjecting them to the controul of *any* American tribunal; for even admitting that they were guilty to the full extent of those offensive acts charged against them, they were not of such a character as to be within the pale of American jurisdiction: Spain was the only power invested with authority, to take cognizance of offences committed by the violaters of her peace.

The Indian nations, though independent communities to a certain extent, are yet considered as subjects, owing a peculiar allegiance to the power, within whose territorial limits they reside; and that such has been the invariable opinion, is evident, from the spirit and language of those treaties, in which the protection and restraint of the Indian nations, residing within their jurisdiction, have been stipulated and provided for, by the powers claiming controul over them.

Arbuthnot was an Indian trader, admitted by the Spanish authorities, to trade within the limits of their command; he was therefore an alien, owing a local and temporary allegiance to Spain, and, if guilty of exciting the inhabitants of the Floridas to war against the United States, was clearly liable to the penalties imposed upon those who levy war, without the consent of the king, in England deemed a high offence, against the dignity and prerogatives of the sovereign power.

Ambrister was certainly differently situated, he was taken in arms, in open hostility to the United States, yet it must be recollected, he was within the Spanish territory, and was authorised by the local allegiance he owed (as a temporary resident) to Spain,* to oppose the progress of invaders, the king's enemies; and, that the American army were such invaders, is evident, from their intrusion into the territory of a friendly power, unauthorised by a competent authority, and without the legitimate pretence of sanctioned hostility. It may be urged, by the apologists of the American Executive, that the hostility of the Indians pre-

---

* This doctrine is expressly admitted in the English law.—" Local allegiance is due from an alien or stranger born, for so long time as he continues within the king's dominions and protection."— 7 Rep. 6.

" Local allegiance.—That allegiance is a debt due from the subject, upon an implied contract with the prince, that so long as the one affords protection, so long the other will demean himself faithfully."— Black. Com. Book, 1, p. 370.

sented no other alternative to their operations, but
that immediate and summary vengeance was necessary, to punish and controul their savage enemies;
so far as this could be effected within their own
territory, the American executive possessed an undoubted and constitutional authority, to direct their
arms to that object, but having done so, to the
limits of their union, they were bound by the faith
of treaties, and the usual delicacy practised by
civilized communities, to respect the neutrality of
those states beyond their boundary, until their demands upon such friendly power, for the execution
of the stipulations of their treaties should be respected, or their neglect should warrant a breach
of that neutrality.

But, admitting for the sake of argument, that
the right of trying those offences, charged against
Arbuthnot and Ambrister, was in the American
general, (though I believe, the fallacy of that
doctrine is self evident) the evidence adduced, by
no means justified the judgment of the court-martial.

It will be seen, on reference to the evidence produced, to substantiate the first charge against
Arbuthnot, that it was principally supported by the
testimony of an individual, who swore *solely from
memory*, to the existence of a letter to the Indian

Chief, little Prince, in which Arbuthnot advised the harmony and union of the Upper and Lower Creeks, and their resistance of the terms of the treaty of Fort Jackson,* imposed upon them by the Americans, which he (Arbuthnot) conceived to be contravening the treaty of Ghent; but, neither the letter nor an attested copy were produced before the court, to confirm the allegation. To this mode of proof, Arbuthnot strenuously, but unavailingly objected, in his defence, on the ground that it was solely dependent upon " *the vagrant memory of a vagrant individual.*"

The evidence of Cook was mainly directed to the supply of munitions of war to the Indians, and the extent of his proof was, that a few kegs of powder, and a small quantity of lead was furnished by Arbuthnot: a supply, evidently inconsiderable, and very inadequate to the purposes of war, and scarcely sufficient for the hunting consumption of the Indians and negroes. The residue of this man's testimony

---

* It has been the disgraceful policy of the people and government of the United States, when desirous of possessing any part of the Indian territory, to excite their unsophisticated neighbours to hostility, in order to furnish them with a pretence for war; the superior resources of the United States in those contests, soon determined the victory in their favour, and enabled them to impose such terms of peace, as placed them in possession of the object of the war.

was given in a spirit so obviously hostile to the
prisoner, and his motives so notoriously those of
revenge, that had the members of the court-martial
exercised unbiassed judgments, or been actuated by
the principles of justice, they would have refused it
in toto, or received it with suspicion of its credibility.

The evidence of the next witness, was perfectly
accordant with the temper and disposition of the
court, and their mode of eliciting his testimony,
proves beyond the power of refutation, that the
sacrifice of the prisoner was determined upon, previous to its admission. Hambly* swore without
reservation, to all the charges against the prisoner,

---

* The pre-existing hostility of Hambly, is apparent throughout
the tenor of his correspondence with Arbuthnot, who retorts upon him
the charge of exciting the Indians to hostility, and with justice.
Forbes and Co., of Pensacola, (to whom Hambly was an agent) obtained from the Indians, a considerable grant of lands, upon condition
of introducing English settlers; these lands were then comparatively
of little value, but by stimulating the Americans to hostility, they
were likely to remove their Indian neighbours, and change the sovereignty to the United States, which promised ample advantage: Hambly appears to have imbibed the spirit of his employers, and to have
sacrificed Arbuthnot to his revenge, for having exposed the infamy of
his motives; how far Forbes and Co. succeeded, will be seen. While
Jackson was at Pensacola, Forbes and Co. sold their grant to C. and
Co. of Savannah, (already noticed in this work, as purchasers of the
anticipated conquest of M'Gregor,) for one hundred and twenty thousand dollars.

to which he was directed by the leading question put by the court, in direct violation of the established laws and rules of evidence, recognized by the United States tribunals.

But with all their subornations of perjury, in spite of their deviations from, and contempt of justice, the chain of evidence does not support the decision of the court-martial, and it remains a public record of the infamous prostitution of the members of that court, to the baneful passions of a military despot, marked with a deeper shade of savage criminality, than the worst acts in the violent career of Buonaparte.

To the first charge against Ambrister, he pleaded not guilty. The evidence was confined to the charge of aiding, abetting, and comforting the enemy, &c. but it did not appear that he was engaged in resisting the progress of the United States army, preceding their entry into the Spanish territory. To the second charge he pleaded guilty, and justification; consequently doing away the necessity of citing evidence to support it, but it is somewhat extraordinary, that in his defence, Ambrister omits altogether the ground of the justification he had pleaded, and confesses, *" as the testimony which was introduced in this case was very explicit, and went to every point the prisoner could wish, he has nothing farther to offer in his defence, but puts himself upon the mercy of the honourable court.*"

I should be sorry to believe that the infamy of this transaction was of a deeper dye than that which is apparent, and, God knows, it is sufficiently black and horrible in the catalogue of the crimes of human nature!! yet this omission of his justification, and this cool reliance upon the *mercy* of the court, implies, that hopes and deceitful promises were offered, to lure the victim from the purpose of his plea.

It has been seen that General Jackson refused to recognise the revised sentence of Ambrister, and ordered him for execution, stating this extraordinary doctrine:—

"*It is an established principle of the law of nations, that any individual of a nation making war against the citizens of any other nation, they being at peace, forfeits his allegiance, and becomes an outlaw and pirate; this is the case of Robert Ambrister, clearly shewn by the evidence adduced.*"

Such was the doctrine promulgated, and such the ignorant interpretation of the term pirate, given by the American general, who, in his civil capacity, had long filled the office of a judge in the courts of the Union; and this conservator of the law, to prove his contempt for the institutions of his country, openly defied, and set at nought the provisions of the military code, the sixty-fifth article of which peremptorily declares:—

"No sentence of a general court-martial, in time of peace, extending to the loss of life, shall be carried into execution, until the whole proceedings shall have been laid before the President of the United States, for his confirmation or approval, and orders in the case."

It cannot be contended, that this act was committed in the progress of a war; it wanted an essential requisite, namely, a declaration of hostility from the congress.

General Gaines, the president of the court-martial, was also a lawyer, celebrated hitherto, in the opinion of his countrymen, for the soundness of his judgment, and the integrity of his heart; what will they now say? with this example of profligate injustice, sanctioned by his name, and supported by his authority. Miserable, indeed, must be the destiny of that country, in which the judges and the advocates are thus corrupt and vicious; vain the boasted freedom of their constitution, their rights, their liberties, when the source can be poisoned, and the stream be polluted, at their pleasure and caprice.

If Jackson had executed his victims, without the

intervention of a court-martial, we might have found an apology in the irritation of feeling, and the necessity of prompt example; but the formality of a trial, and the parade of justice, can only be viewed by us, as a more direct insult, and a refinement of savage cruelty.

When those violent measures of the American generals were known at the court of Madrid, they were received with strong feelings of resentment, suited to the occasion; and produced from M. Pizarro, the minister for foreign affairs, the following remonstrance to the ambassador from the United States, expressive of the sentiments of his catholic majesty.

NOTE.

Sir;

In the department confided to me, disagreeable accounts continue to be received concerning the nature and circumstances of the late events in Florida, and the hostile proceedings of the American General Jackson, and the troops under his command, in the territory of these provinces which belong to his Majesty. Besides the facts to which I invited the attention of your excellency, in my notes of the 26th July, and of the 6th and 11th of this month, I have now before me the copy of a capitulation, which, it appears, followed the hostilities committed by that general, against the fortress of Pensacola, and in consequence of which, the Spanish garrison has been conveyed to the Havana. In my preceding notes, I had the honour to inform your excellency, that notwithstanding the particular character of violence which seemed to mark the actions and operations of General Jackson, since his first entrance into the Floridas, his majesty, although willing to consider these proceedings as the arbitrary acts of the said general, was convinced that the government of the United States would no longer delay to disapprove them, as soon as they came to its knowledge; and that proper orders would immediately be given, not only for the evacuation of the territory invaded, but also for the reparation of the damage occasioned, and for the restoration of the property taken, which belonged as well to his majesty, and Spanish subjects, as also to strangers who lived there, under the protection of his majesty's government.

It could not be presumed, without offence to the integrity of the American government, that there would be any delay in giving satisfaction to a friendly power, and to all civilized nations, this testimony of respect for those principles on which the maintenance of social order depends. It is with profound affliction that his majesty learns, from the subsequent report of his minister at Washington, that as the first excesses of General Jackson had not been disapproved, he had not hesitated to continue his acts of violence, and desolated with fire and sword, every thing upon the Spanish territory, when he met with a resistance, which sense of honour prescribed to some small garrisons, which were attacked in the midst of peace by a numerous body of troops. In general the territory of his majesty was attacked in the most revolting manner; the fortresses and depots of arms, have been taken by force, the garrisons made prisoners, and then sent out of the provinces, where his majesty had ordered them to serve. Nay, subjects of powers in friendship with his majesty, have been executed upon Spanish ground, and this act of barbarity cloaked with judicial forms, which in that situation, and in those circumstances, can only be considered as a refinement of cruelty. It cannot be doubted but these excesses are known to the government of Washington; and it does not yet appear that orders are given to put an end to them, or give to the Spanish government the only satisfaction which they admit of. In this situation his majesty considers it to be due to his own dignity, and that of the people whom he governs, to order me, at the same time that I again most solemnly protest against all that has been done by General Jackson, from the day that he set his foot on the territory of Florida, to add further, that your excellency will be pleased to inform your government, that the king is of opinion, that from the nature of the said injuries, and really hostile proceedings, the course of the negociations pending between the two powers, is and must remain interrupted and broken off, till the government of the United States has marked the conduct of General Jackson, in a manner suitable to its honour, and which, it seems, can be no other than to disapprove of the excesses committed; to give orders to place things on the same footing as they were in before the invasion; and to inflict an appropriate punishment on the author of so many disorders.

It is extremely disagreeable to his majesty, to be compelled to this declaration, which is the more necessary consequence of the nature of the affair, than an act of his royal will, whose wishes and endeavours have always been directed to making an equitable arrangement of the matters in debate between the two governments; but the whole impartial world will equally recognize, in the present state of things, the impropriety that must ensue, if negociations, which suppose a state of perfect political friendship, were to be continued, at a time when such insults have been offered without provocation. The occupation of the larger and better part of Florida, in 1810, by the United States, who deprived his majesty, during his captivity, of a country of which he was in peaceable possession, under pretences, which, if they had been even well founded, ought never to have been enforced by violence; and the late improper attack on Amelia island, were facts of the same nature and tendency, equally unjust in their principle, and equally protested against on the part of Spain; but as they were less offensive in their kind, and under the circumstances, his majesty believed at the same time that he gave proofs of his moderation, that he might wait for satisfaction on these points till the definitive arrangement of the points in dispute, which, it was expected, would soon take place. The same is not the case in the present instance. The Americans have no claim, either founded or unfounded, to the territory which General Jackson has attacked; no real or pretended revolution of the inhabitants could serve as a pretext; no previous attack by robbers, which was alledged as a reason for the unjust seizure of Amelia island; the Spanish flag was flying on the fortresses of San Marcos and Pensacola, when they were attacked; and, to complete the measure of insults, that has been taken by violence which his majesty had offered in the pending negociation to cede to the United States in an honourable manner, so that it seems to have preferred to seize it by violence, rather than to acquire it from the generous friendship of the king. These extraordinary circumstances have induced his majesty to take the resolution, that it is incompatable with the dignity of his exalted character to continue negociations, till an affair has been settled and terminated in a suitable manner, which takes the precedence of all other points in dispute between the two governments, and which, from its importance, is calculated essentially to change, in their whole extent, the political relations between the two countries.

At the same time, to give a proof of the peaceable and moderate sentiments which characterized the conduct of the Spanish government, I must acquaint your excellency, that his majesty has, in charging me to communicate to his minister at Washington the declared rupture of the negociations, likewise commanded me to inform him, that if the government of the United States had given or should give, the only satisfaction which the circumstance admits of, and which his majesty may expect from the justice and probity of that government, he may, in this case, continue the negociations begun, without applying to his majesty for new orders to authorize.

In making to your excellency this communication, I cannot omit to state to you, how painful it has been to me, that this unexpected obstacle should occur just at the time when I flattered myself with the hope of seeing the political relations, and the most perfect harmony between the two governments, re-established upon solid and durable foundations. I renew to your excellency the assurance of my distinguished respect, and pray to God to preserve your excellency many years.

Your excellency's most devoted servant,

Madrid, August 29th, 1818.   JOSEPH PIZARRO.

To the Minister of the United States, from His Catholic Majesty.

The foregoing letter, on being forwarded to the executive of the United States, was answered by the following, from Mr. Adams, couched in the language of haughty defiance, apparently reckless of the issue of the correspondence, and obviously intended as an intimidation to the court of Spain.

The Secretary of State of the United States, to the Minister Plenipotentiary of the United States to Spain, at Madrid.

Department of State, Washington, Nov. 28, 1818.

Sir;

Your despatches, to No. 92 inclusive, with their enclosures, have been received at this department. Among these enclosures are the several notes addressed to you by Mr. Pizarro, in relation to the transactions during the campaign of General Jackson, against the Seminole Indians and the banditti of negroes combined with them, and particularly to his proceedings in Florida, without the boundaries of the United States.

In the fourth and last of those notes of Mr. Pizarro, he has given formal notice, that the king, his master, has issued orders for the suspension of the negociation between the United States and Spain, until satisfaction shall have been made by the American government to him, for these proceedings of General Jackson; which he considers as acts of unequivocal hostility against him, and as outrages upon his honour and dignity; the only acceptable atonement for which, is stated, to consist in a disavowal of the acts of the American General thus complained of, the infliction upon him of a suitable punishment for his supposed misconduct, and the restitution of the posts and territories taken by him from the Spanish authorities, with indemnity for all the property taken, and all damages and injuries, public or private, sustained in consequence of it.

Within a very few days after this notification, Mr. Pizarro must have received, with copies of the correspondence between Mr. Onis and this department, the determination which had been taken by the president to restore the place of Pensacola, with the fort of Barrancas, to any person properly authorised on the part of Spain to receive them ; and the fort of St. Mark's to any Spanish force, adequate to its protection against the Indians, by whom its forcible occupation had been threatened, for the purpose of hostility against the United States. The officer commanding at the post, has been directed to consider 250 men as such adequate force; and in case of their appearance, with proper authority, to deliver it up to their commander accordingly.*

From the last-mentioned correspondence, the Spanish government must likewise have been satisfied that the occupation of these places in Spanish Florida, by the commander of the American forces, was not by virtue of any order received by him from this government to that effect, nor with any view of wresting the province from the possession of Spain, nor in any spirit of hostility to the Spanish government; that it arose from incidents which occurred in the prosecution of the war against the Indians; from the imminent danger in which the fort of St. Mark's was, of being seized by the Indians themselves; and from the manifestations of hostility to the United States by the commandant of S. Mark's and the governor of Pensacola; the proofs of which were made known to General Jackson, and impelled him, from the necessities of self-defence, to the steps of which the Spanish government complains.†

It might be sufficient to leave the vindication of these measures upon those grounds, and to furnish, in the enclosed copies of General Jackson's letters, and the vouchers by which they are supported, the evidence of that hostile spirit on the part of the Spanish commanders, but for the terms in which Mr. Pizarro speaks of the

---

* This is an extraordinary mode of dictation to a sovereign and independent state, and is an unhappy assumption of power in a *virtuous republic.*

† This declaration is extremely suspicious, in the face of the instructions given to General Jackson and Gaines.

execution of two British subjects, taken, one at the fort of St. Mark's, and the other at Suwany, and the intimation that these transactions may lead to a change in the relations between the two nations, which is doubtless intended to be understood as a menace of war.

It may be, therefore, proper to remind the government of his Catholic majesty, of the incidents in which this Seminole war originated, as well as of the circumstances connected with it, in the relations between Spain and her ally, whom she supposes to have been injured by the proceedings of General Jackson; and to give to the Spanish cabinet some precise information of the nature of the business, peculiarly interesting to Spain, in which these subjects of her allies, in whose favour she takes this interest, were engaged, when their projects of every kind were terminated, in consequence of their falling into the hands of General Jackson.

In the month of August, 1814, while a war existed between the United States and Great-Britain, to which Spain had formerly declared herself neutral, a British force, not in the fresh pursuit of a defeated and flying enemy, not overstepping an imaginary and equivocal boundary, between their own territories and those belonging, in some sort, as much to their enemy as to Spain, but approaching by sea, and by a broad and open *invasion* of the Spanish province, at a thousand miles or an ocean's distance from any British territory, landed in Florida, took possession of Pensacola and the Fort of Barrancas, and invited by public proclamations, all the runaway negroes, all the savage Indians, all the pirates, and all the traitors to their country, whom they knew or imagined to exist within reach of their summons, to join their standard, and wage an exterminating war against the portion of the United States immediately bordering upon this neutral and thus violated territory of Spain. The land commander of this British force was a certain Colonel Nicholls, who, driven from Pensacola by the approach of General Jackson, actually left to be blown up the Spanish fort of Barrancas, when he found it could not afford him protection, and, evacuating that part of the province, landed at another, established himself on the Appalachicola River, and there erected a fort, from which to sally forth, with his motley tribe of black, white, and red combatants, against the defenceless borders of the United States in that vicinity. A part of this force consisted of a corps of colonial marines, levied in the British colonies, in which George Woodbine was a captain, and Robert Christe Ambrister was a lieutenant.

As between the United States and Great-Britain, we should be willing to bury this transaction in the same grave of oblivion with other transactions of that war, had the hostilities of Colonel Nicholls terminated with the war. But he did not consider the peace which ensued between the United States and Great-Britain, as having put an end either to his military occupations, or to his negotiations with the Indians, against the United States. Several months after the ratification of the treaty of Ghent, he retained his post and his party-coloured forces in military array.

By the 9th article of that treaty, the United States had stipulated to put an end, immediately after its ratification, to hostilities with all the tribes or nations of Indians with whom they might be at war at the time of the ratification, and to restore to them all the possessions which they had enjoyed in the year 1811. This article had no application to the Creek nation, with whom the United States had already made peace, by a treaty concluded on the 9th day of August, 1814, more than four months before the treaty of Ghent was signed. Yet, Colonel Nicholls not only affected to consider it as applying to the Seminoles of Florida, and the outlawed Red Sticks, whom he had induced to join him there, but actually persuaded them that *they* were entitled, by virtue of the treaty of Ghent, to all the lands which had belonged to the *Creek* nation, within the United States, in the year 1811, and that the government of Great Britain would support them in that pretension. He asserted also this doctrine in a correspondence with Col. Hawkins, then the agent of the United States with the Creeks, and gave him notice, in their name, with a mockery of solemnity, that they had concluded a treaty of alliance, offensive and defensive, and a treaty of navigation and commerce with Great Britain, of which more was to be heard after it should be ratified in England. Col. Nicholls then evacuated his fort, which, in some of the enclosed papers, is called the Fort at Prospect Bluff, but which he had denominated the British post on the Appalachicola ; took with him the white portion of his force, and embarked for England, with several of the wretched savages whom he was thus deluding to their fate, among whom was the Prophet Francis, or Hillis Hadjo ; and left the fort, amply supplied with military stores and ammunition, to the Negro department of his allies. It afterwards was known by the name of Negro Fort. Col. Hawkins immediately communicated to this government the correspondence between him and Nicholls, here referred to, upon which Mr. Munroe, then secretary of state, addressed a letter to Mr. Baker, the British chargé d' affaires, at Washington, complaining of Nicholls's conduct, and showing that his pretence, that the 9th article of the treaty of Ghent could have any application to his Indians, was utterly destitute of foundation. Copies of the same correspondence were transmitted to the minister of the United States then in England, with instructions to remonstrate with the British government against these proceedings of Nicholls, and to show how incompatible they were with the peace which had been concluded between the two nations. These remonstrances were accordingly made, first in personal interview with Earl Bathurst and Lord Castlereagh, and afterwards in written notes, addressed successively to them. Lord Bathurst, in the most unequivocal manner, confirmed the facts, and disavowed the misconduct of Nicholls ; declared his disapprobation of the pretended treaty of alliance, offensive and defensive, which he had made ; assured the American minister that the British government had refused to ratify that treaty, and would send back the Indians whom Nicholls had brought with him, with advice to make their peace on such terms as they could obtain. Lord Castlereagh confirmed the assurance that the treaty would not be ratified ; and if, at the same time that these assurances were given, certain distinctions of public notoriety were shown to the Prophet Hillis Hadjo, and he was actually honoured with a commission, as a British officer, it is to be presumed that these favours were granted him as rewards of past services, and not as encouragement to expect any support from Great Britain, in a continuance of savage hostilities against the United States, all intention of giving any such support having been repeatedly and earnestly disavowed.

The Negro fort, however, abandoned by Col. Nicholls, remained on the Spanish territory, occupied by the banditti to whom he had left it, and held by them as a post, from whence to commit depredations, outrages, and murders, and as a receptacle for fugitive slaves and malefactors, to the great annoyance both of the United States and Spanish Florida. In April, 1816, General Jackson wrote a letter to the governor of Pensacola, calling upon him to put down this common nuisance to the peaceable inhabitants of both countries. That letter, together with the answer of the governor of Pensacola, have already been communicated to the Spanish minister here, and by him, doubtless, to his government. Copies of them are, nevertheless, now again enclosed; particularly as the letter from the governor explicitly admits, that this fort, constructed by Nicholls, in violation both of the territory and neutrality of Spain, was still no less obnoxious to his government than to the United States; but that he had neither sufficient force, nor an authority, without orders from the governor-general of the Havannah, to destroy it. It was afterwards, on the 27th of July, 1816, destroyed by a cannon-shot from a gun-vessel of the United States, which, in its passage up the river, was fired upon from it. It was blown up, with an English flag still flying as its standard, and immediately after the barbarous murder of a boat's crew belonging to the navy of the United States, by the banditti left in it by Nicholls.

In the year 1817, Alexander Arbuthnot, of the island of New Providence, a British subject, first appeared, as an Indian trader in Spanish Florida; and as the successor of Colonel Nicholls, in the employment of instigating the Seminole and outlawed Red Stick Indians to hostilities against the United States, by reviving the pretence that they were entitled to all the lands which had been ceded to the Creek nation by the United States, in August, 1814.* As a mere

---

* This assertion is unsupported—Arbuthnot, doubtless, conceived the United States were trenching upon the rights of the Indians (provided for by the treaty of Ghent) in the treaty of Fort Jackson, and advised their refusal to ratify; but it was solely the inventive malice of his enemies which implicated him in exciting Indian hostility.

Indian trader, the intrusion of this man into a Spanish province was contrary to the policy observed by all the European Powers in this hemisphere, and by none more rigorously than by Spain, of excluding all foreigners from intercourse with the Indians within their territories.* It must be known to the Spanish government, whether Arbuthnot had a Spanish license for trading with the Indians in Spanish Florida or not; but they also know that Spain was bound by treaty to restrain by force all hostilities on the part of those Indians, against the citizens of the United States, and it is for them to explain how, consistently with those engagements, Spain could, contrary to all the maxims of her ordinary policy, grant such a license to a foreign incendiary, whose principal, if not his only object, appears to have been to stimulate those hostilities which Spain had expressly stipulated by force to restrain. In his infernal instigations he was but too successful. No sooner did he make his appearance among the Indians, accompanied by the Prophet Hillis Hadjo, returned from his expedition to England, than the peaceful inhabitants on the borders of the United States were visited with all the horrors of savage war; the robbery of their property, and the barbarous and indiscriminate murder of woman, infancy, and age.†

After the repeated expostulations, warnings, and offers of peace, through the summer and autumn of 1817, on the part of the United States, had been answered only by renewed outrages, and after a detachment of forty men, under Lieutenant Scott, accompanied by seven women, had been way-laid and murdered by the Indians,

---

* Mr. Adams could not be ignorant that Panton, Leslie and Co. formerly of St. Augustine, Forbes and Co. of Pensacola, and others, were licensed by the Spaniards as traders with the Indians; and that *all foreigners* were freely admitted into the Floridas, and even permitted to hold lands under Spanish grants, until the aggressions of the people of the United States induced Spain to exclude them *particularly*.

† The conclusion of Mr. Adams is by no means supported, even by the evidence offered at the *mock trial* of Arbuthnot. There was no direct testimony to overt acts, but the mere vague opinion of an infamous witness, elicited by questions *illegally put*.

orders were given to General Jackson, and an adequate force was placed at his disposal, to terminate the war. It was ascertained that the Spanish force in Florida was inadequate for the protection even of the Spanish territory itself, against this mingled horde of lawless Indians and negroes; and, although their devastations were committed within the limits of the United States, they immediately sought refuge within the Florida line, and there only were to be overtaken. The necessity of crossing the line was indispensable; for it was from beyond the line that the Indians made their murderous incursions within that of the United States. It was there that they had their abode, and the territory belonged in fact to them, although within the borders of the Spanish jurisdiction. There it was that the American commander met the principal resistance from them;[*] there it was, that were found the still bleeding scalps of our citizens, freshly butchered by them; there it was that he released the only *woman* who had been suffered to survive the massacre of the party under Lieutenant Scott. But it was not anticipated by this government, that the commanding officers of Spain, in Florida, whose especial duty it was, in conformity to the solemn engagements contracted by their nation, to restrain by force those Indians from hostilities against the United States, would be found encouraging, aiding, and abetting them, and furnishing them with supplies for carrying on such hostilities. The officer in command immediately before General Jackson, was, therefore, specially instructed to respect, as far as possible, the Spanish authority, wherever it was maintained, and copies of these orders were also furnished to General Jackson upon his taking the command. In the course of his pursuit, as he approached St. Mark's, he was informed, direct from the governor of Pensacola, that a party of the hostile Indians had threatened to seize that fort, and that he apprehended the Spanish garrison there was not in strength sufficient

---

[*] It is by no means a matter of surprise that the American commanders met with the principal resistance to their progress within the Spanish lines. The Indians were defending all that is dear to man, savage or civilised—their homes, their families, and their country!

to defend it against them. This information was confirmed from other sources, and by the evidence produced upon the trial of Ambrister, it proved to have been exactly true.* By all the laws of neutrality and of war, as well as of prudence and of humanity, he was warranted in anticipating his enemy, by the amicable, and that being refused, by the forcible occupation of the fort. There will need no citations from printed treatises on international law, to prove the correctness of this principle. It is engraved in adamant on the common sense of mankind : no writer upon the laws of nations ever pretended to contradict it; none of any reputation or authority ever omitted to assert it.†

At Fort St. Mark's, Alexander Arbuthnot, the British Indian trader from beyond the seas, the firebrand, by whose torch this Negro Indian war against our borders had been rekindled, was found an inmate of the commandant's family ; and it was also found that, by the commandant himself, councils of war had been permitted to be held within it, by the savage chiefs and warriors :— that the Spanish store-houses had been appropriated to their use ; that it was an open market for cattle, known to have been robbed by them from citizens of the United States, and which had been contracted for and purchased by the officers of the garrison :— that information had been afforded from this fort by Arbuthnot, to the enemy, of the strength and movements of the American army : that the date of the departure of express had been noted by the Spanish commissary, and ammunition, munitions of war, and all necessary supplies furnished to the Indians.‡

---

* Surely Mr. Adams must have overlooked the small force, with which it was asserted, Ambrister proposed to storm St. Mark's : it was too ridiculous to entertain it. At any rate, it was no ordinary courtesy in the American general to force his protection upon the unwilling governor.

† The American secretary appears aware of his inability to defend the conduct of the Seminole war, and therefore rejects the interposition and authority of the writers upon international law : we shall see by-and-bye how far he is consistent.

‡ It has been already shown, how Arbuthnot became an inmate of the family of the governor of St. Mark's, and how *honourably* he was decoyed into the power of his enemies to their eternal infamy.

The conduct of the governor of Pensacola was not less marked by a disposition of enmity to the United States, and by an utter disregard to the obligations of the treaty, by which he was bound to restrain, by force, the Indians from hostilities against them.*— When called upon to vindicate the territorial rights and authority of Spain, by the destruction of the Negro fort, his predecessor had declared it to be not less annoying and pernicious to the Spanish subjects in Florida, than to the United States, but had pleaded his inability to subdue it. He himself had expressed his apprehensions that Fort St. Mark's would be forcibly taken by the savages, from its Spanish garrison; yet, at the same time, he had refused the passage up the Escambia river, unless upon the payment of excessive duties, to provisions destined as supplies for the American army, which, by the detention of them, was subjected to the most distressing privations.† He had permitted free ingress and egress at Pensacola to the avowed savage enemies of the United States. Supplies of ammunition, munitions of war, and provisions had been received by them from thence. They had been received and sheltered there from the pursuit of the American forces, and suffered again to sally thence, to enter upon the American territory, and commit new murders. Finally, on the approach of General Jackson to Pensacola, the governor sent him a letter, denouncing his entry upon the territory of Florida as a violent outrage upon the rights of Spain, commanding him to depart and withdraw from the same, and threatening, in case of his non-compliance, to employ force to expel him.

It became, therefore, in the opinion of General Jackson, indispensably necessary to take from the governor of Pensacola the

---

* Spain was certainly bound to restrain the Indians; but it was an implied contract that the people of the Union should withhold from violating the territorial limits of Spain, and disturbing the peace of her Indian subjects.

† The mode of reasoning pursued by Mr. Adams, defies all practical rules. Assuredly it was in the exercise of an undoubted right, that the Spanish governor of Pensacola refused a passage for the supplies to the American army.

means of carrying his threat into execution. Before the forces under his command, the savage enemies of his country had disappeared; but he knew that the moment those forces should be disbanded, if sheltered by Spanish fortresses, if furnished with ammunitions and supplies of Spanish officers, and if aided and supported by the instigation of Spanish encouragement, as he had every reason to expect they would be, they would re-appear; and fired, in addition to their ordinary ferociousness, with revenge for the chastisement they had so recently received, would again rush with the war hatchet and scalping knife into the borders of the United States, and mark every footstep with the blood of their defenceless citizens. So far as all the native resources of the savage extended, the war was at an end; and General Jackson was about to restore to their families and their homes, the brave volunteers who had followed his standard, and who had constituted the principal part of his force. This could be done with safety, leaving the regular portion of his troops to garrison his line of forts, and two small detachments of volunteer cavalry, to scour the country round Pensacola, and sweep off the lurking remnant of savages who had been scattered and dispersed before him. This was sufficient to keep in check the remnant of the banditti against whom he had marched, so long as they should be destitute of other aid and support. It was, in his judgment, not sufficient, if they should be suffered to rally their numbers under the protection of Spanish forts, and to derive new strength from the impotence or the ill-will against the United States of the Spanish authorities.

He took possession, therefore, of Pensacola, and of the fort of Barrancas, as he had done of St. Mark's, not in a spirit of hostility to Spain, but as a necessary measure of self-defence; giving notice that they should be restored, whenever Spain should place commanders and a force there, able and willing to fulfil the engagements of Spain and the United States, of restraining by force the Florida Indians from hostilities against their citizens. The president of the United States, to give a signal manifestation of his confidence in the disposition of the king of Spain, to perform with good faith this indispensable engagement, and to demonstrate to the whole world, that neither the desire of conquest, nor hostility to

Spain, had any influence in the councils of the United States, has directed the unconditional restoration to any Spanish officer, duly authorised to receive them, of Pensacola and the Barrancas, and that of St. Mark's to any Spanish force, adequate for its defence against the attacks of the savages. But the president will neither inflict punishment, nor pass a censure upon General Jackson, for that conduct, the motives for which were founded in the purest patriotism, of the necessity for which he had the most immediate and effectual means of forming a judgment, and the vindication of which is written in every page of the law of nations, as well as in the first law of nature, self-defence. He thinks it, on the contrary, due to the justice which the United States have a right to claim from Spain; and you are accordingly instructed to demand of the Spanish government, that inquiry shall be instituted into the conduct of Don Jose Mazot, Governor of Pensacola, and of Don Francisco C. Luengo, commandant of St. Mark's, and a suitable punishment inflicted upon them, for having, in defiance and violation of the engagements of Spain with the United States, aided and assisted these hordes of savages, in those very hostilities against the United States which it was their official duty to restrain.* This inquiry is due to the character of those officers themselves, and to the honour of the Spanish government. The obligation of Spain to restrain by force the Indians of Florida from hostilities against the United States and their citizens, is explicit, is positive, is unqualified. The fact, that for a series of years they have received shelter, assistance, supplies, and protection, in the practice of such hostilties from the Spanish commanders in Florida, is clear and unequivocal. If, as the commanders both at Pensacola and St. Mark's have alleged, this has been the result of their weakness rather than of their will; if they have assisted the Indians against the United States, to avert their hostilities from the province, which they had not sufficient force to defend against them, it may serve

---

* With singular felicity the American secretary turns round upon the Spanish government, and takes the place of the accuser; but he vainly attempts by such finesse, to get rid of the charges against the United States.

in some measure to exculpate, individually, those officers; but it must carry demonstration irresistible to the Spanish government, that the right of the United States can as little compound with impotence as with perfidy; and that Spain must immediately make her election, either to place a force in Florida, adequate at once to the protection of her territory and to the fulfilment of her engagements, or cede to the United States a province of which she retains nothing but the nominal possession ; but which is, in fact, a derelict, open to the occupancy of every enemy, civilised or savage, of the United States; and serving no other earthly purpose than as a post of annoyance to them.

That the purposes, as well of the Negro Indian banditti, with whom we have been contending, as of the British invaders of Florida, who first assembled and employed them, and of the British intruding and pretending traders, since the peace, who have instigated and betrayed them to destruction, have been not less hostile to Spain than to the United States, the proofs contained in the documents herewith enclosed, are conclusive. Mr. Pizarro's note of 29th of August, speaks of his catholic majesty's profound indignation at the " sanguinary executions on the Spanish soil, of the subjects of powers in amity with the king," meaning Arbuthnot and Ambrister. Let Mr. Pizarro's successor take the trouble of reading the enclosed documents, and he will discover who Arbuthnot and Ambrister were, and what were their purposes: that Arbuthnot was only the successor of Nicholls, and Ambrister the agent of Woodbine, and the subaltern of M'Gregor. Mr. Pizarro qualifies General Jackson's necessary pursuit of a defeated savage enemy, beyond the Spanish line, as a *shameful invasion of his majesty's territory*; yet that territory was the territory also of the savage enemy ; and Spain was bound to restrain them by force from hostilities against the United States ; and it was the failure of Spain to fulfil this engagement, which had made it necessary for General Jackson to pursue the savages across the line. What then was the character of Nicholl's invasion of his majesty's territory? and where was his majesty's profound indignation at that ? Mr. Pizarro says, his majesty's forts and places have been violently seized on, by General Jackson. Had they not been seized on, nay, had not the principal of his forts been blown up by Nicholls, and a British fort on the same Spanish territory been erected during the war, and left standing as a negro fort, in defiance of Spanish authority, after the peace? Where was his majesty's profound indignation at that? Has his majesty suspended formally all negotiation with the sovereign of Colonel Nicholls, for the shameful invasion of his territory, without colour of provocation, without pretence of necessity, without the shadow or even avowal of pretext? Has his majesty given solemn warning to the British government, that these were incidents " of transcendent moment, capable of producing an essential and thorough change in the political relations of the two countries? Nicholls and Woodbine, in their invitations and promises to the slaves, to run away from their masters and join them, did not confine themselves to the slaves of the United States; they received with as hearty a welcome, and employed with equal readiness, the fugitives from their masters in Florida, as those from Georgia. Against this special injury the Governor of Pensacola did earnestly remonstrate with the British Admiral Cockburn; but against the *shameful invasion* of the territory, against the violent seizure of the forts and places, against the blowing up of the Barrancas, and the erection and maintenance under the British banners, of the negro fort on Spanish soil; against the negociation by a British officer in the midst of peace, of pretended treaties, offensive and defensive, and of navigation, and commerce upon Spanish territory, between Great-Britain and Spanish Indians, whom Spain was bound to controul and restrain; if a whisper of expostulation was ever wafted from Madrid to London, it was not loud enough to be heard across the Atlantic, nor energetic enough to transpire beyond the walls of the palaces from which it issued, and to which it was borne.

The connection between Arbuthnot and Nicholls, and between Ambrister, Woodbine, and M'Gregor, is established beyond all question by the evidence produced at the trials before the court-martial. I have already remarked to you on the very extraordinary circumstance, that a British trader from beyond the sea should be permitted by the Spanish authorities to trade with the Indians of Florida. From his letter to Hambly, dated 3d May,

1817 (see the documents marked G in the proceedings of the court-martial), it appears that his trading was but a pretence; and that his principal purpose was to act as the agent of the Indians of Florida, and outlaws from the Creeks, to obtain the aid of the British Government in their hostilities against the United States. He expressly tells Hambly there, that the chief of those outlaws was the principal cause of his, Arbuthnot's, being in the country; and that he had come with an answer from Earl Bathurst, delivered to him by Governor Cameron, of New Providence, to certain Indian talks, in which this aid of the British Government had been solicited. Hambly himself had been left by Nicholls as the agent between the Indians and the British Government; but having found that Nicholls had failed in his attempt to prevail upon the British Government to pursue this clandestine war in the midst of peace, and that they were not prepared to support his pretence; that half a dozen outlawed fugitives from the Creeks were the Creek nation;—when Arbuthnot, the incendiary, came, and was instigating them, by promises of support from Great Britain, to commence their murderous incursions into the United States. Hambly, at the request of the Creeks themselves, wrote to him, warning him to withdraw from among that band of outlaws, and giving him a solemn foreboding of the doom that awaited him from the hand of justice, if he persevered in the course that he pursued. Arbuthnot, nevertheless, persisted; and while he was deluding the wretched Indians with the promise of support from England, he was writing letters for them to the British minister in the United States, to Governor Cameron, of New Providence, to Colonel Nicholls, to be laid before the British Government; and even to the Spanish Governor of St. Augustine, and the Governor-general of the Havanna, soliciting in all quarters aid and support, arms and ammunition, for the Indians against the United States; bewailing the destruction of the Negro fort, and charging the British Government with having drawn the Indians into war with the United States, and deserting them after the peace.

You will remark, among the papers produced on his trial, a power of attorney dated 17th June, 1817, given him by twelve Indians, partly of Florida, and partly of the fugitive outlaws from the United States. He states, that this power, and his instructions, were to memorialize the British Government and the Governor-general of the Havannah. These papers are not only substantially proved, as of his hand-writing, on the trial, but in the daily newspapers of London, of the 24th and 25th of August last, his letter to Nicholls is published (somewhat garbled), with a copy of Hambly's above-mentioned letter to him, and a reference to this Indian power of attorney to him, *approved by the commandant of St. Mark's, S. C. Luengo.* Another of the papers is a letter written in the name of the chiefs, by Arbuthnot, to the Governor-General of the Havannah, asking of him permission for Arbuthnot to establish a ware-house on the Appalachicola; bitterly and falsely complaining that the Americans had made settlements on their lands, within the Spanish lines, and calling upon the Governor-General to give orders to displace them, and send them back to their own country. In this letter they assign as a reason for asking this licence for Arbuthnot, the want of a person to put in writing for them, their talks of grievances against the Americans; and they add, " the commander of the fort of St. Mark's has heard all of our talks and complaints. He approves of what we have done, and what we are doing; and it is by his recommendation we have thus presumed to address your excellency." You will find these papers in the printed newspapers enclosed, and in the proceedings of the court-martial; and will point them out to the Spanish Government, not only as decisive proofs of the unexampled compliances of the Spanish officers in Florida to foreign intrusive agents, and instigators of Indian hostilities against the United States, but as placing beyond a doubt, that participation of this hostile spirit in the commandant of St. Marks, which General Jackson so justly complains of, and of which we have so well-founded a right to demand the punishment. Here is the commandant of a Spanish fort, bound by the sacred engagements of a treaty to restrain by force the Indians within his command, from committing hostilities against the United States, conspiring with those same Indians, and deliberately giving his written approbation to their appointment of a foreigner, a British subject, as their agent, to solicit assistance and supplies from the Governor-General of the Havannah.

and from the British government, for carrying on these same hostilities.

Let us come to the case of Ambrister. He was taken in arms, leading and commanding the Indians, in the war against the American troops; and to that charge, upon his trial, pleading guilty. But the primary object of his coming there was still more hostile to Spain than the United States. You find that he told three of the witnesses, who testified at his trial, that he had come to this country upon Mr. Woodbine's business at Tampa Bay, to see the negroes righted; and one of them, that *he had a commission in the patriot army, under M'Gregor*, and that he expected a captaincy. And what was the intended business of M'Gregor and Woodbine at Tampa Bay? It was the conquest of Florida from Spain, by the use of those very Indians and negroes, whom the commandant of St. Mark's was so ready to aid and support in war against the United States. The chain of proof that establishes this fact, is contained in the documents communicated by the president to congress, at their last session, relating to the occupation of Amelia island by M'Gregor. From these documents you will find, that while M'Gregor was there, Woodbine went from New Providence, in a schooner of his own, to join him; that he arrived at Amelia island just as M'Gregor, abandoning the companions of his atchievements there, was leaving it; that M'Gregor, quitting the vessel in which he had embarked at Amelia, went on board that of Woodbine, and returned with him to New Providence; that Woodbine had persuaded him they could yet accomplish the conquest of Florida, with soldiers to be recruited at Nassau, from the corps of colonial marines, which had served under Nicholls during the late war with the United States, which corps had been lately disbanded; and with negroes to be found at Tampa Bay, and 1,500 Indians, already there engaged to Woodbine, who pretended that they had made a grant of all their lands there to him. Among the papers, the originals of which are in our possession, in M'Gregor's own hand-writing, instructions for sailing into Tampa Bay, with the assertion that he calculated to be there by the last of April or first of May, of the present year; a letter, dated 27th December last, to one of his acquaintance in this country, disclosing the same intention; and the extract of a proclamation which was to have been issued at Tampa Bay, to the inhabitants of Florida, by the person charged with making the settlement there, before his arrival, announcing his approach, for the purpose of liberating them from the despotism of Spain, and of enabling them to form a government for themselves. He had persuaded those who would listen to him here, that his ultimate object was to sell the Floridas to the United States.* There is some reason to suppose that he had made indirect overtures, of a similar nature, to the British government.—This was Ambrister's business in Florida. He arrived there in March, the precursor of M'Gregor and Woodbine; and immediately upon his arrival, he is found seizing upon Arbuthnot's goods, and distributing them among the negroes and Indians: seizing upon his vessel, and compelling its master to pilot him, with a body of armed negroes, towards the Fort of St. Mark's, with the declared purpose of taking it by surprise, in the night: writing letters to Governor Cameron, of New Providence, urgently calling for supplies of munitions of war, and of cannon, for the war against the Americans; and letters to Colonel Nicholls, renewing the same demands of supplies; informing him that he is with 300 negroes, 'a few of our Bluff people,' who had *stuck to the cause*, and were relying upon the faith of Nicholls's promises. Our Bluff people were the people of the negro fort, collected by Nicholls's and Woodbine's proclamations, during the American and English war; and the *cause* to which they stuck, was the savage, servile, exterminating war against the United States.

Among the agents and actors of such virtuous enterprises as are here unveiled, it was hardly expected that there would be found remarkable evidences of their respect, confidence, and good faith towards one another. Accordingly, besides the violent seizure and distribution, by Ambrister, of Arbuthnot's property, his letters to Governor Cameron, and to Nicholls, are filled with the distrust and suspicions of the Indians, that they were deceived and betrayed by

---

* Surely this detail of occurrences in Florida, by M'Gregor and his partisans, is foreign to the subject of discussion.

Arbuthnot; while in Arbuthnot's letters to the same Nicholls, he accuses Woodbine of having taken charge of poor Francis the prophet, or Hidlis Hadjo, upon his return from England to New Providence, and under pretence of taking care of him and his affairs—of having defrauded him of a large portion of the presents which had been delivered out from the king's stores to him, for Francis's use. This is one of the passages of Arbuthnot's letter to Nicholls, *omitted* in the publication of it last August in the London newspapers.

Is this narrative of dark and complicated depravity; this creeping and insidious war, both against Spain and the United States; this mocker of patriotism; these political philters to fugitive slaves and Indian outlaws; these perfidies and treacheries of villains incapable of keeping their faith even to each other, all in the name of South American liberty, of the rights of runaway negroes, and the wrongs of savage murderers—all combined and projected to plunder Spain of her provinces, and to spread massacre and devastation along the borders of the United States;—is all this sufficient to cool the sympathies of his Catholic Majesty's government, excited by the execution of these two " subjects of a power in amity with the king?" The Spanish government is not at this day to be informed that, cruel as war in its mildest forms must be, it is, and necessarily must be, doubly cruel, when waged with savages; that savages make no prisoners, but to torture them;— that they give no quarter; that they put to death without discrimination of age or sex; that these ordinary characteristics of Indian warfare have been applicable, in their most heart-sickening horrors to that war, left us by Nicholls, as his legacy, reinstigated by Woodbine, Arbuthnot, and Ambrister, and stimulated by the approbation, encouragement, and aid of the Spanish commandant at St. Mark's. Is proof required? Entreat the Spanish minister of state, for a moment, to overcome the feelings which details like these must excite, and to reflect, if possible, with composure, upon the facts stated in the following extracts from the documents enclosed:

Letter from sailing-master Jairus Loomis to Commodore Daniel

T. Patterson, 13th August, 1816, reporting the destruction of the Negro Fort.

"On examining the prisoners, they stated that Edward Daniels, O. S. who was made prisoner in the boat on the 17th July, *was tarred and burnt alive.*"

Letter from Archibald Clarke to General Gaines, 26th February, 1817. (Message of the President of the United States to Congress, 25th March, 1818.)

"On the 24th inst. the house of Mr. Garrett, residing in the upper part of this county, near the boundary of Wayne county, Georgia, was attacked, during his absence, near the middle of the day, by this party (of Indians), consisting of about 15, who shot Mrs. Garrett in two places, and then despatched her by stabbing and scalping. Her two children, one about 3 years, and the other 2 months, were also murdered, and the eldest scalped: the house was then plundered of every article of value, and set on fire." *

Letter from Peter B. Cook (Arbuthnot's clerk) to Eliz. A. Carney, at Nassau, dated Suwahnee, 19th Jan. 1818, giving an account of their operations with the Indians, against the Americans, and their massacre of Lieutenant Scott and his party.

"There was a boat that was taken by the Indians, that had in her 30 men, 7 women, 4 small children. There were 6 of the men got clear, and 1 woman saved, and all the rest of them got killed. The children were took by the leg, and their brains dashed out against the boat."

---

* No one can for a moment attempt to justify the barbarities of the Indians—humanity shudders at their recital; but it behoves the people of the Union to refrain from exciting and imitating those atrocities: but that the backwoodsmen do practice them is beyond a doubt. While in the United States, I received a letter from East Florida, stating that the surveyor-general of that province, on an excursion up the river St. John's, had been suddenly recalled to a district under his command, by an account of the murder of four persons. This atrocity was imputed to the fugitive Indians, put in motion by the advance of General Jackson, but it was subsequently proved to be the act of some American borderers, who had scalped their victims, in order to throw the odium upon the Indians.

If the bare recital of scenes like these cannot be perused without shuddering, what must be the agonized feelings of those whose wives and children are, from day to day, and from night to night, exposed to be the victims of the same barbarity? Has mercy a voice to plead for the perpetrators and instigators of deeds like these? Should enquiry hereafter be made, why, within three months after this event, the savage Hamathli Micco, upon being taken by the American troops, was, by order of their commander, immediately hung, let it be told that savage was the commander of the party by which those women were butchered, and those helpless infants were thus dashed against the boat. Contending with such enemies, although humanity revolts at entire retaliation upon them, and spares the lives of their feeble and defenceless women and children, yet mercy herself surrenders to retributive justice the lives of their leading warriors taken in arms—and still more the lives of the foreign white incendiaries, who, disowned by their own governments, and disowning their own natures, degrade themselves beneath the savage character, by voluntarily descending to its level. Is not this the dictate of common sense? Is it not the usage of legitimate warfare? Is it not consonant to the soundest authorities of national law? " When at war (says Vattel) with a ferocious nation, which observes no rules and grants no quarter, they may be chastised in the persons of those of them who may be taken; they are of the number of the guilty; and by this rigour the attempt may be made of bringing them to a sense of the laws of humanity." And again: " As a general has the right of sacrificing the lives of his enemies to his own safety or that of his people, if he has to contend with an inhuman enemy, often guilty of such excesses, he may take the lives of some of his prisoners, and treat them as his own people have been treated." * The justification of these principles is found in their salutary efficacy, for terror and for example. It is thus only that the barbarities of Indians can be successfully encountered. It is thus only that the worse than Indian

---

* Mr. Adams cites authority, only when it supports his arguments; he had previously set at defiance the writers on national law.

barbarities of European impostors, pretending authority from their governments, but always disavowed, can be punished and arrested. Great Britain yet engages the alliance and co-operation of savages in war. But her government has invariably disclaimed all countenance or authorization to her subjects to instigate them against us in time of peace. Yet so it has happened, that from the period of our established independence to this day, *all* the Indian wars with which we have been afflicted have been distinctly traceable to the instigation of English traders or agents, always disavowed, yet always felt, more than once detected, but never before punished. Two of them, offenders of the deepest dye, after solemn warning to their government, and individually to one of them, have fallen, *flagrante delicto,* into the hands of an American general; and the punishment inflicted upon them has fixed them on high as an example, awful in its exhibition, but, we trust, auspicious in its results, of that which awaits unauthorised pretenders of European agency, to stimulate and interpose in wars between the United States and the Indians within their control.

This exposition of the origin, the causes, and the character of the war with the Seminole Indians and part of the Creeks, combined with M'Gregor's mock patriots and Nicholls's negroes, which necessarily led our troops into Florida, and gave rise to all those incidents of which Mr. Pizarro so vehemently complains, will, it is hoped, enable you to present other and sounder views of the subject to his Catholic Majesty's government. It will enable you to show that the occupation of Pensacola and St. Mark's was occasioned neither by a spirit of hostility to Spain, nor with a view to extort, prematurely, the province from her possession;—that it was rendered necessary by the neglect of Spain to perform her engagements of restraining the Indians from hostilities against the United States, and by the culpable countenance, encouragement, and assistance given to those Indians, in their hostilities, by the Spanish governor and commandant at those places:—that the United States have a right to demand, as the President does demand, of Spain, the punishment of those officers for this misconduct; and he further demands of Spain a just and reasonable indemnity to the United States for the heavy and necessary expenses which they have been compelled to incur, by the failure of Spain to perform her engagement, to restrain the Indians, aggravated by this demonstrated complicity of her commanding officers with them, in their hostilities against the United States;—that the two Englishmen executed by order of General Jackson were not only identified with the savages with whom they were carrying on the war against the United States, but that one of them was the mover and fomenter of the war, which, without his interference and false promises to the Indians of support from the British government, never would have happened—that the other was the instrument of war against Spain as well as the United States, commissioned by M'Gregor, and expedited by Woodbine, upon their project of conquering Florida, with these Indians and negroes; that, as accomplices of the savages, and, sinning against their better knowledge, worse than savages, General Jackson, possessed of their persons and of the proofs of their guilt, might, by the lawful and ordinary usages of war, have hung them both without the formality of a trial; but to allow them every possible opportunity of refuting the proofs or of showing any circumstance in extenuation of their crimes, he gave them the benefit of a trial by a court-martial of highly respectable officers: that the defence of one consisted, solely and exclusively, of technical cavils at the nature of part of the evidence against him, and the other confessed his guilt.* Finally, that in restoring Pensacola and St. Mark's to Spain, the President gives the most signal proof of his confidence, that hereafter her engagement to restrain, by force, the Indians of Florida from all hostilities against the United States, will be effectually fulfilled; that there will be no more murders, no more robberies within our borders, by savages prowling along the Spanish line, and seeking shelter within it, to display in the villages the scalps of our women and children, their victims, and to sell, with shameless effrontery, the plunder from our citizens in Spanish forts and cities; that we shall hear no more apologies from Spanish governors and commandants, of

---

* If such are the benefits of American justice, I very sincerely pray God, to avert their protection.

their inability to perform the duties of their office and the solemn contracts of their country; no more excuses for compliances to the savage enemies of the United States, from the dread of their attacks upon themselves; no more harbouring of foreign impostors, upon compulsion; that a strength sufficient will be kept in the province to restrain the Indians by force, and officers empowered and instructed to employ it effectually to maintain the good faith of the nation by the effective fulfilment of the treaty.— The duty of this government to protect the persons and property of our fellow-citizens on the borders of the United States is imperative—it must be discharged; and if, after all the warnings that Spain has had—if, after the prostration of all her territorial rights and neutral obligations, by Nicholls and his banditti during war, and of all her treaty stipulations, by Arbuthnot and Ambrister, abetted by her own commanding officers, during peace, to the cruel annoyance of the United States—if the necessities of self-defence should again compel the United States to take possession of the Spanish forts and places in Florida, declare, with the candour and frankness that becomes us, that another unconditional restoration of them must not be expected; that even the President's confidence in the good faith and ultimate justice of the Spanish government will yield to the painful experience of continual disappointment; and that, after unwearied and almost unnumbered appeals to them, for the performance of their stipulated duties, in vain, the United States will be reluctantly compelled to rely, for the protection of their borders, upon themselves alone.

You are authorised to communicate the whole of this letter, and the accompanying documents, to the Spanish government.

I have the honour, &c.
JOHN QUINCY ADAMS.

The sentiments conveyed in this letter of Mr. Adams, incontestibly prove the feelings of the American government towards Spain; but did Mr.

Adams in the adoption of such language, imagine that Spain was the only power to whom the American government was responsible for those violences? I can scarcely believe that a mind so constituted as that of the American secretary, well acquainted with the character and feelings of the British government and people, near whose court he had for some time resided, could conceive, or for one moment suspect, that they would so far forget their own dignity, as to pass over in silence this gross iusult on their honour, and the wanton sacrifice of Englishmen. Our doctrine of allegiance and protection is of this peculiar character, that the constitution extends its fostering care over the subject, to the remotest region. An Englishman can never relieve himself from the natural allegiance due to the institutions of his country;* and he has an undoubted and admitted right to claim their protection and support, (for protection is co-extensive with allegiance,) when peaceably demeaning himself, and respecting the established laws of the country, in which he becomes a temporary resi-

---

* Natural allegiance is a debt of gratitude, which cannot be forfeited, cancelled or altered, by any change of time, place or circumstance, nor by any thing but the united concurrence of the legislatine.

2 P. Wms. 124.

dent;* but if he engages in domestic rebellion against the government of the foreign state in which he is a resident, and is found fighting in the ranks of the insurgents, he is liable to be treated as a rebel, and is without the pale of British protection; for his local allegiance is a primary duty, and forms one exception to the doctrine of protection. In the American revolutionary war the Baron de Kalb, La Fayette, and other foreign officers in the ranks of the American army, incurred the penalties of rebellion. This doctrine is applicable to the situation of all foreigners, who enter the armies of the Spanish American revolutionists, and is worthy of the reflection of those individuals who engage in that desperate service; few of whom, and I speak from personal experience, are aware of the extent of their responsibility.

The people of the United States, in their contemptuous indifference to the resentment of Spain, have calculated upon her weakness, in a spirit of egotism perfectly national, but by no means complimentary to their political foresight. Spain in her

---

* As, therefore, the prince is always under a constant tie to protect his natural born subjects, at all times and in all countries, for this reason their allegiance due to him is equally universal and permanent. Black Com. b. 1. c. 10. p. 370.

European possessions, is too remote to dread the hostility of the union, her commerce across the Atlantic is already too nearly destroyed, by the numerous cruisers under the various republican flags, to make her vulnerable in that particular. The North American government may seize upon the Floridas, may, perhaps, reduce them into possession, yet, neither their financial resources, nor their effective and disposable forces, are equal to a farther territorial aggrandizement. In the mean time, a war between the two countries would be popular with the maratime nations of Europe, from whose numerous ports swarms of privateers would traverse the ocean, commissioned by, and under the flag of Spain, capturing the American ensign in every direction, while the navy of the union, too few for their protection over the extensive seas they navigate, would fruitlessly pursue their enemies. It remains, therefore, for the people of the union, seriously to reflect, whether it be politic to place the means of accommodation beyond their reach, whether by an obstinate support of a military despot, they will compromise their national character; and by tolerating this disgraceful outrage, establish a precedent, more dangerous to their boasted liberties than formidable as an example of terror to their enemies.

FINIS.

NOTES.

Note A. page 39.

In consequence of the outrageous conduct of the passengers in the " *Two Friends*," at Madeira, the *Dowson* and other ships, on a similar destination, were refused permission to land their passengers, but were supplied from the shore with those articles required.

Note B. page 50.

O. and the Irish apothecary, with several brother adventurers proceeding for the Oronoco, were captured by a Spanish schooner, off Grenada. The whole number, amounting to twelve, were inhumanly beheaded.

Note C. page 109.

The following letters were published in the American papers, noticing M'Donald's arrival at Amelia Island :—

Extract of a letter from Mr. Clark, collector of St. Mary's, to Mr. Crawford.

" *Collector's Office, St. Mary's, Georgia, Nov.* 1, 1817.

" Hon. W. H. Crawford ;

" SIR—I hasten to communicate the following information received from a gentleman residing on St. John's river, East Florida. The subject, in its bearings, presents considerations of the first importance as to our political relations with Spain. The following is extracted from the same:

"*Pablo River, St. John's, Oct.* 24, 1817.

"About sun-set a yawl boat arrived at the landing, when seven persons came from her, who requested shelter for the night, and some refreshments, stating that they were half-pay British officers, of the army and navy, from the Island of St. Thomas, on their way to England, *via* the United States; that they had mistaken this bar for the St. Mary's; that they left the schooner in the offing under that impression, and intended to send her a pilot by the return of the boat. After staying all night, they embarked at daylight, having procured a negro pilot to conduct them inland to Fernandina.

"Colonel M'Donald, thanking me for the hospitality he had received, said he felt bound, as a gentleman, to be candid, and accordingly informed me that he had lately arrived from London at St. Thomas's, in the ship *"Two Friends,"* with a great number of officers, and munitions of war in abundance; that he had with him thirty officers on board the schooner; that he would command in this quarter; that they would have men sufficient, and a profusion of every thing necessary for active operations; that they wanted a war with Spain, and that he had power to draw on England for 100,000*l.* sterling; that they would have a fine park of artillery, and that all these supplies were actually on their way, or shipping; that a number of gun-brigs and sloops would leave England, reported for the East Indies, but were bound directly here and to South America. That they were much disappointed at learning M'Gregor had left Amelia Island, and that the capture of Amelia was known prior to their leaving England.

"These officers have a soldier-like and genteel appearance, and all have their commissions; they said their object in leaving the schooner was to reconnoitre. They have all since arrived at Fernandina.

"I have the honour to remain, &c.

"ARCHIBALD CLARK."

Note D. *page* 116.

Washington, Jan. 10, 1818.

Mr. Middleton, from the committee on so much of the Message of the President of the United States, as relates to the illicit introduction of slaves from Amelia Island into the United States, made the following report :—

The committee, to whom was referred so much of the President's Message, as relates to the illicit introduction of slaves from Amelia Island, having carefully taken the matter committed to them into consideration, respectfully report—

That having applied to the department of state for information respecting the illicit introduction of slaves into the United States, they were referred by the Secretary of State to the documents transmitted to this house, by the President's Message of the 15th of December last, consisting of various extracts of papers on the files of the departments of State, of the Treasury, and of the Navy, relative to the proceedings of certain persons who took possession of Amelia Island in the summer of the past year, and also relative to a similar establishment previously made at Galveston, near the mouth of the river Trinity.

Upon a full investigation of these papers, with a view to the subject committed to them, your committee are of opinion, that it is but too notorious that numerous infractions of the law, prohibiting the importation of slaves into the United States, have been perpetrated with impunity upon our southern frontier ; and they are further of opinion that similar infractions would have been repeated with increasing activity, without the timely interposition of the naval force under direction of the executive of our government. In the course of the investigation, your committee have found it difficult to keep separate the special matter given into their charge, from topics of a more general nature, which are necessarily interwoven therewith. They, therefore, crave the indulgence of the house while they present some general views connected with the subject, which have developed themselves in the prosecution of the enquiry.

It would appear from what had been collected from these papers, that numerous violations of our laws have been latterly committed by a combination of freebooters and smugglers, of various nations, who located themselves in the first instance upon an uninhabited spot, near the mouth of the river Trinity, within the jurisdictional limits of the United States, as claimed in virtue of the treaty of cession of Louisianna by France.

This association of persons organised a system of plunder upon the high seas, directed chiefly against Spanish property, which consisted frequently of slaves from the coast of Africa ; but their conduct appears not always to have been regulated by a strict regard to the national character of vessels falling into their hands, when specie or any other very valuable articles formed part of the cargo. Their vessels generally sailed under a pretended Mexican flag, although it does not appear that the establishment of Galveston was sanctioned by, or connected with, any government. The presumption, too, of any authority ever having been given for such an establishment, is strongly repelled as well by its piratical character, as by its itinerant nature; for the first position at Galveston was abandoned on or about the 5th of April last, for one near Matagorda, upon the Spanish territory, and at a later period this last was abandoned, and a transfer made to Amelia Island, in East Florida, a part of which had been previously seized by persons, who appear to have been equally unauthorised, and who were, at the time of the said transfer, upon the point, it is believed, of abandoning their enterprise, from the failure of resources, which they expected to have drawn from within our limits, in defiance of our laws. There exists on the part of these sea rovers, an organised system of daring enterprise, supported by force of arms, and it is only by a correspondent system of coercion, that they can be met and constrained to respect the rights of property, and the law of nations. It is deeply to be regretted that practices of such a character, within our immediate neighbourhood, and even within our jurisdictional limits, should have prevailed unchecked for so long a time ; more especially as one of their immediate consequences was to give occasion to the illicit introduction of slaves from the coast of Africa into these UnitedStates, and thus to revive a traffic repugnant to humanity and to all sound principles of policy, as well as severely punishable by the laws of the land.

By the 7th section of the Act, prohibiting the importation of slaves, passed in 1807, the President is fully authorised to employ the naval force to cruize on any part of the coast of the United States, or territories thereof, where he may judge attempts will be made to violate the provisions of that Act, in order to seize and bring in for condemnation, all vessels contravening its provisions to be proceeded against according to law.

By the joint resolution of the Senate and House of Representatives, of the 15th of January, 1811, and the act of the same date, the President is fully empowered to occupy any part, or the whole of the territory lying east of the river Perdido, and south of the State of Georgia, in the event of an attempt to occupy the said territory, or any part thereof, by any foreign government or power; and by the same resolution and act, he may employ any part of the army and navy of the United States, which he may deem necessary, for the purpose of taking possession and occupying the territory aforesaid, and in order to maintain therein the authority of the United States.

Among the avowed projects of the persons who have occupied Amelia Island, was that of making the conquest of East and West Florida, professedly for the purpose of establishing there an independent government; and the vacant lands in those provinces have been from the origin of this undertaking, down to the latest period, held out as lures to the cupidity of adventurers, and as resources for defraying the expences of the expedition. The greater part of West Florida being in the possession of the United States, this project involved in it, designs of direct hostility against them, and as the express object of the resolution and act of 15th of January, 1811, was to authorise the President to prevent the province of East Florida from passing into the hands of any foreign power, it became the obvious duty of the President to exercise the authority vested in him by that law. It does not appear, that among these itinerant establishers of republics, and distributors of Florida lands, there is a single individual inhabitant of the country where the republic was to be constituted, and where lands were to be thus bestowed : the project was, therefore, an attempt to occupy that territory by a foreign power. Where the profession is in such direct opposition to the fact; where the venerable forms by which a free people constitute a frame of government for themselves, are prostituted by a horde of foreign freebooters for purposes of plunder ; if, under colour of authority from any of the provinces contending for their independence, the Floridas, or either of them, had been permitted to pass into the hands of such a power, the committee are persuaded, it is quite unnecessary to point out to the discernment of the House, the pernicious influence which such a destiny of the territories in question must have had upon the security, tranquillity, and commerce of this union.

It is a matter of public notoriety, that two of the persons who have successively held the command at Amelia Island, whether authorised themselves by any government or not, have issued commissions for privateers, as in the name of the Venezuelan and Mexican governments, to vessels fitted out in the ports of the United States, and chiefly manned and officered, by our countrymen, for the purpose of capturing the property of nations with which the United States are at peace.

One of the objects of the occupation of Amelia Island, it appears, was to possess a convenient resort for privateers of this description, equally reprobated by the laws of nations, which recognise them only under the denomination of pirates, and by several of the treaties of the United States with different European powers, which expressly denominate them as such. *

---

* See the treaty of peace with France, 1778, Art. 21, U. S. laws, vol. I. page 88 ; with the Netherlands, 1782, Art. 19, vol. I. p. 162 ; with Sweden, 1783, Art. 23, vol. I. p. 190 ; with Great Britain, 1794, Art. 21, vol. I. p. 218 ; with Prussia, 1785, Art. 20, vol. I. p. 238, and 1797, Art. 20, p. 256 ; with Spain, 1795, Art. 14, vol. I. p. 270.

It was against the subjects of Spain, one of the powers with which the United States have entered into stipulations, prohibiting their citizens from taking any commission from any power with which she may be at war, for arming any ships to act as privateers, that these vessels have been commissioned to cruise, though, as the committee have observed, no flag, even that of our own country, has proved a protection from them.

The immediate tendency of suffering such armaments, in defiance of our laws, would have been to embroil the United States with all the nations, whose commerce with our country was suffering under these depradations, and if not checked by all the means in the power of the government, would have authorised claims from the subjects of foreign governments for indemnities, at the expense of this nation, for captures by our people, in vessels fitted out in our ports, and as could not fail of being alledged, countenanced by the very neglect of the necessary means for suppressing them. The possession of Amelia island as a port of refuge for such privateers, and of illicit traffic, in the United States, of their prizes which were frequently, as before stated, slave ships from Africa, was a powerful encouragement and temptation to multiply these violations of our laws, and made it the duty of the government to use all the means in its power, to restore the security of our own commerce, and of that of friendly nations upon our coasts, which could in no other way more effectually be done than by taking from this piratical and smuggling combination their place of refuge.

In order, therefore, to give full effect to the intentions of the legislature, and in pursuance of the provisions of the above recited resolution and acts, it became necessary, as it appears to your committee, to suppress all establishments of the hostile nature of those above described, made in our vicinity, the objects of which appear to have been the occupation of the Floridas, the spoliation of peaceful commerce upon and near our coasts, by piratical privateers, the clandestine importation of goods, and the illicit introduction of slaves within our limits.

Such establishments, if suffered to subsist and strengthen,

would probably have rendered nugatory all provisions made by law for the exclusion of prohibited persons.

The course pursued on this occasion, will strongly mark the feelings and intentions of our government, upon the great question of the slave trade, which is so justly considered, by most civilized nations, as repugnant to justice and humanity, and which, in our particular case, is not less so to all the dictates of sound policy.

Your committee anticipate beneficial results from the adoption of those measures by the executive, in the promotion of the security of our southern frontier, and its neighbouring seas, and in the diminution of the invasions, latterly so frequent, of our revenue and prohibitory laws. The experience of ten years has, however, evinced the necessity of some new regulations being adopted, in order effectually to put a stop to the farther introduction of slaves into the United States.

In the act of congress prohibiting this importation, the policy of giving the whole forfeiture of vessel and goods to the United States, and no part thereof to the informer, may justly be doubted.

This is an oversight which should be remedied. The act does indeed give a part of the personal penalties to the informer, but these penalties are generally only nominal, as the persons engaged in such traffic are usually poor, the omission of the States to pass acts to meet the act of congress, and to establish regulations in aid of the same, can only be remedied by congress legislating directly on the subject themselves, as it is clearly within the scope of their constitutional powers to do.

For these purposes your committee beg leave respectfully herewith to report a bill.

Note E. page 147.

Three days after the banishment of the prisoner, the Morgianna fell in with a British brig, bound to Philadephia, on board of which Captain Liers put his captive. I subsequently met him at Charleston. At that time Aury arrived off the bar of that harbour in the brig *Mexico Libre*, to receive some recruits. Not satisfied with the treatment he had already experienced in the service of Aury, he once more became his partisan, and sailed with him as his second lieutenant.

Note F. page 207.

From the National Intelligencer. —" By the Commodore Porter we learn that the United States corvette John Adams, Commodore Henly, briggs Enterprize and Saranac, and Schooner Lynx, with one gun boat, arrived off Amelia island, on the 18th ult. On the 22d, Commodore Aury was summoned, in the name of the United States, to surrender the island to the United States force, ordered there for that purpose. Which summons was complied with on the 23d, when 250 United States troops from Point Petre, took possession of the island."

A messenger to Washington, dispatched by Commodore Aury, arrived in the Commodore Porter, and furnishes a copy of the following document.

The Answer of General Aury, to a Letter from the American Officers, demanding the surrender of Fernandina.

H. Q. Fernandina, December 22d, 1817.

GENTLEMEN;

I have received your official letter of this day, by which, in the name of the government of the United States, you summon me to evacuate this place with the troops under my command, as soon as it will be convenient, as possession thereof is to be taken by the forces under your command, under certain conditions specified in your said letter.

Neither this republic, that of Mexico, nor any other of South America, being at war with the United States, obliges me to state to you, that the contents of your letter greatly surprised this government and the people of this state. You have, nevertheless, intimated, that in case of our acquiescense in your demand, we shall be *permitted* to evacuate this island, which neither is, nor ever has been, a part of the United Srates.

Allow me to observe to you, Gentlemen, that from the moment we took Fernandina by the force of our arms, we entered into the full possession of all the rights appertaining to our enemy, and to this day we have supported these rights, at the risk of our lives and fortunes.

The boundaries between the Floridas and the United States, having been fairly settled on the 27th October, 1795, we are at a loss how to ascertain your authority to interfere in our internal concerns.

Our surprise increases when we reflect, that your communication comes as authorised by the government of a people, who, in this respect, glory in the rights of nations, whether great or small, and who, no doubt, sympathise with their southern brethren in the struggle for liberty and independence in which they are engaged, as were the United States forty years ago.

On the other hand, you promise to hold sacred such of our property, as unquestionably belongs to our citizens. Who is to be the judge in that case? The United States? They can by no means claim any kind of jurisdiction from the source of the river St. Mary's down to the ocean, on this side the centre of the channel. We entertain too much veneration to believe for a single moment, that you, (supposed already in possession of this island, which has never been ceded by the King of Spain, or by its inhabitants. to the United States,) can bring with you a competent tribunal to decide upon this question. The only law you can adduce in your behalf, is that of force, which is always repugnant to a republican government, and to principles of a just and impartial nature. The same observation may be applied to your interference for the property of the inhabitants, which we have always respected and considered as sacred.

You order us also, as if we were subjects of your government, to leave behind, when Fernandina is evacuated, all the public property that was found at its surrender. This demand is directly contrary to the public rights, by which public property captured from the enemy, is avowedly that of the captors, when not otherwise stipulated. Are you acting in the name of the King of Spain or his allies? As we consider the people of the United States to be unquestionably the only free people on the surface of the globe, we cannot admit that you have already arrived to such a point of degradation. Otherwise your demand is inadmissable and unjustifiable in the ages of the world; and if we must submit to it, all the blame rests with you.

Permit me, therefore, gentlemen, to request you to lay before the President of the United States, these remarks, in order that a matter of so serious tendancy may be duly considered. We have read his excellency's message at the opening of congress, with the utmost concern, and have concluded that the political situation of this republic has been greatly misrepresented in the United States, through the intrigues of our enemies. We have certainly a right to be heard, for which purpose I shall have the honour of forwarding to your government the necessary documents. If you are not disposed to let the thing remain in *statu quo*, I am authorised to assure you that we respect and esteem too highly, the people of the United States, to carry matters to extremities.

I have the honour to remain, with the highest consideration,

Gentlemen, yours, &c.

AURY.

S. L. HOLME, Secretary.

To Commodore Henly, and Colonel Bankhead.

Note G. page 208.

Washington, 14th January, 1818.

The following message was this day delivered to both Houses of Congress, from the President.

To the Senate, and House of Representatives, of the United States.

I have the satisfaction to inform congress, that the establishment at Amelia island, has been suppressed, and without the effusion of blood.

The papers which explain this transaction, I now lay before congress.

By the suppression of this establishment, and of that at Galverton, which will soon follow, if it has not already ceased to exist, there is good cause to believe that the consummation of a project, frought with much injury to the United States, has been prevented.

When we consider the persons engaged in it, being adventurers from different conntries, with very few, if any, of the native inhabitants of the Spanish colonies, the territory in which the establishments were made, one as a portion of that claimed by the United States, westward of the Mississippi, the other on a part of East Florida, a province in negotiation between the United States and Spain; the claim of their leader as announced by his proclamation in taking possession of Amelia island, comprising the whole of both the Floridas, without excepting that part of West Florida, which is incorporated into the state of Louisiana, their conduct while in the possession of the island, making it instrumental to every species of contraband, and, in regard to slaves, of the most odious and dangerous character ; it may fairly be concluded, that if the enterprise had succeeded on the scale on which it was formed, much annoyance and injury would have resulted from it, to the United States.

Other considerations were thought to be no less deserving of attention, the institution of a government by foreign adventurers in the island, distinct from the colonial government of Buenos Ayres, Venezuela, or Mexico, pretending to sovereiguty, and exercising its highest offices, particularly in granting commissions to privateers, were acts which could not fail to draw after them, the most serious consequences. It was the duty of the executive, either to extend to this establishment all the advantages of that neutrality, which the United States had proclaimed, and have observed in favour of the colonies of Spain, who by the strength of their own population and resources, had declared their independance, and were affording strong proof of their ability to maintain it, or to make the discrimination which circumstances required. Had the first course been pursued, we should not only have sanctioned all the unlawful claims and practices of this pretended government, in regard to the United States, but have countenanced a system of privateering in the gulf of Mexico, and elsewhere, the ill effects of which might, and probably would, have been deeply and very extensively felt. The path of duty was plain from the commencement, but it was painful to enter upon it, while the obligation could be resisted. The law of 1811, lately published, and which it is therefore proper now to mention, was considered applicable to the case, from the moment that the proclamation of the chief of the enterprise was seen, and its obligation was daily increased by other considerations of high importance, already mentioned, which were deemed sufficiently strong in themselves to dictate the course which has been pursued.

Early intimations having been received, of the dangerous purposes of these adventurers, timely precautions were taken, by the establishment of a force near the St. Mary's, to prevent their effect, or it is probable that it would have been more sensibly felt.

To such establishments, made so near to our settlements, in the expectation of deriving aid from them, it is particularly gratifying to find, that very little encouragement was given.

The example so conspicuously displayed by our fellow citizens, that their sympathies cannot be perverted to improper purposes, but that a love of country, the influence of moral principles, and a respect for the laws, are predominent with them, is a sure pledge that all the very flattering anticipations, which have been formed of the success of our institutions, will be realized.

This example has proved, that if our relations with foreign powers are to be charged, it must be done by the constituted authorities, who, alone, acting on a high responsibility, are competent to the purpose; and, until such change is thus made, that our fellow citizens will respect the existing relations by a faithful adherence to the laws which secure them.

Believing that the enterprise, though undertaken by persons, some of whom may have held commissions from some of the colonies, was unauthorised by and unknown to the colonial governments, full confidence is entertained that it will be disclaimed by them, and that effectual measures will be taken to prevent the abuse of their authority, in all cases, to the injury of the United States. For these injuries, especially those proceeding from Amelia Island, Spain would be responsible, if it was not manifest, that although committed in the latter instance through her territory, she was utterly unable to prevent them. Her territory ought not, however, to be made instrumental, through her inability to defend it, to purposes so injurious to the United States. To a country over which she fails to maintain her authority, and which she permits to be converted to the annoyance of her neighbours, her jurisdiction for the time necessarily ceases to exist, The territory of Spain will, nevertheless, be respected, so far as it may be done consistently with the essential interests and safety of the United States.

In expelling these adventurers from these ports, it was not intended to make any conquest from Spain, or to injure in any degree the cause of the colonies. Care will be taken that no part of the territory contemplated by the law of 1811, shall be occupied by a foreign government of any kind, or that injuries of the nature of those complained of, shall be repeated; but this it is expected will be provided for, with every other interest, in a spirit of amity, in the negotiation now depending with the government of Spain.

JAMES MUNROE.

Note H. page 247.

An English gentleman travelling towards the Alabama territory, in company with some back-woodmen, saw in passing a swamp, a solitary Indian. One of the party, without provocation, immediately levelled his rifle, and shot the unfortunate being dead, exclaiming, "there goes another of your damned race."

This outrage was never punished.

Note I. page 254.

The following order from General Jackson, for the extermination of the Indians, between the Escambia and Appalachicola rivers, appeared in the National Intelligencer, on the 16th of July, 1818, and was copied into other papers of the union without comment!!!

Head-Quarters, Division of the South,
Adjutant-General's Office, 25 miles west of
Pensacola, May 31, 1818.

Captain M'Girt, of the territory of Alabama, is authorised and instructed to raise one company of volunteer mounted men, for the period of six months, unless sooner discharged, to consist of two subalterns, and sixty privates, to be under his command as captain. As soon as Captain M'Girt raises thirty men, he will proceed directly to the Perdido, and scour the country; putting to death every hostile warrior that may be found, preserving the women and children, and delivering them to the commanding officer at Pensacola.

The subalterns will be left to raise the balance of the company, and will immediately join him at Pensacola, where the officer commanding will be instructed regularly to muster them into service.

Captain Boyle, of said territory, is in like manner authorised and instructed to raise a company, and will proceed with Captain M'Girt, in raising thirty men, to aid in executing the wishes of the major-general, leaving his subalterns to raise the balance of his company, who will be instructed to join at Pensacola, and be mustered into service.

These companies, on reaching Pensacola, will be furnished with provisions by the commanding officer, and will then proceed to scour the country between the Escambia and Appalachicola rivers, destroying any hostiles as above directed, and on their application at Fort Gadsden or Scott, provisions will be issued to them by the respective commanding officers.

The quarter-master's department at either of the foregoing posts will furnish forage on their regular returns.

Captains M'Girt and Boyle will report to Colonel King, in writing, a statement of all occurrences which may be worthy of note.

By order,
ROBERT BUTLER, Adjutant-General.

To the patriotism of the young men on Tombeckbe!

Captain M'Girt will leave a confidential subaltern at Dale ferry, on the Alabama, in readiness to accept the services of all who may feel disposed to protect the frontier from the depredations of these hordes of outlying savages that infest the frontier It is hoped that this appeal to the patriotism of the citizens, will not be made in vain, that the noble spirit of the Alabamians will be roused on this occasion, and that every young man that has a horse, will immediately repair to the rendezvous.

PRINTED BY W. SMITH, KING STREET, SEVEN DIALS.

INDEX.

Adams, John Quincy, **22**, 197, 207, 286, 292, 294, 295, 306, 309
Alabama, 203, 210, 326, 327, 328
Alachua (Lahheway), 236
Alligators, 159
Allison, Capt. John S., 252
Altamaha River, **12**, 86
Ambrister, Robert Christie, **22**, 196, 207, 215, 234, 245, 251, 257, 258, 260, 261, 262, 265, 266, 267, 270, 272, 274, 275, 276, 279, 280, 289, 294, 298, 299, 302, 303, 304, 309
Amelia Island, 1, 5, 10, **14**, **15**, **16**, **17**, **18**, **19**, **20**, 53, 65, 66, 77, 79, 87, 89, 90, 92, 93, 95, 115, 122, 127, 128, 140, 148, 149, 150, 209, 284, 285, 302, 313, 314, 315, 316, 317, 318, 319, 321, 323, 324, 326
América Libre, privateer, **16**
American consul, St. Thomas, **12**, 53
"American" party, Amelia Island, **16**, **17**, **18**
Anastasia Island, 117
Angostura, Venezuela, 42, 46, 186
Apalachee Bay, 82
Apalachee River, 231
Apalachicola River, **9**, **21**, 199, 200, 201, 217, 219, 222, 237, 260, 288, 290, 301, 326, 327
Apiny, 222, 230, 231
Arana, Luis, **28***n*26
Arbuthnot, Alexander, **22**, 196, 207, 210, 211, 212, 215, 216, 218, 219, 220, 222, 225, 228, 229, 231, 233, 244, 247, 258, 259, 261, 262, 264, 266, 267, 268, 269, 272, 274, 276, 277, 278, 291, 292, 294, 298, 299, 300, 301, 303, 304, 305, 309

NOTE: Boldface numbers refer to Griffin's introduction; arabic numbers in roman type refer to the *Narrative*.

Arbuthnot, John J., 212, 216, 256, 267
Aresmendez, Gen., 183–84
Artillery, U.S. Corps of, 214
Atlantic Ocean, 157
Aury, Luis, **15, 16, 17, 18, 19, 20**, 78, 80, 95–97, 98–100, 102–4, 106, 108–9, 112–13, 127, 129, 135, 147, 148, 151, 188, 320, 321, 323

Bagot, Charles, 213, 219, 220, 227, 228, 241
Bagpipes, 36
Bahama Islands, 66, 78, 96, 218
Bain, Dunshee, and Co., 219
Baker, British chargé d'affaires, 290
Baltimore, **12**
Bankhead, Maj. James, **19, 20**, 147, 150, 323
Barataria, **16**
Barbuda, island, 38
Barrancas, fort at Pensacola, 202, 287, 288, 296, 297, 299
Bartram, John, **25**
Bathurst, Earl, 227, 231, 290, 300
Bebb, W. W., 210
Big Warrior, 226
Biscay, Bay of, 13
Blackbeard, pirate, 57–63
Blowgun, 170
Bolívar, General Simón, **2, 11**, 29, 42, 43, 44, 85, 184, 187, 191
Bonaparte, Napoleon, 2
Bowlegs, Seminole chief, 178, 212, 217, 218, 220, 221, 223, 225, 227, 234, 235, 239, 244, 249
Bowman, Charles H., Jr., **28**
Boyle, Capt., 327, 328
British Colonial Marines, 252
"British" party, Amelia Island, **17**
Brown, Col. Thomas, 171
Buenos Ayres, republic, **14**, 78, 89, 93, 188, 191, 324
Buffon, Comte de, 165
Butler, Col. Robert, 267, 328

C. and Co., Savannah merchants, 86–87, 278
Cameron, Gov. Charles, 212, 213, 218, 219, 226, 227, 230, 231, 235, 237, 238, 241, 253, 257, 259, 261, 262, 300, 303
Campbell, Commodore, USN, **8**, 122
Camp Crawford, 227
Canary Islands, 49–50
Cancer, Tropic of, 34
Canoe, 152, 153, 217
Cappachimicco. *See* Kinhigee
Caracas, Venezuela, 45
Carney, Elizabeth A., 305
Carnival season, 163–64
Cassava flour, **26**, 138

Castillo de San Marcos. *See* Fort St. Marks
Castlereagh, Lord, 290
Cattle, 167, 175, 227, 232, 236, 294
Cedar Key Bay, 218
Chance, schooner, 253, 254, 264
Charleston, S.C., **12**, **20**, 85, 101, 113, 129, 145, 146, 150, 182, 320
Charles Tuctonoky, 233, 234
Charlotte Harbor, 82
Chattahoochee River, 227, 235
Chehaw, Indian village, 203, 204
Chesapeake, U.S. frigate, 150
Chili, republic of, 188
Choctaw Indians, 241
Choctohachy River, 227, 232
Cienfugas, Spanish Captain-General, 92
City gate, St. Augustine, **24**, 161, 162–63
Clark, Archibald, 313–14
Clarke, Archibald, 305
Clarke, George J. F., **10**, **18**
Clemente, Lino de, **12**, **19**
Clock, 162
Cockburn, Adm., 299
Codazzi, Augustin, 16
Commodore Porter, ship, 321
Congress, Secret Act of 1811, **6**, **20**, 84, 317, 325
Cook, Peter B., 215, 216, 234, 239, 249, 250, 253, 258, 262, 277, 305
Coppinger, José, Spanish governer, **13**, **14**, **15**, **18**, **25**, **26**, 90, 92, 94, 120, 127–28, 235
Corn, 155, 158–59, 167
Cotton, 125, 155–56
Coweta, 219, 226
Cowford, village, **13**, **26**, 130, 133, 135, 140
Crawford, W. H., 313
Creek Indians, 9, 142, 180, 211, 212, 215, 218, 219, 220, 222, 225, 226, 229, 231, 233, 235, 236, 237, 238, 244, 252, 289, 291, 300, 307
Crittenden, Capt., Kentucky volunteers, 214
Cruz, Ramón de la, **24**
Cuba, royal regiment of, **14**, **15**, 93, 118, 120
Cumberland Island, Ga., 87

Dale ferry, on Alabama River, 328
Dancing, 122
Daniels, Edward, 305
Dany, interpreter, 230
Darien, Ga., 86
de Kalb, Baron, 311
Dogs, 131, 132, 140
Dolphins, 74
Dowson, ship, 313
Doyle, Edmund, 213, 219, 226, 232, 240, 255

Drawbridge, St. Augustine, 23, 24, 162–63
Duels, 29–30, 35–36, 51–53
Dyer, Col., Tennessee volunteers, 214

Eachallaway, town, 225
East Florida, 1, 7, 8, 9, 10, 12, 18, 76, 79, 81, 86, 90, 150, 157, 305, 313, 317, 324
East Florida militia (Spanish), 15, 93, 94
East Florida Rangers (Loyalist), 172
Elliott, Col., Tennessee volunteers, 214
Elton, Capt. John H., USN, 14, 111–12
Embargo Act of 1807, 10
Enterprise, U.S. brig, 19, 147, 150, 321
Erving, George William, 197, 207
Escambia River, 295, 326, 327
Estrada, Juan de, 8

Fanning, Maj. A. C. W., 214, 267
Fernandina, 1, 7, 8, 9, 10, 11, 13, 14, 15, 16, 17, 19, 20, 78, 79, 87, 93, 95, 99, 108, 128, 314, 321, 322
Firing of woods, 135, 162
Flint River, 222, 227, 235
Folch, Juan Vicente, 6, 7
Food, 135–36, 141
Forbes, James, 11
Forbes and Co., 219, 226, 227, 229, 232, 278, 292
Fort Clairborne, 202
Fort Gadsden, 21, 327
Fort Gaines, 225, 227, 230, 242
Fort George Island, Fla., 152
Fort Jackson, Treaty of, 212, 277, 291
Fort Mitchell, 235
Fort St. Marks (Castillo de San Marcos), 8, 24, 116–18
Fort St. Marks (San Marcos de Apalachee), 21, 197, 200, 201, 206, 210, 211, 212, 216, 224, 231, 232, 241, 251, 254, 255, 259, 262, 263, 264, 266, 285, 287, 288, 293, 294, 295, 296, 297, 301, 302, 303, 304, 307, 308
Fort San Carlos, 11, 13
Fort Scott, 209, 241, 327
43d Regiment, British, 64
4th Infantry, U.S., 214
Fowl Town, 220, 222, 223, 224
Francis, Milly, 202
Francis the Prophet. *See* Hillis Hadjo
"French Party," on Amelia Island, 16, 17, 97, 99
Fulton, William, 243
Funchal, Madeira, town, 21, 22
Funchal Bay, Madeira, 19

Gaines, Gen. Edmund P., 199, 207, 208, 209, 210, 214, 217, 219, 220, 222, 223, 251, 266, 267, 272, 281, 287, 305
Galveston Bay, **15**, **16**, 89, 315, 316, 324
Garrett, Mr. and Mrs., 305
Georgia, **8**, 76, 81, 84, 86, 91, 101, 122, 149, 196, 198, 199, 203, 218, 227, 305, 317
Georgia militia, 199, 203, 204, 214
Ghent, Treaty of, 212, 277, 289, 290
Gibson, Col., Tennessee volunteers, 214
Gladwin, schooner, 185
Glassel, Lt. J. M., 213, 214, 251, 253, 266
Grapes, 159
Graziers, 131, 141
Grenada, 313
Gual, Pedro, **12**, **15**, **16**
Gun-boat No. 168, **19**

Haitian mulattoes, **16**
Hall, Judge, 180
Hambly, William, 212, 213, 219, 225, 226, 229, 230, 231, 232, 234, 238, 239, 249, 250, 255, 278, 299, 300, 301
Hammock, 37
Harrison, Jacob, 263
Harvey, Adm., 6
Havana, 88, 92, 127–28, 163, 203, 228, 231, 282, 291, 300, 301
Hawkins, Col. Benjamin, 289, 290
Hemattlemico (Himathlo Mico), 201, 217, 306
Henley, Commodore J. D., USN, **19**, **20**, 147, 321, 323
Hillis Hadjo (Francis the Prophet), 201, 202, 217, 220, 224, 226, 227, 233, 234, 241, 257, 260, 262, 290, 292, 304
Himashy Miso Chattchichy, 220
Hoes, 155
Holme, S. L., 323
Horses, 23, 67, 130, 136, 138, 157, 159, 160, 161, 181, 240, 260
House of Representatives, U.S., 206
Houses, 22, 56, 117, 133, 141, 159, 167
Howratule, 233, 234
Hubbard, Ruggles, **13**, **16**, **17**, **18**, 95, 97, 103

Imatchlacle, 233, 234
Indians, **26**, 126, 142, 154, 164–79, 180, 186, 213, 216, 217, 222, 288, 326
Inhemocklo (Inhimarthlo), 222, 224, 233, 234
Inhimatcchucle, 233, 234
Irwin, Jared, **13**, **16**, **17**, 91, 99–100, 108–10, 114, 151
Isle of Wight, 13

Jackson, General Andrew, **9**, **20**, **21**, **22**, **23**, 178–81, 196, 197, 200, 201, 202, 203, 205, 206, 207, 208, 209, 210, 211, 212, 216, 217, 220, 223, 267, 268, 272, 278, 280, 281, 282, 283, 284, 286, 287, 288, 291, 293, 295, 296, 297, 298, 301, 305, 308, 326

John Adams, U.S. frigate, **19**, 147, 321

Kearney, Capt., USN, 150
Kentucky, 179, 180, 200, 203, 204, 214
Kindelan, Sebastian, **8**, **10**
King, Col. William, 214, 328
King Hatchy. *See* Kinhigee
Kingsley, Zephaniah, **10**, 152
King's Road (Royal Road), 130
Kinhigee (Kinhijah), 217, 220, 221, 222, 223, 225, 227, 229, 233, 234, 236, 241, 243, 244

Lafayette, Marquis de, 311
Lafitte, Jean, **16**, 89
Lane, Capt., 54
Lawrence, Capt., USN, 150
Lewis, Capt., 253
Liers, Capt., **17**, 78, 103, 320
Lindsay, Col. William, 214
Little prince, the (Seminole chief), 211–12, 215, 246, 247
Lohoe, Itamatchly, 233, 234
Loomis, Jairus, 304
Louisiana, 316, 324
Louisiana Purchase, **2**
Luengo, Don Francisco C., commandant Fort St. Marks, 210, 211, 224, 231, 232, 294, 297, 301, 302, 304
Lynx, U.S. schooner, **19**, 147, 321

Maclure, William, 25
McClure's Hill, Amelia Island, 93
McDonald, Col., **4**, **5**, 14, **17**, **18**, **20**, 20, 28, 32, 33, 40–42, 52, 67, 71–73, 78, 80, 98–99, 107, 186, 313, 314
McGirt, Captain, 327, 328
MacGregor, Sir Gregor, **1**, **5**, **11**, **12**, **13**, **14**, **15**, **17**, **20**, **21**, 53, 67, 78, 81, 85–95, 148–49, 187–88, 259, 298, 299, 302, 303, 307, 308, 314
McIntosh, John Houston, **7**, **8**, **9**, **19**
McKrimmon, captive of Indians, 202
McQueen, Peter, 217, 229, 234
Madeira, island, **4**, **12**, **17**, 18–30, **23**, 49, 313
Madison, James, **6**
Mandihoca, **26**, 138
Mappalitchy, 230
Margarita (Margaretta) Island, **4**, **8**, 45, 183, 184
Mary, schooner, **5**, 54
Masot, Don José, governor of Pensacola, 202, 217, 293, 295, 297, 299
Matagorda Bay, **16**, 316
Matanzas Inlet, 117
Mathews, Gen. George, **7**, **8**, 122, 124
Mendez, Don Luis Lopez, 3, 9, 33, 73, 184, 191
Mexico, Gulf of, 89, 95, 157, 325

Mexico, republic of, **12**, **15**, **16**, 89, 95, 151, 188, 316, 318, 321, 324
Mexico Libre, privateer brig, 95, 320
Miasma, 156–57
Mikasuki (Mickasucky, Michaseky), town, 217, 238, 241, 253, 254, 257
Miller, John, **3**
Miller, Gen. William, **3**
Minorcans, **5**
Minton, Maj., Georgia militia, 214
Miranda, Francisco de, **11**
Mitchell, Gen. David Brydie, **8**, 222, 224, 235, 236, 241, 243, 244
Mobile, Ala., 66
Monakatapa, Seminole chief, 178
Monastery, Dominican, Madeira, 25–26
Monroe, James, **6**, **19**, **21**, 290, 326
Montgomery, Maj. Elijah, 214
Moodie, Benjamin, 219, 228
Moosa Old Fort, **8**
Morales, Don Francisco de, **13**
Morelos (Morales), José Maria, 44
Morgiana, privateer brig, **13**, **17**, 78, 93, 106, 110, 320
Morillo, Gen. Pablo, Spanish, 191
Morning Chronicle, newspaper, 191
Mosquitoes, insect, 56
Mounater Creek, 218
Muhlenburg, Maj. Peter, Jr., 214

Napoleonic Wars, **1**, **3**
Nassau, New Providence, 79, 92, 225, 226, 302, 305
Nassau River, Fla., 152
Negroes, as Indian allies, 216, 221, 222, 234, 235, 249, 254, 258, 260, 286, 288, 290, 294, 298, 307
Negro Fort, **9**, 290, 291, 295, 299, 303, 305
Nero, 258
Nevis, island, 38
New Grenada, **12**, **15**
New Orleans, battle of, 64, 180, 218
New Providence, Bahamas, 212, 220, 231, 233, 243, 253, 255, 260, 291, 300, 302, 303, 304
New Providence Gazette, 215
New Smyrna, Fla., **6**
New York, 54, 95
Nichols (Nicholls), Col. Edward, 201, 225, 236, 238, 259, 260, 288, 290, 291, 298, 299, 300, 301, 302, 303, 304, 307, 309
Niles' Weekly Register, **22**
North River, Fla., **23**, 154, 159, 160

Ocklocknee Sound, 226, 229, 233, 240, 242
Ocmulgee River, 230
Ocnacone Tuctonoky. *See* Opony
Okeefenokee (Okeyfenokey) Swamp, 142

Olis Micco (Otus Mico), 225, 233, 234
Onís, Luis de, 287
Oparthlomico, 234
Opony, 233, 234
Opy Hatch, 230
Oranges, 21, 118, 159
Ord, George, 25
Orinoco River, 46, 184, 185, 186, 313
Oso Hatjo Choctawhacy, 220

Pablo Creek, Fla., 154, 314
Panton, Leslie and Co., 292
Patriot War, 7–9, **11**, 122–24
Patterson, Commodore Daniel T., 305
Pazos, Vicente, **16, 18,** 20
Peale, Titian, 25
Pensacola, 9, **22**, 197, 202, 203, 204, 206, 267, 278, 282, 285, 287, 288, 291, 292, 293, 295, 296, 297, 299, 307, 308
Perdido River, **6**, 84, 317, 327
Persat, Maurice, **16**
Phenix, John Lewis, 215, 245, 253, 263
Philadelphia, **12**, 54
Philadelphia Academy of Natural Sciences, 25
Piar, Gen. Manuel, 44
Picolata, 25
Pigs, 39
Pizarro, Joseph, 282, 285, 286, 287, 298, 307
Plantations, 123, 152, 154–59, 160
Point Petre, Ga., 147, 152, 321
Portsmouth, England, 4, 9, 10, 11
Posen (Posey?), Col., 87, 91
Potatoes, 155, 167
Prince, Spanish non-commissioned officer, 123
Prometheus, U.S. brig, **19**
Prospect Bluff, on Apalachicola R., 217, 218, 219, 229, 238, 289, 303
Puerto Rico, 55

Red Sticks, 289, 291
Republic of the Floridas, **18**
Republic of West Florida, **6**
Rice, 125, 155–56, 167
Rio de la Plata, **12**
Rolle, Dennis, 153, 154
Royal road, 130

Saba, island, 38
St. Augustine, 5, 7, **8, 14, 15, 18, 23, 25, 26**, 77, 78, 88, 90, 92, 94, 115, 116–23, 129, 130, 151, 152, 162–64, 181, 235, 292, 300
St. Bartholomew, island, 38
St. George, lake, 125

St. John's, island in West Indies, 38
St. Johns, town, 153
St. Johns River, 9, **13**, **25**, 77, 78, 94, 125, 129, 130, 133–34, 136–37, 152–54, 209, 227, 305, 313, 314
St. Kitts, island, 38
St. Marks, fort. *See* Fort St. Marks
St. Marks River, 200, 217
St. Marys, town, 7, **17**, **18**, 101, 113–14, 129, 145, 151
St. Marys River, 7, 8, **14**, **15**, 76, 77, 87, 111, 112, 143–44, 314, 322, 325
St. Thomas, island, **4**, **5**, 9, **12**, **23**, 38, 40–63, 183, 314
Salt production, 66
San Nicholas, post of, **13**, **26**
Santa Catherina Island, 188
Santa Cruz (St. Croix), Virgin Islands, 41, 54
Santo Domingo (St. Domingo), 3, 44, 72, 126, 185
Saranac, U.S. brig, **14**, **17**, **19**, 77, 147, 321
Satilla River, Ga., 198, 199, 208, 240
Savannah, Ga., **12**, 86
Say, Thomas, 25
Scott, Lt. Richard W., 199, 292, 293, 305
Scott, Gen. Winfield, 199
Secret Act of 1811. *See* Congress
Seminole Indians, 9, **21**, **26**, 142, 154, 164–79, 196, 199, 200, 208, 209, 220, 221, 227, 228, 240, 242, 286, 289, 291, 307
Seminole War, **22**, 198, 205, 294
7th Infantry, U.S., 214
Sharks, 75
Shipwrecks, 157
60th regiment, British, 21
Slavery, **13**, **14**, **18**, 86, 125–27, 149, 158, 167, 181, 315, 316, 317, 319, 324
Smilax, **26**
Smith, Col. Thomas, **8**, **9**, 122
Smuggling, **13**, **19**, 77, 149, 316, 324
Sombrero, island, 38
Spanish Bluff, 217
Spanish Indians, 299
Sugar, 125
Surveyor-general of East Florida, 113
Suwannee River, **21**
Suwany, Indian town(s) (Sahwahnee), 212, 216, 217, 218, 219, 221, 227, 238, 241, 243, 244, 245, 249, 250, 253, 255, 256, 257, 258, 260, 262, 264, 288, 305

Talbot Island, Fla., 79, 92, 152
Tampa Bay, **20**, 82, 254, 256, 259, 302, 303
Tamuches Haho. *See* McQueen, Peter
Taverns, **11**, 21, 135
Taxes, 158
Telégrafo de las Floridas, El, **18**

Tennessee, 179, 180, 200, 203, 204, 214
Thompson, Martin, 12
Thugart, interpreter, 226
Tiger Island, Fla., 111, 144
Tombigbee (Tombeckbe), 328
Tortola, island, 38
Trinidad, island of, 185
Trinity River, Texas, 89, 315, 316
Turks Island, 5, 54, 66–67
29th Regiment, British, 119
Two Friends, ship, **4**, **5**, 4, 5, 8, 9, 48, 54, 145, 183–85, 313, 314

Uniforms, 15, 21, 46

Vashon, Capt. George, 214
Venezuela, republic of, **2**, 3, **4**, **11**, **12**, 42, 89, 95, 151, 188, 191, 318, 324
Villaret, Augusto Gustavo, **16**
Virgin Gordas, islands, 38

Walton, W., 3
War of 1812, **2**, **9**
Washington Square, Fernandina, 109
Warterloo, Battle of, **1**
Wayne County, Ga., 305
Wellington, Lord, 7, 51
West Florida, **6**, **12**, 201, 317, 324
Wexford, Ireland, 121
White, Enrique, **10**
Williams, Col., Tennessee volunteers, 214
Winslett, John, 214, 246, 247
Woodbine, Capt. George, 226, 254, 256, 258, 259, 289, 298, 299, 302, 303, 304, 308
Wright, Capt. Obed, 203–4

Yellow fever, 101
Yonge, Henry, **10**

Zamia, 26